CRITICAL
INSIGHTS
Southern Gothic
Literature

CRITICAL INSIGHTS

Southern Gothic Literature

Editor
Jay Ellis
University of Colorado Boulder

SALEM PRESS
A Division of EBSCO Publishing
Ipswich, Massachusetts

GREY HOUSE PUBLISHING

Cover Photo: Angel statue on top of a tombstone, Bonaventure Cemetery, Savannah, Georgia. (Peter Johansky)

Critical Insights: Southern Gothic Literature, 2013, published by Grey House Publishing, Inc., Amenia, NY, under exclusive license from EBSCO Publishing, Inc.

∞ The paper used in these volumes conforms to the American National Standard for Permanence of Paper for Printed Library Materials, Z39.48-1992 (R1997).

Library of Congress Cataloging-in-Publication Data

Southern gothic literature / editor, Jay Ellis, University of Colorado.
    pages cm. -- (Critical insights)
    Includes bibliographical references and index.
    ISBN 978-1-4298-3823-8 (hardcover)
    1. Gothic fiction (Literary genre), American--History and criticism. 2. American fiction--Southern States--History and criticism. 3. Gothic revival (Literature)--Southern States. 4. Horror tales, American--History and criticism. I. Ellis, Jay, 1963- editor of compilation.
    PS374.G68S78 2013
    813'.0872909975--dc23
                                                                                2012049040

ebook ISBN: 978-1-4298-3839-9

PRINTED IN THE UNITED STATES OF AMERICA

Contents_____

About This Volume

Jay Ellis

No single book comprehensively covers a literary genre, so the field of Gothic studies, now well established, naturally proceeds in two directions: multiple foci on smaller facets of Gothic, and larger claims for its reflections in our—which is to say global—culture. In parallel, study of Southern Literature long ago evolved its contextual concerns. Both fields now recognize global and comparative (transnational) readings and myriad subspecialties. But work on each genre began at the large-scale job of definition and taxonomy. In that process, Southern Gothic and its study got buried, in separate pieces, under each of its respective terms. It is time to dig out.

With this volume, whole books addressing the compound genre "Southern Gothic" remain rare, even as the subset refuses to be subsumed—or people would not continue to use the full term so widely. Here we sometimes treat Southern Gothic as a subgenre, but also makes larger claims. Of the few books already focused on our generic category, nearly all perform comparative study of one or two authors in terms of "Southern Gothic." Google Scholar returns only sixty entries for the compound term—by far finding most in article and dissertation titles. MLA International Bibliography finds only two dozen articles or chapters with our compound in their titles.

Writing one of very few book-length studies of Southern Gothic has been rewarding but daunting. The primary works considered here nonetheless represent Southern Gothic across literary genres. In addition to exemplary novels from established writers, works explored here include poetry, a play, a fairy tale novella, and a novel that—although honored by the French forty years ago—American literary circles, certainly syllabi, largely forgot. While the works on which we focus certainly fit most definitions of *Southern* Gothic, I am also happy that out of our eleven scholars, four either live outside the United States or were born abroad.

Gothic itself seems to be making a play as a nearly normative mode, at least in popular US culture, which continues to be a major cultural export. In *Gothicka: Vampire Heroes, Human Gods, and the New Supernatural* (2012), Victoria Nelson argues that Gothicka proceeds in the twenty-first century beyond the darker genre of Gothic through the twentieth. Nelson's Gothicka poses nothing less than a post-Christian—if not quite posthumanist—resolution of otherwise incommensurable contradictions and the cognitive dissonance they occasion, between our sense of life understood scientifically and rationally, yet permeated with unfathomable mystery. Instead of the historical Gothic that bumps our fears awake in the night, Gothicka presents us with often optimistic narratives of empowerment beyond the constrictions of inherited identities of race, gender, sexuality, and religion—and even seems comfortable in daylight. As I notice in the introduction that follows, however, Nelson seems to have missed how much of the newer Gothicka she finds is inarguably *Southern*. While less sunny in our forecast, our study of Southern Gothic hopes at least to contribute to its acceptance as more than a buried relative in the South, and many of our chapters do find the darkest clouds fairing off.

Defining genres remains a complicated task, and the introductory essay attempts to triangulate between its constitutive terms the location, geographically and metaphorically, of Southern Gothic. Our critical context essays continue the difficult task of defining and locating, then assessing past assessments of, Southern Gothic. Two essays then determine critical contexts for Gothic elements within Southern fiction.

Bridget Marshall helps dig up our buried genre, observing that Southern Gothic's lineage of "contested boundaries" derive ultimately from British Gothic, yet noting its other origins. She rightly nods to Potter Stewart's famous definition for pornography, that we know it when we see it. As impossible a means of legal definition as this continues to be for our courts, it appeals to individual sensibility. When we read, we feel we recognize differences of genre the way a record store owner (I know one still in business), or even a computer's database system for recommending what you might "like," makes assessments based on details of the artifact. The rest is argument for what belongs where, and as Marshall finds the substitution of spaces linked to slavery, the haunting of our genre becomes clear.

Perhaps, as new scholarship reveals the degree of cognitive dissonance (allowing moral hypocrisy) in the ironies of the writing of the United States as a place where all (people) are created equal, Southern Gothic will cease to be seen as the buried child of its American progenitor, but rather the other way around. Not merely Southern, but the dominant culture of the entire country bears the guilt of slavery. Interesting, then, that our genre remains—at least in earlier scholarship— the lesser of an already degenerate one. Marshall locates the centrality of slavery to Southern Gothic, and thereby suggests an ironically foundational relationship to other Gothic genres.

As Chris Walsh points out in his chapter on critical reception, the boundaries of *Beloved* (1987) figure into the problem of what constitutes Southern literature; much of the novel occurs in Ohio, yet the traumatic events haunting it crossed over the Ohio River. That line of demarcation (actually the line of the Missouri Compromise, and therefore the real line between slave and free states, rather than the popularly remembered Mason-Dixon) suggests the fuzziness even of the North-South border. Where Marshall focuses on the "Gothic" half of our genre, Walsh provides deeper exploration into its "Southern" provenance. As with those boundary difficulties, Walsh outlines the arguments over the importance of slavery to our understanding of an evolving South, and therefore to studies of Southern Literature—especially its Gothic genre.

Henry Carrigan provides any writer looking into the Gothic heart of a contemporary Southern writer a path to its provenance in tradition. Impressively, he sketches the parallel histories of Harry Crews with the much better known Flannery O'Connor without actually naming William Faulkner; as Carrigan makes clear in his excellent later chapter on Faulkner for our critical readings section, however, uninitiated readers quickly discover the Faulknerian foundation to all Southern Gothic. In his compare and contrast essay on Flannery O'Connor and Harry Crews, Carrigan finds the surprisingly numerous affinities between otherwise remarkably different writers. O'Connor died of lupus at thirty-nine after living much of her life in bed, or near it. A deeply religious writer whose eye remained skeptical of the term "Southern Gothic," O'Connor shares with Crews, a tattooed Korean War marine veteran and ex-boxer whose work embraced the genre, a love of grotesque characters laid bare for truth, even as each writer finds that truth leading in different directions.

The final critical contexts essay employs some of the rich scholarship on zombies alongside a key horror film of the 1970s to deepen its close reading of Cormac McCarthy's *The Road* (2006). Although—as is the case with all strong works of literature—*The Road* cannot be reduced to a generic reading, aspects of Southern Gothic not only inform the book, but also suggest the New Southern Gothic whose economic and potentially posthumanist concerns rise to the surface of the text more readily than in many Southern Gothic works.

Our first critical readings essay, by Ronja Vieth, traces guilt in short and long fiction by Charles Chesnutt, *The Conjure Woman* (1899) and *The Marrow of Tradition* (1901). Vieth compellingly follows her claim of the centrality of guilt to Southern Gothic with Leslie Fiedler's of the centrality of the Gothic to the American novel. By extension, therefore, we find that not only does Southern Gothic rise to its own importance beyond that of a subgenre, but it has also informed—or at least a parallel guilt over slavery and Reconstruction informed— American novels from well outside the South. Readers may be tempted to connect Vieth's attention to buried guilt in Chesnutt's work, with works explored in other chapters, where figurative disinterments, figurative zombies, and literal ghosts carry with them reminders of otherwise suppressed accountability. Chronology ordered the essays for our critical readings, yet Vieth's argument proved perfect to contextualize those that follow.

Writing after Chesnutt, William Faulkner's attention to the guilt of slavery receives some of its less direct attention in *The Sound and the Fury* (1929)—until we follow Henry Carrigan's reading of its concluding fourth part. Readers newer to Southern Gothic and, for that matter, to Southern literature will find a sound mapping of Faulkner's literary railroad and the postage stamp to which it returns. Those quite familiar with the bard of Oxford, however, will then appreciate Carrigan's sensitive treatment of the religious feeling in Dilsey's section. Without a direct avowal of any particular religious faith, Faulkner conveys the depth of religious belief in his most moral character. Carrigan first contextualizes *The Sound and the Fury* in terms of the larger biblically-informed metanarrative of the Compsons, then helps readers challenged by the novel's polyvalent structure, ultimately revealing the depth of religious feeling that—whatever Faulkner himself believed—the novel allows readers to see in Dilsey.

Julieann Ulin situates her reading of Carson McCullers in spatial terms amenable to many of our essays. Exploring the fallen boardinghouse setting of *The Heart is a Lonely Hunter* (1940), Ulin finds that ruined space hospitable to an affirmation of New Southern identity. Southern Gothic here, for all its saturation in guilt, proves to be more positive than typical Gothic constructions of space. McCullers presents readers with a Bakhtinian carnivalesque that allows, through its grotesques, a positive site for regrowth. Recontextualizing the boardinghouse in McCullers, Ulin breaks ground for a more persuasive reading than has been historically allowed most Southern Gothic texts when critics reduce their complexity to stereotypes of decay and fall.

Not long after the publication of *The Heart is a Lonely Hunter*, Eudora Welty's *The Robber Bridegroom* (1942) appeared, drawing on European fairy tales, Victorian Gothic, and Welty's own loose history of her region for its "Southern Fried" story. As Tanya Jones demonstrates, Welty worked freely with her source materials to create her "monomyth." The Brothers Grimm, Hans Christian Anderson, and Charles Perrault's stories and folktales all provided Welty with ingredients for a Southern Gothic recipe, and readers will find in this reading a reliable connection from Welty back to previous iterations of Gothic, as well as another way to understand how Southern Gothic becomes greater than the sum of its ingredients. Welty's use of fairy tales points us to another genre for Tennessee Williams.

Suddenly Last Summer (1958) serves an example as strongly as any novel of quintessential Southern Gothic. Tanfer Tunc traces the roots of this Tennessee Williams play about deviance and cannibalism to both the Gothic of the Old South and the resurfacing decrepitude in the New South. The plantation in the play figures both literally and figuratively as the haunted physical and mental space for its character conflicts. As Marshall notes the replacement of the European aristocrat with the slave master, Tunc finds the all-consuming Sebastian—himself consumed by those he would sexually exploit—absent before the play begins, and therefore haunting it much as the Old South haunts the new. Where Vieth had established guilt as the pervasive warp of the fabric in Southern Gothic, Tunc finds the pressure to keep that guilt secret the perpendicular thread woven through this sometimes-atypical Williams play. Distilled to an impossible degree that collapses the color and gender binaries of the dominant culture, whiteness in *Suddenly Last Summer* becomes another commodity—eventually a meat as literal as that in *The Road*. Ultimately, the last secret hidden by Sebastian proves to be the implication of the women around him in his predations. Tunc's excellent focus on the power of secrecy about the South's ongoing economy of predation helps readers see the richness in what can be misperceived as a relatively hyperbolic work for Williams, while connecting Sebastian to the vampire legends of more direct Gothic horror. As Tunc finds, regardless of orientation or gender, survivors of the South must betray the secrets of this Williams play.

David Rothman then provides another excellent corrective to what would have been a collection limited to fiction. His essay on Southern Gothic poetry traces all Gothic back to the earliest literature, especially for poets, who often took their Gothic straight, as it were, from classical Greece. As Rothman points out, Gothic elements arose in the earliest Greek poetry—and in the Old English poem *Beowulf.* Gothic spaces originate in poetry because poetry has always been a first genre for literature, relying initially on the exigencies of repeated verbal performance and oral memory. As Rothman puts it, "poetry always comes first." The difference he finds in his chapter here, however, between the oldest sources of Gothic elements and their reappearance in the Southern Gothic of modern poetry, lies in the space between belief in "literal, historical, or legendary" stories, and in the "symbolic and aesthetic rebellion against Enlightenment rationality" that most readily explains all modern Gothic and grew particularly in Southern poetry.

Michal Svěrák continues our attention to poetry in one sense. His reading of *Dagon* draws welcome attention to a writer better known now as a poet, and the first of our living writers within these critical readings. Poet laureate of North Carolina Fred Chappell's 1968 novel provides a solidly Southern Gothic version of Dagon mythology by way of a better-known practitioner of fantasy and horror, H. P. Lovecraft. The French Academy awarded *Dagon* its Best Foreign Book of the Year prize in 1972—probably years after it would have been hard to find a copy of *Dagon* in an American bookstore. Lovecraft's Cthulhu Mythos can be daunting for readers unacquainted with that mystical New Englander's work. Readers less disposed to enjoy his fantastic elements may find Lovecraft's hyperbolic style, freighted with heavy adjectives and adverbs, a final impediment. How wonderful, then, that our Czech contributor brings Chappell's sharply written novel to wider attention. Svěrák helps readers understand Cthulhu Mythos, and thereby, Lovecraft's influence on Chappell's novel, while recovering a beautifully written book whose every sentence bears the hard facets of a poet's craft. Any volume dedicated to representing a movement or genre must address canonical works, yet should also expand our sense of its categories. That *Dagon* will find a higher place not only among horror fiction (where its reputation remains strong), but among representative works of Southern Gothic, any reader of this initially decadent but ultimately highly spiritual work is bound to agree.

That the family of *Dagon*'s Peter Leland seems to have lorded over their poorer neighbors remains in the background of the novel's mythological and spiritual concerns. But Leland does seem to be a scion of landed gentry in North Carolina. His counterpart in Cormac McCarthy's highly autobiographical *Suttree* (1979) has renounced his birthright before the novel begins. The fall of Leland may shock us in the depths of its depravity; Cornelius Suttree—without a glimpse yet of even a posthumanist god of mindless indifference and indolence—has hit a fairly hard bottom when his novel begins, and he keeps falling. Chris Walsh's reading follows the alcoholic Cornelius Suttree's Joycean wanderings through a miasma of guilty self-abuse (and occasional meanness to others) while Suttree attempts to help the denizens of a Gothic Knoxville. Walsh meanwhile provides an excellent overview of the Gothic features of the novel's setting, and a critical yet fair assessment of the novel's treatment of race and class.

McCarthy's father was the lead attorney for the Tennessee Valley Authority (TVA), and while Suttree's father's occupation remains vague, he reproaches the son early on. Of all the sites of dispossession in the novel, the bar of Ab Jones, an African American whose beating by the police Suttree attempts to avenge, stands out as especially freighted with symbols of oppression. Sitting in the bar with a blind friend, Suttree asks the man to read the names written on the undersides of the tables. We realize the tabletops for drinking away one's senses are the displaced tombstones from whole communities uprooted—and disinterred—to make way for the flooding waters of the TVA's reservoirs.

Prosopopoeia—bringing forward the mask of the dead or otherwise absent figure—recurs without the need for the titular headstone in Toni Morrison's *Beloved*. In *The Body Embarrassed: Drama and the Disciplines of Shame in Early Modern England* (1993), Gail Kern Paster identifies an "early modern English culture's complex articulation of gender—the weaker vessel as the leaky vessel" (24). Sharon Decker finds Morrison's powerful poetic evocation of reclaiming Sethe's body through her refusal to continue providing milk for children not her own; instead, Sethe "has rewritten in milk and blood." Decker's readings remain strong as she traces the river's power, and ultimately, the power of "rememory" as nothing less than a national project. Here, too, we see Southern Gothic as critical beyond study of a mere subgenre. Decker's sure-footed close reading of this novel argues for its place within, as well as beyond, Southern Gothic.

The "symbolic and aesthetic rebellion" Rothman notes in Southern Gothic poetry proves true of all the works examined here. That rebellion can occur in the imagination anywhere when confronted with the darkness on the other side of rationality. The American South has its universal share of the Gothic in common with universal mythology. Then of course, we find its European Gothic heredity, and, especially in its modern development into a more distinct genre, its more particular American Gothic influence. But this volume ultimately finds the genre sufficient unto itself. Like Freud's layers of Rome upon Rome in *Civilization and Its Discontents* (16–17), we can imagine layers of Gothic in the South.

Put in a pleasurable way, anyone who has reached the bottom of a Kentucky Derby mud pie (primarily chocolate, pecans, and bourbon) knows what the compression of layers can do to enrich an experience. More seriously, the South has its graves upon graves, a figurative layering up from its influences. The essays here should provide an excavation of what promises to be an undying form of literature.

Works Cited

Freud, Sigmund. *Civilization and Its Discontents*. Trans. and ed. James Strachey. New York: Norton, 1961. Print.

Paster, Gail Kern. *The Body Embarrassed: Drama and the Disciplines of Shame in Early Modern England*. Ithaca: Cornell UP, 1993. Print.

On Southern Gothic Literature

Jay Ellis

> All great fiction has been allegorical
> in the sense that the instances presented in it
> reverberate in a more general world of types.
>
> Robert Scholes 269

Don't open that door. This remains one of the primary feelings manipulated in the viewer of horror films, just as opening that door remains the most difficult chore to give to a young child: "Go down in
the basement and bring back—". The underground space, that place at
the bottom of the rabbit hole, need not literally be found under the floor
of the house. Where I grew up, we had no basements. But the bike shed
beyond reach of the floodlight at the corner of the backyard shop, any
place out there in the dark outside the warm light of the house, that was
where cat litter got dumped over the fence into the alley before a quick
run back inside. "Down in the basement" need not be literal.

The Gothic, as a genre, continually takes us out there, below
ground, and behind the door we would rather leave closed. Even if
that dark space smelling more of earth and death is found over a fence.
If not always literally, our sense of Gothic space remains subterranean; psychologically, sociologically, politically, and, as this volume
often suggests, especially geographically when we attach the prefix
"Southern." In many ways, Southern Gothic originated on its own,
but always as extensions of other Gothic pathways, and not always
geographically "down." Down from its relative Northern predecessors, but also up from the Caribbean, and over from Africa and Europe in the more direct passages of slaves and slave owners, from the
folktales of Europe through Scottish and Irish immigrants, and with
direct connections through books made of books (such as the classical
influences on Gothic poetry)—extending from its influences, Southern

Gothic becomes a site of flux and mixture. Although the Gothic certainly includes less obvious figures than the monsters of what we call "horror," it as certainly includes them. If we trace the immigration of just two monsters to Southern Gothic, we will see the need to triangulate its spatial history.

That history remains too complex to cover in this introduction, but I attempt to sketch it in three ways: first, following the tracks of a representative subgenre of the Gothic, zombie narratives; second and third, retracing the geographical and generic ways in which Southern and Southern Gothic have been configured through a regular trope of "below." We will find Southern Gothic as a triangulation of space and genre after a quick test of one of its typical characters. How universal and central its features might therefore be, will be the ultimate argument of this essay. Why does the Gothic threaten to become an aspect of literature and culture that reaches well beyond genre? If it does, why does American Gothic so regularly remain especially "Southern"— even when scholars miss noting this?

Monstrous Origins

While zombie narratives remain too rich to be confined to regional readings of their literature, the provenance of their mythic graves remains mostly Southern. They may, as Gilles Deleuze and Félix Guattari, and now countless newer scholars argue, represent so many things in our culture as to be overdetermined—uncontrollable as the zombie hordes within any such narrative. But the critical task of remembering includes tracing history where the documents and artifacts maintain more specific accuracy than some of the looser so-called postmodernist critical moves tend to bother with. Through Haiti, but also through the particular aspects of the American Southern history of slavery, Jim Crow laws (including those against miscegenation), and the fragile constructions of gender against which William Faulkner's novels play out, zombies and their most cherished victims prove to be especially Southern, and thus, especially Southern Gothic.

Zombies now seem to come from everywhere and nowhere. Created by magic, mesmerism, neurotoxins, nuclear fallout, a virus or a bite, they now seem global citizens, which is why Deleuze and Guattari see them as pandemic to capitalism and its normative generation and satisfaction of the "death instinct" proposed by Freud: "The only modern myth is the myth of zombies—mortified schizos, good for work, brought back to reason" (368). In their typically quick reasoning, Deleuze and Guattari connected the zombie with the condition of every modern person, as given the surplus of capitalism, "so many unemployed are needed, so many deaths, the Algerian War doesn't kill more people than weekend automobile accidents" (368). We recognize something in this, as soon as we discipline our attention away from the latest horrific murder and dismemberment to the larger statistics on automotive deaths. And then given the way we see the zombie figure appropriated for any situation—from Occupy zombie walks to online dating sites—it is easy to feel a simple (or complicated theoretically imagined) history of the zombie must be impossible. As Steven Shaviro describes them,

> the sheer exorbitance of the zombies defies causal explanation, or even simple categorization. The living dead don't have an origin or a referent; they have become unmoored from meaning. They figure a social process that no longer serves rationalized ends, but has taken on a strange and sinister life of its own. (84)

But the zombie's importation and immigration into Southern Gothic, while complicated, turns out to be a rich path of scholarship. As Deleuze and Guattari note in passing, Freud's development of a theory of the death instinct derived in part from "World War I, which remains the model of capitalist war" (368). Freud's idea also had its historical moment to follow, as World War II began just nineteen years after publication of *Beyond the Pleasure Principle* in 1920. And what of the first mention of zombies in Southern Literature? In 1929, William Buehler Seabrook, an alcoholic reporter born in Maryland, publishes the first widely read work of American literature mentioning zombies, a travel memoir called *The Magic Island*. Jennifer Fay follows Seabrook's experiences writing the book to his description of American-owned Haitian American Sugar Company, and the zombies he hears were created for work in the sugar cane fields. Seabrook's book directly influenced the screenplay for the 1932 American film *White Zombie*, with actor Bela Lugosi as Murder Legendre, the owner of a sugar cane mill. Fay reads the most startling moment of the film well.

Rather than the sounds of an industrial factory, the film provides early sound effects of "the monotonous moan of creaking wood" as men turn the stiles of a shredding machine cutting up the cane that others, above, dump into it from baskets (Fay 86). When "one of the workers falls into the sieve and is quietly processed with the rest of the harvest," the viewer realizes "that these are but the shells of men"; Fay notes that only then do we see the faces of the zombies at work, noting that "the introduction to labor in this gothic factory satisfies the Hollywood convention of gradually revealing monstrosity. But in suspending our knowledge of the worker's revivified state, the film intentionally conflates deadening, low-wage, factory work with work performed by zombies" (86).

More disturbing to viewers is the sound we do not hear: the man who falls into the blades of the shredder makes no sound at all. A shot of the shredder's blades turning, quite slowly, their battered forge marks visible, precedes the zombie's fall into it. It is 1932, and we see no blood, nothing at all of the man after he falls, only the zombies below, continuing to turn the revolving handles of the shredder. But with no other sound—not even music—the repetitive, near-human groaning of the wooden and iron machinery continues. This moment of a human being—or the zombified remains of one—being processed by the machinery of an empire's sweet tooth is horrific. It also reaches back, as Fay finds, through the colonial history of Haiti and its manipulation even well after its revolution. Indeed, Fay notes that, while the "magic behind [zombie labor] is not black or even Haitian, but white and European," the zombies in Legendre's sugar mill are not all Haitian blacks, and include any personal enemies of Legendre, including anyone "connected to the occupation" of Haiti (86–87).

Fay points out that in *White Zombie*, zombies are used for more than cheap agricultural slave labor, remarking that "zombification is domesticated and deployed as a technology of forgetting." She then notes that the American occupation of Haiti has itself been forgotten in recent discussions in favor of a focus on the "'successes' of U.S. occupation in postwar Germany and Japan" (87). Lest we forget, watching *White Zombie* means reading Southern Gothic, in as much as the history of slavery remains so close to the dark provenance of Southern Gothic. So, too, as Harilaos Stecopoulos reminds us, is the US history of imperial interventions to the south of the South. Remembering both the slave origins of much zombie mythology as well as the capitalist and imperialist critiques noted by most scholars of the zombie, we can remember as well the southern writer whose book generated the film *White Zombie*. By the time we follow the zombie figure all the way to its most recent popular appearance—in the New Southern setting of the long-arc television series *The Walking Dead*—we have come full circle to Southern Gothic.

Still set in the South, this series (which premiered in 2010) was based on one from Southern Gothic literature, a comic book series created by Robert Kirkman and Tony Moore in 2003. In both stories, the main character awakens in a hospital room in Kentucky to find the world overrun with zombies. As the action follows him and a revolving group of non-zombie survivors, the settings enact a virtual tracing of force movement during the American Civil War, running to Washington but then back six miles to the South, to Alexandria, Virginia. Although racial identity in zombie narratives can seem complicated (such as the variety of faces among the zombie workers in *White Zom-bie*) Ann Kordas notes the variety of zombie masters includes non-Africans, but never whites unless they presented other threats: "While white southerners employed Jim Crow laws to control the south's black population, white, native-born Americans in the industrialized north sought to control another group of potentially dangerous people—immigrants from southern and eastern Europe" (22). Thus, the famous accent of Bela Lugosi in *White Zombie* presents a similar threat to his characterization of Dracula in the Todd Browning film: fear of the dark European other.

Not only a reemergent memory of slavery, but an expression of wider xenophobic fears of the other as well, the zombie narrative frequently revives especially Southern fears involving gender. Gerry Canavan sees in *The Walking Dead* comics an

> uncritical relationship to a particular pre-feminist narrative about the need to "protect" women and children. . . . "Proper" control over wombs, and anxiety that they will somehow be captured, polluted, or compromised, is a kind of Ur-myth for the apocalyptic genre in general and the zombie sub-genre in particular. (444)

Surprisingly, Canavan does not note the Southern provenance of this Ur-myth. To be sure, the fear of loss of control by the male of the female power of birth arises from a landscape larger than the South. (Mary Shelley's *Frankenstein*, in which the good doctor takes far longer to create a living creature from dead men than it would take to marry his fiancée and make one in the usual method, can be read in this way.) But as Faulkner tells us in the appendix for Quentin in *The Sound and the Fury* (1929), his sister's "maidenhead [is] a miniature replica of all the whole vast globy earth" (207).

As Quentin's father lectures further in *Absalom, Absalom!* (1936), the maidenhead remained the absurd idea on which the South rested, an invented value of distinction that in Faulkner's words join constructions of race to those of gender. The South to Mr. Compson was,

> a milieu where the other sex is separated into three sharp divisions, separated (two of them) by a chasm which could be crossed but one time and in but one direction—ladies, women, females—the virgins whom gentlemen someday married, the courtesans to whom they went while on sabbaticals to the cities, the slave girls and women upon whom that first caste rested and to whom in certain cases it doubtless owed the very fact of its virginity. (112)

Within the primary text here we already see more complexity and irony in the absurd taxonomic distinctions of gender and race always in terms of control (here, that valued "virginity" that "rested" on the putative other) than critics often understand. No wonder the reverberations of such cultural constructions turn so regularly Gothic in the South. In zombie narratives, this construction of the feminine remains one to be protected and, thereby, controlled.

By comparison, a similar provenance of vampire mythology in its most recent manifestations in popular culture also retains its racial, gendered, and economic origins in the South, but where zombie narratives usually fail to find improvised domestic safety against the raging monsters out there, vampire narratives have begun to point to liberation. In *Gothicka: Vampire Heroes, Human Gods, and the New Supernatural*, Victoria Nelson sees a new development in Gothic (thus the added "ka") away from the decadent past to a new generic direction of wish fulfillment and imaginative retracing of identity. Nelson's arguments run at the pace of more recent vampires and zombies—fast. These monsters, and her readings, have been to Starbucks. To be fair, Nelson takes on an impressive scope of argument and often convinces: Gothicka moves beyond the historical Gothic. Surprisingly, however, the reader looking for "Southern Gothic" is referred simply to "American Gothic."

But reading into that blur may prove the argument that American Gothic is often the same thing as Southern, but put the other way around, that the Gothic still finds its locations readily in the South. In her chapter on vampires, Nelson moves from Bram Stoker's *Dracula* (1897) and its precedents to Anne Rice and, eventually, Charlaine Harris's Sookie Stackhouse novels,[1] focusing on their adaptation as *True Blood* for HBO as another long-arc television series. Quoting producer Alan Ball on what Nelson deems "the quintessential post-2000 Gothick position," Nelson notes his attempt to move away from the "supernatural" to "something that was almost like a deeper manifestation of nature" (Ball qtd. in Nelson 130). Nelson then observes the move forward—at least "forward" by fewer restrictions of sexuality and identity: "By its fourth season, *True Blood* had added werewolves, fairies, witches, and other supernatural creatures, all of whom, in a mad display of Gothick hybridity, engage in sex with humans and each other" (130). So much for waging losing wars to protect virginity in an untenable construction of gender distinctions.

What Nelson understandably does not have time to notice, however, is that of four prominent film or television series following novels or comics that bring zombies, vampires, and werewolves to renewed popularity in the culture, three are Southern. Only the comparatively chaste *Twilight* series by Stephenie Meyer is not; Anne Rice's vampire novels, *The Walking Dead* comics, and *True Blood*—as well as their reemergence as video and film productions—are steeped in Southern Gothic. The tracks of our most popular and obvious Gothic monsters run circles in, or back to, the South.

Southern Genre and Geography

We may trace the steps of obvious monsters of the Gothic (even as they are us) and find them regularly Southern even for the larger United States. But it also helps to see the historical forces within the dominant literary discourse of the United States, which was determinedly

Northeastern before that could even get around its insecurities in comparison with Europe, nonetheless have situated "Southern" as "below."

Southern literature had been noted as of course geographically, but also canonically, "below" the level of value deemed "mainstream" in American literature. Geographically, Jennifer Rae Greeson finds that before the Civil War, Ralph Waldo Emerson "inscribes New England as a silent norm, as a universal center" (148). Emerson "cycl[es] through historical incarnations of the South" (147) as a means to expand the reach of his famous "'transparent eyeball' of *Nature*" in a "dream of an absolute, singular, and omniscient subjectivity, which cannot itself be perceived or objectified" (145). What Emerson saw as an "ascendancy of Commerce" in the North over "Feudalism" in the South becomes an "ascendance of Industrial North over Slave South" (153). Greeson sees the resulting complex but insistent dream of empire resulting from Emerson's differentiation of North and South as connected to the emancipation of slaves in the British West Indies in 1833 (156).

That Emerson further differentiated between the American South still under slavery and the further South of the West Indies only reinforces the hierarchical tendency in Emerson: that South is visually below North on maps has only to do with the historical accidents of technology and power resulting in the dominance of maps made by Northern peoples. But Greeson makes clear, in Emerson, the South remains below the North, even as she finds Emerson dodging a direct confrontation with the problem of slavery.

Not only in Emerson, but also in Edgar Allan Poe, Greeson finds a corollary to this geographical judgment. More darkly, Poe senses the inevitability of American expansion to the South, resulting in but also derived from "the abjection of the U.S. South before the cultural hegemony of New England Transcendentalism and the terms under which U.S. expansion across the continent (and beyond) is being ideologically assimilated into national discourse" (168). What Greeson identifies as an "American Universal Geography" therefore not only entails a "struggle for dominance out onto formerly Mexican territory" but also contains within its expanding body a subjugated American South (168). Harilaos Stecopoulos similarly traces Southern identity as irrevocably bound up in the project of United States imperialism, particularly during Reconstruction.

Our "below" trope, therefore becomes on a map, "out there," in geopolitical terms, just as "below ground" within Gothic imaginative spaces regularly shifts to "out there" beyond the fence. Beyond the normative expectations of boundaries that promise safety, but that regularly betray us, we double back only to find those boundaries unreliable. As Bridget Marshall points out in her 2011 book, *The Transatlantic Gothic Novel and the Law, 1790–1860*, scholars of the Gothic have regularly found the genre "fragmentary, unstable, hybrid, transnational, and transhistorical" (1). Spatially as well as generically, we find the same psychological and sociological instability of boundaries and definitions for the Gothic, and yet, as particularly so in the "Southern" of Southern Gothic, we yet triangulate to the region. Like the Jesuit monks who, with nothing but canoe strokes with which to measure, produced a map of the shores of Lake Superior that held up for a hundred years (Hall 24), we paddle hope to find the location with at least a practical degree of accuracy.

Geographical configurations that place the South extending always below the North indeed resulted in frequent canonical barriers to literature deemed merely "Southern," in a way that Emerson, for instance, was not deemed merely "Northern," let alone merely the product of relatively tiny "New England." Admissions into the canon therefore depended on exceptions to an awareness of Southern literature's provenance as a product of a region—part of a larger whole assumed to be more nationally important than that part.

James Tuttleton, a great close reader and rescuer of so-called "domestic fiction" from its place (for decades near the turn of the nineteenth century to the later twentieth) below the value level of a lasting canon of American literature, was prone to writing off any author with regional aspects to their work who lacked sufficient aesthetic achievement, as a mere "local colorist" (182). In the classes where I heard Tuttleton level that harsh judgment, however, the exceptions made, not only for Faulkner, but also for Kate Chopin in the phrase cited above, rested on assessments of aesthetic and philosophical achievement. Tuttleton might complain that politically motivated readers were reading Chopin for the wrong reasons, and misreading her, but this writer from Missouri who lived and wrote from New Orleans receives equitable comparisons with Herman Melville because, as Tuttleton convinces, her description of "a desire to merge with the universe" ends in "a horrific surprise: self-annihilation by drowning" (202). In agreement with Melville, *The Awakening* (1899) becomes Chopin's entry to the canon.

These distinctions may now seem silly. But old arguments, and book sales, have repeatedly fallen out into presumed camps between novels addressing social ills and novels once called "romances." As the American novel grew in its originality (see especially Charles Brockden Brown's *Edgar Huntly*), found slightly more economic viability with changes in copyright law, and became more popular, romances did not mean titillating stories veering to or toward sex, but rather what most people now think of as novels. So, too, what detractors might have called "suasion fiction," i.e. stories meant didactically to enact a rhetorical function, certainly qualify as novels as well. This, too, may seem silly in an age when the growth of the memoir, a never-ending uneasiness in American life about what constitutes a true story, and questions of the value—sometimes even stated in economic terms—of the imagination in our culture, lead popular culture to a notable obsession with anything labeled "reality." The stakes for the claim of "truth" can be higher, as Marshall notes was the case in narratives of slavery. Frederick Douglass and Harriet Beecher Stowe both "felt compelled to prove to their readers the truth of their tales via documentation, testimony, and outside verification" and their works ultimately enact a legal function (127).

Those old arguments, about what constitutes the proper and true nature of American literature, collapse under scrutiny, as any text worth reading contains too much complexity for admission into strict generic parameters: *Uncle Tom's Cabin* proves to be as full of what Nathaniel Hawthorne claimed as the high ground of "fancy" (imagination) as does *Moby Dick*. Hawthorne's preface to *The House of Seven Gables* serves as part of the historical documentation of a division that should no longer bother us. And yet it does, whenever readers and writers make claims for what ought to matter in literature. What persistently matters, then, for an introduction to Southern Gothic is that we notice the persistence of questions around genre and region, differing claims for truth and invention, putative realism and fantasy. Within academia, scholars of Southern Gothic may no longer need to argue for its relevance. But beyond professional specializations that may be understandably confusing to younger students and to lay readers, the Gothic can too easily be seen merely in terms of popular culture. Ironically, Melville's eventually canonical novel was originally written off as a mere seafaring adventure. Henry Fothergill Chorley deemed *The Whale* (*Moby Dick* in America) "an ill-compounded mixture of romance and matter-of-fact." This is a judgment of genre, here one where genre mixing seems to be the problem.

Gothic, as a subgenre of that earlier generic term, "romance," has therefore often remained low in a "hierarchy of genres" (Fowler 113). Alistair Fowler's phrase, from his "Genre and the Literary Canon," may be as out of fashion as the phrase "literary canon." But Fowler did convincingly trace at least the prevailing hierarchical attitudes governing relative value in what one should read. Careful readers will notice in nearly every word of the preceding sentence rather old-fashioned and time-worn assumptions of how dominant voices in a culture decide who gets read, and who does not. This volume on Southern Gothic certainly comes from a more enlightened age (as any age must feel itself to be), and ideas of "canon" have thankfully undergone extensive revision since Fowler's article in 1979—thirty-three years before the writing of this introduction. But when one takes a class, or prepares a syllabus, or assembles chapters from various scholars on various writers somehow grouped together, the phrase "time's the enemy" comes to mind. With only so many weeks in a semester, hours in a day, one still runs into moments of choice: what to include, and what to leave out? As I noted in the preface, this volume could not be inclusive on its subject; none could. But what Fowler tackled remains worth tackling: what does one read—and read again; what will be read in other ages, and why? As problematic assumptions around identity have factored into questions of canonicity, so have matters of genre.

If the Gothic carries with it at least a small hint of shame, writers with deeply ambivalent feelings about their identity as "Southern" (often, but at all always "white") often embrace that. The Southern identity that Stecopoulos finds always in relation not only to the North, but also to the rest of the world, he finds in Carson McCullers in particular:

> McCullers herself thought that the gothic mode well suited writers from the region that Jake Blount of *The Heart is a Lonely Hunter* (1940) dubs "the most uncivilized area on the face of this globe." As she argued in 1940 [in "The Russian Formalists and Southern Literature"], the gothic, a brutal form of "moral realism," enabled southern artists to "transpose the painful substance of life around them as accurately as possible." Yet if McCullers believed that the South warranted its own "Gothic school" of literary expression, she also understood that such a school might connect a local literature to national and international themes. (101; McCullers, *Heart* 254; *Russian* 258, 252).

Stecopoulos goes on to list the characters McCullers created from oppressed situations across the globe, from Nazi Germany to the Philippines (101).

We can see again how Southern Gothic therefore must be located not only in relation to a historically hierarchical dominance of an American North within the United States, but also globally. That said, as Walsh and Marshall also make clear in this volume, the legacy of slavery remains endemic to the problematic identity of the South, so that its location seems once again more relatively local, and again relational to the North. Naming that "geography of race and region," Thadious Davis chooses "southscape" as a term that

> references landscape in broad geographical-social contexts and mediated symbolic structures. As a concept, "southscape" has both subjective and objective elements, but primarily it acknowledges the connection between society and environment as a way of thinking about how raced human beings are impacted by the shape of the land. (2)

Davis sees the "politics of location" as making possible "a connection . . . between a spatial organization and racialized voices and, by means of that connection, a reformulation of marginalization and domination form an alternative perspective" (3).

If we put this in terms of Southern Gothic, we might imagine an ironically privileged view (something called "standpoint epistemology" in feminist philosophy of science), here from the bottom up. Not only the racial other, but the even more generally deviant other that erupts against the putative rationality of "marginalization and domination," comes back to haunt, as it were, the dominant culture of slavery and segregation, but also the relatively mild dehumanization of rampant consumerism we began with above, with Deleuze and Guattari.

Such an appropriation of Davis's "southscapes" risks the offense of burdening and simultaneously stealing from a primarily "racialized" vision for a larger project. But what Davis achieves in a spatial, rather than chronological, identification of southscape promises much. Davis reads segregation as the primary subject for New Southern studies. Understanding segregation in spatial terms means understanding the creation of putative binaries of race, to be sure. In as much as those binaries prove to be, as Davis notes, unstable, we may nonetheless hope for a spatial attention to the South in larger terms that might bring together previously incommensurable narratives of the South as a place lost to its people, whatever their identity, in other than regionally confining spatial terms.

Many Gothic texts set in the South do just that, such as the DC Comics *Swamp Thing* read by Qiana J. Whitted. As she notes, the creature Swamp Thing began as a white scientist transformed by a lab explosion, but Alan Moore "reconceptualiz[es] the character's physiological structure as sentient plant matter," retaining nothing of the white scientist except this: his *"consciousness."* The creature therefore becomes a racialized memory wholly identified with the "swamps he was the Thing of," as Whitted quotes Moore (187). This renders the character a spatial memory and, indeed, Whitted goes on to connect the function of the character with Morrison's "rememory" in *Beloved* (188)—which is discussed in this volume by Sharon Decker. For Whitted, "Swamp Thing's encounter with the South ultimately furnish[es] the material horrors of black enslavement with psychological resonance. Multiple codes of signification . . . coalesce around the discourses of nature, moral reciprocity, and memory that are central" to this comic series (189).

Spatially, of course, this example provides us with another descent, particularly as in swamps, more than in Walden's pond, the bottom is hard to find. Whitted focuses on an American Gothic line of stories in the comic, particularly on episodes where zombie slaves rise up on their former plantation. Her points on zombie identity in this Southern Gothic text will prove relevant to my reading of Cormac McCarthy's *The Road*. Spatially, that book presents the threat of seemingly white zombies both in the open spaces of the novel and in an ironic (and, oddly, a presumably postracial) opposition in the main house of a former plantation. The space of zombies as both monsters and victims is most centrally located in that house's cellar.

Gothic space of course includes attics and other higher architectural places, but even those are places of figurative descent: below the normative, below consciousness, below social control; in this sense, "below" can become "beyond" as well. As the lineage of Gothic works in early American literature often reveal, the Gothic can be found particularly out there in the savage woods—a problematic distinction, of course, but one that recurs in the literature still influenced by Puritans who felt themselves camped out on the edge of wilderness and charged with achieving nothing less than a New Canaan.

Rather than locating a central American Gothic in opposition to some subset we call "Southern," however, we might actually find—by triangulating the historical dominance of both geographical architectonics of value that place the South always below the North, alongside the historical marginalization of genres such as Gothic—the location not only of Southern Gothic, but also of an ironically advantageous point of view for understanding American literature and culture. Not the only one—as any scholar of the American West would be quick to remind us—but certainly one whose tropes and themes (much as those of the American West) so inform the supposedly nongeneric genre of mainstream literature as to have become a central thread.

As New Southern scholars have found race, gender, and geographical concerns well beyond the borders of the United States to be critical in understanding Southern literature, so too have scholars of Southern Gothic. We end up spatially inside out, finding our culture so regularly trading in Gothic—and often Southern Gothic—tropes and images that the old hierarchies of genre and regionalism fall away. And if Nelson is right, a new Gothicka of promise will continue, its postapocalyptic zombie walks and other attempts at outmaneuvering capitalist subsumption as desperate, perhaps, as the inhabitants of a house beset by zombies.

Poorly crafted works of any art, regardless of geographic origin or generic classification, may find temporary audiences, but not long-lasting ones. Put another way, all great works transcend their region and their genre, even if they retain the most powerful aspects of their regional origin and their generic features. Most of the works studied in this volume have already stood that test of time; others we have bet on by including attention to them here.

Generally, Specifically, and Relatively *South*

The Gothic itself proves to be universal. Like the tunnels of Guillermo del Toro's horrifically dark 2006 film *Pan's Labyrinth* and Hayao Miyazaki's beautiful 1988 film *My Neighbor Totoro*, dark spaces have always run under the quotidian. As with darker backyards, socioeconomically and educationally depressed neighborhoods, and lightless alleys, that darkness need not be spatially below its lighter complement—though, as much writing on the Gothic finds, it often is. It can simply lie there in the apparently undisturbed grass on a walk home through a field, like the severed human ear found by the main character of *Blue Velvet*. The director of that 1986 movie, David Lynch, spent formative years in the South, and although his family moved frequently, he claims a happy childhood. But describing a cherry tree from his childhood, Lynch found "millions of red ants crawling all over it. I discovered that if one looks a little closer at this beautiful world, there are *always* red ants underneath. Because I grew up in a perfect world, other things were a contrast" (Rodley 1, 11).

Many who grew up in the South, myself included, would not dream of describing our particular neighborhoods, and certainly not the darkness beyond our fences, as "perfect." Dark tunnels and passages run everywhere, but the South also has, for many reasons, an extra share of them. Both from within the region's generative historical and cultural legacy (that is to say, in both positive and negative mythology), and from without, as the regional South became the scapegoat, among an entire national history of slavery and only slightly more subtle subjugation, for that horror. Not only in terms of race, but also every other aspect of social identity and conflict, the South has become the synecdochic repository for sexism, ignorance, willful anti-intellectualism, poverty, rural parochialism, and sexual deviance. If aimed and coded carefully enough, jokes at the expense of a few of its poorest people remain one of the few acceptable clichés allowed by otherwise proper audiences. Even so, the worst appeals to the persistent racism, sexism, and fear among many of those people (and we more enlightened readers and viewers) continue to find resonance in larger popular culture.

Wherever the readers of this volume grew up, they will find in the dark spaces of the complex works explored here monsters we are all tempted to see as the other. But as is always the case with monsters, they turn out to be us. So, too, the South remains one of the underground passages of America, a Gothic passage where what we would prefer to forget will not stay buried. Where we end up reveals more than a mere trip down South; more than mere celebration, condemnation, or even commemoration, Southern Gothic provides a means of looking deeply around the larger, still dark neighborhood we all share.

Notes

1. See Harris, Charlaine. The "Sookie Stackhouse" novels, twelve as of this writing.

Works Cited

Blue Velvet. Dir. David Lynch. Screenplay by David Lynch. 1986. MGM, 2000. DVD.

Brown, Charles Brockden. *Edgar Huntly Or, Memoirs of a Sleep-Walker*. New York: Penguin, 1988. Print.

Canavan, Gerry. "'We *Are* the Walking Dead': Race, Time, and Survival in Zombie Narrative." *Extrapolation: A Journal of Science Fiction and Fantasy* 51.3 (2010): 431–53. Print.

Chorley, Henry Fothergill. Rev. of *Moby Dick; or, The Whale*, by Herman Melville. *Athenaeum* 25 Oct. 1851: 112–13. Print.

Davis, Thadious M. *Southscapes: Geographies of Race, Region, & Literature*. Chapel Hill: U of North Carolina P, 2011. Print.

Deleuze, Gilles, and Félix Guattari. *Anti-Oedipus: Capitalism and Schizophrenia*. Trans. Robert Hurley, Mark Seem, and Helen R. Lane. Minneapolis: U of Minnesota P, 1983. Print.

Faulkner, William. *The Sound and the Fury*. Ed. David Minter. 2nd ed. New York: Norton, 1994. Print.

___. *Absalom, Absalom!: The Corrected Text*. New York: Modern Lib., 1993. Print.

Fay, Jennifer. "Dead Subjectivity: *White Zombie*, Black Baghdad." *CR: The New Centennial Review* 8.1 (2008): 81–101. Print.

Fowler, Alastair. "Genre and the Literary Canon." *New Literary History* 11.1 (1979): 97–119. Print.

Freud, Sigmund. *Beyond the Pleasure Principle*. Trans. and ed. James Strachey. New York: Norton, 1989. Print.

Greeson, Jennifer Rae. *Our South: Geographic Fantasy and the Rise of National Literature*. Cambridge: Harvard UP, 2010. Print.

Hall, Stephen S. *Mapping the Next Millennium: The Discovery of New Geographies*. New York: Random, 1992. Print.

Hawthorne, Nathaniel. *The House of Seven Gables*. Ed. Robert Levine. New York: Norton, 2005. Print.

Kirkman, Robert, writer. *The Walking Dead*. Berkeley: Image Comics, 2003–2010. Print.

Kordas, Ann. "New South, New Immigrants, New Women, New Zombies: The Historical Development of the Zombie in American Popular Culture." *Race, Oppression and the Zombie: Essays on the Cross-Cultural Appropriations of the Caribbean Tradition*. Ed. Christopher M. Moreman and Cory James Rushton. Jefferson: McFarland, 2011. Print.

Marshall, Bridget M. *The Transatlantic Gothic Novel and the Law, 1790–1860*. Burlington: Ashgate, 2011. Print.

McCullers, Carson. *The Heart is a Lonely Hunter*. Boston: Houghton, 1940. Print.

___. "The Russion Formalists and Southern Literature." *The Mortgaged Heart*. Ed. Margarita Smith. New York: Mariner, 2001. Print.

Moore, Alan, writer. "Strange Fruit." *Swamp Thing #42*. Art by John Totleben and Ron Randall. New York: DC Comics, 1985. Print.

Moore, Alan, writer. "Southern Change." *Swamp Thing #41*. Art by Stephen Bissette, and Alfredo Alcala. New York: DC Comics, 1985. Print.

My Neighbor Totoro [*Tonari no Totoro*]. Dir. Hayao Miyazaki. Screenplay by Hayao Miyazaki. 1988. Disney, 2010. DVD.

Nelson, Victoria. *Gothicka: Vampire Heroes, Human Gods, and the New Supernatural*. Cambridge: Harvard UP, 2012. Print.

Pan's Labyrinth [*El Laberinto del fauno*]. Dir. Guillermo del Toro. Screenplay by Guillermo del Toro. 2006. New Line, 2007. DVD.

Rodley, Chris, ed. *Lynch on Lynch*. Boston: Faber, 1997. Print.

Scholes, Robert. "On Realism and Genre." *NOVEL: A Forum on Fiction* 2.3 (1969): 269–71. Print.

Seabrook, William B. *The Magic Island*. New York: Lit. Guild of Amer., 1929. Print.

Shaviro, Steven. *The Cinematic Body*. Minneapolis: U of Minnesota P, 1993. Print.

Stecopoulos, Harilaos. *Reconstructing the World: Southern Fictions and U.S. Imperialisms, 1898–1976*. Ithaca: Cornell UP, 2008. Print.

Tuttleton, James. *Vital Signs: Essays on American Literature and Criticism*. Chicago: Dee, 1996. Print.

Walking Dead, The. AMC. 2010–2012. Television.

White Zombie. Dir. Victor Halperin. Screenplay by Garnett Weston. Perf. Bela Lugosi. 1932. Roan, 1999. DVD.

Whitted, Qiana J. "Of Slaves and Other Swamp Things: Black Southern History as Comic Book Horror." *Comics and the U.S. South*. Ed. Brannon Costello and Qiana J. Whitted. Jackson: UP of Mississippi, 2012. Print.

CRITICAL
CONTEXTS

Defining Southern Gothic_____

Bridget M. Marshall

The term "Southern Gothic" has long been used to refer to a particular subspecies of American Gothic, which itself is a subspecies of the Gothic, a genre of much-contested boundaries. Dating back to Horace Walpole's *The Castle of Otranto* (1764), the Gothic typically featured moldering castles, treacherous villains, distressed damsels, and dark secrets; the Gothic has proven to be a remarkably flexible genre that has adapted and flourished in a variety of countries across many centuries. Just as the term "Gothic" was originally used as a pejorative (in the sense that it was perceived as barbaric and superstitious), the earliest use of the term "Southern Gothic" was similarly dismissive. The phrase "the Southern Gothic school" first appeared in 1935 in a *Saturday Review* article by novelist Ellen Glasgow, who used the term negatively to refer to the writings of Erskine Caldwell and William Faulkner, which she believed were filled with "aimless violence" and "fantastic nightmares" (360, 357).[1] The negative connotation initially was so strong that some authors even wished to not be included in the category of Southern Gothic at all; Eudora Welty, for one, insisted, "They better not call me that!" (qtd. in Donaldson 567). But "Southern Gothic," like the Gothic more generally, eventually came to be a less derogatory term and is now much more widely used and generally applied to literature dating back to the nineteenth century. David Punter and Glennis Byron describe Southern Gothic as "investigating madness, decay and despair, and the continuing pressures of the past upon the present, particularly with respect to the lost ideals of a dispossessed Southern aristocracy and to the continuance of racial hostilities" (116–17). While "Southern Gothic" is a term readily recognized in popular culture, it has not been the focus of extensive literary criticism.[2]

Scholars of the Gothic point to the time period of 1760 to 1820 as the heyday of the "classic" British Gothic;[3] these "classics" include such titles as Ann Radcliffe's *The Mysteries of Udolpho* (1794) and

The Italian (1797), Matthew Lewis's *The Monk* (1796), Mary Shelley's *Frankenstein* (1816), and Robert Maturin's *Melmouth the Wanderer* (1820), among many, many others. This rise was followed by a secondary rise in the 1890s, consisting of Robert Louis Stevenson's *Strange Case of Dr Jekyll and Mr Hyde* (1886), Oscar Wilde's *The Picture of Dorian Gray* (1891), and Bram Stoker's *Dracula* (1897), among others. Some of the earliest American Gothic texts include the novels of Charles Brockden Brown —in particular *Wieland* (1798) and *Edgar Huntly* (1799)—and those of Nathaniel Hawthorne, particularly *The House of the Seven Gables* (1851). Southern Gothic then sprouts from this American Gothic in the mid-nineteenth century, with both long- and short-form fiction written by Edgar Allan Poe, William Gilmore Simms, and others.

Gothic features are also apparent in many texts that may not entirely fit the traditional model of the Gothic novel. Both fiction and nonfiction texts of the mid-nineteenth century focused on slavery, as in Harriet Beecher Stowe's *Uncle Tom's Cabin* (1852) and William and Ellen Crafts's *Running a Thousand Miles for Freedom* (1860).[4] Although many critics view the Gothic as primarily (some would say exclusively) a prose form, the Gothic also features in poetry and in drama; both poetry (especially that of Poe) and drama (especially that of Tennessee Williams) are essential to an understanding of Southern Gothic, as David Rothman and Tanfer Emin Tunc argue in other essays in this collection. Southern Gothic continued to expand across multiple forms in the early- and mid-twentieth century, particularly in the fiction of William Faulkner, Carson McCullers, and Flannery O'Connor, and in the poetry of Donald Justice and James Dickey; the genre has continued to flourish into the twenty-first century.

Numerous early critics of the Gothic proposed satirical "recipes" for Gothic novels that pointed to the conventional settings, plots, and characters of the genre; one such recipe from 1797 proposed the following elements as essential ingredients:

- An old castle, half of it ruinous

- A long gallery, with a great many doors, some secret ones.

- Three murdered bodies, quite fresh.

- As many skeletons, in chests and presses.

- An old woman hanging by the neck; with her throat cut.

- Assassins and desperadoes '*quant suff.*'

- Noise, whispers, and groans, threescore at least. ("Terrorist Novel Writing" 183)

A Southern take on this recipe only requires a few substitutions and adjustments. Much as the English might not recognize the Southern beverage known as "sweet tea" as being any relative to the British institution of tea, Southern Gothic is perhaps a distant cousin of its British ancestor, but it still nonetheless shows a family resemblance. As the following sections will detail, changes in the setting, the villain, and the victim all allow for the transportation of an iconic British Gothic genre to the American South. Southern Gothic also evinces a particular focus on the South's history of slavery, a fixation with the grotesque, and a tension between realistic and supernatural elements.

The Gothic Setting: From Castle to Plantation

British Gothic novels frequently placed the horrors of their tales not in England, but on foreign soil, likely Italy or France. Early writers in the Southern Gothic tradition also engaged in a similar displacement of the setting onto foreign shores. In "The Oval Portrait" (1842), Poe not only sets his story in Italy, but also references classic Gothic novelist Ann Radcliffe as the story opens with the narrator describing "one of those piles of commingled gloom and grandeur which have so long frowned among the Appenines [*sic*], not less in fact than in the fancy of Mrs. Radcliffe" (*Selected Writings* 296). Poe's "The Cask of Amontillado" (1846) is set in Italy, and his "The Masque of the Red Death" (1842) similarly appears to be set in medieval or Renaissance Europe, where Prince Prospero can retire to his well-protected (he thinks) "castellated abbeys" (*Selected Writings* 300). William Gilmore Simms sets one of his chilling Gothic tales, "Matilda; or, The Spectre of the Castle" (1846) in Germany. While later Southern Gothic, especially from the twentieth and twenty-first centuries, is identified by its specific setting within the American South, that was not always a necessary element of the Gothic for writers who called the American South home.

British Gothic novels derive a considerable amount of their gloom-and-doom mood from the location of the action: Gothic heroines frequently await their fate (whether good or bad) in dark, dreary halls of ancestral palaces, cloisters, monasteries, or other large and imposing architectural structures. Indeed, the literary term "Gothic" is related to the architectural style described as Gothic, which is seen primarily in churches; the primary feature of Gothic architecture is its well-known pointed arches. The Gothic architectural style was revived in the late eighteenth century, with Horace Walpole serving as its principal champion at the same time that he was the instigator of the literary genre, which he christened the "Gothic story." Even his book's title—*The Castle of Otranto*—makes clear that the architecture itself is essential to the tale. Walpole's novel is filled with details about the castle that prove important to its plot, particularly its "subterraneous passage," "several intricate cloisters," its doors with "rusty hinges," and so on (82). These aspects of the setting add to the dark, creepy mood and heighten the anxiety of the protagonists (and the readers). Kate Ferguson Ellis argues that the Gothic "can be distinguished by the presence of houses in which people are locked in and locked out" (3). Thus, the specific design of the building—whether a cloister, abbey, castle, or other form—is not as important as the fact that the building itself can be a source of terror, as it represents powerful social and economic structures that have survived over several generations.

What the American South lacks in medieval castles, it makes up for with plantations, often sprawling and in varying degrees of decrepitude.

The physical architecture of these once grand plantations also works metaphorically, alluding to the dark history of these buildings and grounds. Gothic tales typically include a backstory that reveals the true history of such buildings, including the torture, rape, and other crimes committed against black slaves by their white masters. Actual slave plantations, as well as their renderings in Gothic fiction, frequently featured secret rooms and even spaces specifically used for the punishment of slaves. Secret rooms that hide evidence of criminal acts (frequently dead bodies) are the stock in trade of the Gothic. The Southern Gothic provides numerous examples for secret rooms, as in William Gilmore Simms's *Castle Dismal; or, The Bachelor's Christmas* (1844), in which the narrator must spend a night in a "haunted chamber" of an ancestral mansion. These rooms are also seen in several of Poe's works, including "The Tell-Tale Heart" (1843), with the body under floorboards; "The Black Cat" (1843), with the woman's body walled up (along with the cat) in the basement; or "The Cask of Amontillado," in which the narrator walls up his nemesis in the catacombs of his palazzo. There are literal skeletons in the closet (or in the secret rooms) of the Southern Gothic. This feature echoes later in Southern Gothic in tales such as William Faulkner's "A Rose for Emily" (1930).

The Southern plantation also serves well as a replacement for the more traditional Gothic castle because of its symbolic reference to a fallen aristocracy. Much as decrepit castles allude to an earlier generation's fall from wealth and power, so the destitute state of the Southern plantation in the post–Civil War period refers to the history of the planter class and, indeed, of the American South more generally. The physical space of the plantation (like that of the castle) echoes the fallen nature of the inhabitants with its many rooms, once beautiful but now disintegrating. These buildings hearken back to a lost past; the fact that they will never be restored, but only continue to decay often motivates the offspring of the aristocratic class and serves as a visible punishment to the untamed and ultimately ruinous power of the earlier generation. Critic Margie Burns cites the prevalence throughout

Southern Gothic of "secretive enclosures: darkened rooms with drawn blinds and wisteria crawling over their windows, New Orleans-style wrought-iron grillwork sheltering yet-undescribed Creole mysteries, shadowy verandas and backyards behind massed azaleas, distant woods at the edges of fields of stubble, and so forth" (117). Such details create the "local color" of the American South, which provides a more local—and even realistic—setting for an American version of the Gothic.

The Gothic Villain: From Aristocrat to Master

The typical British Gothic villain is a man with a considerable amount of social power, prestige, and sometimes wealth; Gothic villains are often of noble lineage (or at least are believed to be so). The villain of Walpole's *Otranto* is the king, Manfred; Radcliffe's *The Italian* features friar Schedoni and her *Mysteries of Udolpho* features Montoni (who pretends to be an Italian nobleman) and Count Morano (who is an Italian nobleman without means); Lewis's *The Monk* features Ambrosio, a highly regarded monk of the Catholic Church. These men—and they are usually, though not always, men—engage in a range of villainy that is typically motivated at least in part by pride—pride in their own family line or power or pride simply in their own ability to manipulate and victimize others. As inaugurated by Walpole's novel, a primary theme of the Gothic is a concern that "the sins of fathers are visited upon their children" (61). Thus, readers see villains who have usurped power, who are descended from those who have usurped power, or who are otherwise overreaching in their position of privilege.

Typically, villains in British Gothic violate not merely laws of state, but also profound social taboos that are seen as violations against nature—in particular, the crime of incest. Walpole's Manfred plans to divorce his wife and marry his son's fiancée in an attempt to maintain his family's ill-gotten legacy, which his great-grandfather usurped by killing the real ruler of Otranto. Ann Radcliffe's Schedoni has killed his brother in the past and plans to kill Ellena, who he later believes to be his daughter (but who turns out to be his niece). Lewis's Ambrosio kills a woman who turns out to be his mother, and rapes and kills a woman who he later finds out is his sister. Such incestuous crimes—and the lack of recognition of one's own family members—are frequently the focus of Southern Gothic, in no small part because the system of slavery in the American South encouraged masters to rape slaves, and the offspring of those slaves were often raped as well. The sexual violation of slaves was further aggravated by the fact that masters would frequently sell the offspring of their slaves, even when they knew these offspring to be their own children. The Gothic's obsession with the "sins of fathers" and with the revelation of unknown or obscured family trees fits well with the severely damaged family situations that resulted from the system of American slavery. William Faulkner's masterpiece of Southern Gothic, *Absalom, Absalom!* (1936), features Thomas Sutpen, a classic Southern Gothic villain, who attempts to create his own Southern dynasty but ultimately is the cause of ruin for his estate and his heirs.

Gothic villains are frequently mesmerizing. While they commit terrible acts, they are often seen as compelling figures; other characters within the stories, as well as the readers, are frequently taken in by the often handsome, always domineering Gothic villain. Sometimes called the "Byronic villain," this figure is attractive and able to dissemble so as to entrap his victim. A Southern Gothic version of this figure can be seen in characters such as Poe's Montresor, who, in "The Cask of Amontillado," befriends and "smile[s] in [the] face" of his nemesis, who "did not perceive that my smile *now* was at the thought of his immolation" (*Selected Writings* 415). Villains who disguise themselves as innocents are that much more terrifying, as with the creepy villain of Flannery O'Connor's "Good Country People" (1955); when the victim meets him, she believes she is "face to face with real innocence" (202), but in fact, the man leads her to a secluded place and steals her glasses and prosthetic leg. O'Connor's villains are typically men who act heartlessly and often violently, without any compunction, as with her character the Misfit, the murderer who appears in her story "A Good Man is Hard to Find" and explains that there is "no pleasure but meanness" (22). There are numerous variations on the villain in the Southern Gothic, but a central "meanness" runs throughout these characters.

Southern Gothic—and indeed, American Gothic generally and later Gothic altogether—takes a turn toward the psychological in its portrayal of the minds of villains. As early as Poe's writing, we can see this development, particularly in his "Berenice" (1835), "The Tell-Tale Heart," or "The Black Cat," all of which feature first-person narration from the point of view of a character wrestling with mental disorder and committing violence against innocents. Faulkner's novels and short stories also frequently feature characters who are wrestling with mental illness, which can be both the cause and the result of Gothic horrors. Both villains and victims are often beset with psychological stresses that lead to mental collapse, and these symptoms are typically antagonized by the pressures of the grim, even terrifying Gothic setting. Both villains and victims in the Southern Gothic frequently suffer from mental illness, which typically worsens over the course of the story, sparking further violence and death. The blurring of the line between villain and victim is a key development of Southern Gothic.

The Gothic Victim: From Maiden in Peril to . . . Maiden in Peril

The traditional Gothic villain would have no fun at all if it were not for the (usually feminine) screams of his victim. Southern Gothic, too, typically features victims of the female sex. Poe's stories and poems frequently feature beautiful but doomed women, as with Madeline in "The Fall of the House of Usher" (1839), Lenore in "The Raven" (1845), and the title character of "Annabel Lee" (1849); many of these poor ladies are also touched with madness, much like the villains of the tales. But the victims in Southern Gothic can also be male: Carson McCullers's character Spiros Antonapoulos in *The Heart is a Lonely Hunter* (1940) exhibits signs of mental illness, after which he is placed in an asylum where his imprisonment could rightfully be described as torture; it eventually kills him. This motif of madness also appears elsewhere in later Southern Gothic, as in Faulkner's "A Rose for Emily," wherein the title character not only kills her lover, but then sleeps with his dead body for many years afterward. While the fact that Emily Grierson committed murder might make her a villain by some standards, we might also see Emily as a victim of her father or even of restrictive gender and social roles in the American South. In any case, she is clearly out of her mind, a feature of many Gothic victims and villains alike.

In the Southern Gothic, perhaps more so than in other strains of the Gothic, the villain often ultimately becomes the victim of his own plans. Faulkner's novels are filled with characters with glorious (often deranged) plans that fail miserably, ruining the protagonist and his family. In this way, some Southern Gothic villains may be considered victims of their own debauchery.

Slavery and the Southern Gothic

The horror of the system of American slavery is perhaps the most insistent and recurrent theme of Southern Gothic. One way or another, America's history of slavery, racial violence, and racial inequality lie at the heart of Southern Gothic. There are gestures toward the issue of slavery in British Gothic; as Meredith Miller explains, "late eighteenth- and nineteenth- century British Gothic drew heavily on the culture of slavery" (135). But in Southern Gothic, it is full-blown and central. Walpole's *Otranto* and many early British Gothics are filled with "domestics" who are superstitious, act foolishly in the face of danger, and provide comic relief for a tension-filled moment. Within some depictions of domestic servants, there were certainly critiques of the social and economic class structures that underpinned the separation of servants and masters. But as the Gothic developed, so too did the genre's ability to develop more serious critiques of profound social problems, particularly the profound injustice of slavery and the slave trade. Among other critics, Kari Winters argues that Gothic novels frequently engaged with the theme of slavery. This is perhaps most notable in the work of Matthew Lewis, author of the infamous *The Monk*, who himself owned a slave plantation. [5] The connections between abolitionist writing about slavery and the depiction of slavery in the Gothic are clear; as Lesley Ginsberg argues in "Slavery and the Gothic Horror of Poe's 'The Black Cat,'" Poe depicts "the struggle between a helpless dependent and an abusive tyrant which figures so prominently in both gothic fictions and abolitionist discourses" (99). The fictional horrors of the Gothic were all too frequently reflecting the real horrors of longstanding social and economic institutions like slavery.

As Robert Martin explains in "Haunted by Jim Crow: Gothic Fictions by Hawthorne and Faulkner," Hawthorne's and Faulkner's novels (representing, perhaps, Northern and Southern strains of American Gothic), both focus on "stolen land and bartered bodies," a fact that "locate[s] the gothic as a national repressed, a series of crimes that are not incidental to but rather constitutive of the nation" (140). American Gothic more generally is haunted by frequent references to the historical crimes of slavery, the institution that physically built the nation. The collective national guilt about this founding crime is typically seen specifically in tales set in the South. As Teresa A. Goddu explains in her key work, *Gothic America: Narrative, History, and Nation*, "the American gothic is most recognizable as a regional form" (3); in particular, "the American South serves as the nation's 'other,' becoming the repository of everything from which the nation wants to disassociate itself" (3–4). But in true Gothic fashion, the horrors of the past continue to dominate the present.

Southern Gothic can also be seen as overlapping with the popular genre of plantation novels, particularly in the case of those by E. D. E. N. Southworth. One of Southworth's most popular novels, *The Hidden Hand* (1888), hits all the required trappings of the Gothic just in the first few pages, which feature a classic Gothic "large old family mansion" (1) and a perfect Gothic villain with "fierce, dark gray eyes," a "hard, harsh face," and a character "arrogant, domineering, and violent" (2). As Dana Luciano suggests in her discussion of Southworth, "the gothic rage that suffuses these domestic narratives has rarely been recognized" (324), yet Southworth—and perhaps many other works of Southern literature that have yet to be discovered—deserves a place in the tradition of American literature and the Southern Gothic.

The Grotesque

The grotesque—in particular, physical disfigurement of the human body—was a longstanding concern of the Gothic, as seen particularly in such texts as Mary Shelley's *Frankenstein* (1818), Bram Stoker's *Dracula* (1897), and Robert Louis Stevenson's *Dr Jekyll and Mr Hyde* (1886). In all of these texts, characters appear severely disfigured (Frankenstein's monster, the vampire Dracula, and the laboratory creation Hyde) and their physical deformities either indicate or are at least presumed to indicate moral deformity as well. These texts (and many more like them) engage with a troubling human assumption about the ways that appearances match reality: the notion that an attractive appearance indicates that someone is morally good, while an appearance that is ugly or somehow outside cultural or social norms is inherently evil. While some texts, like *Frankenstein*, question this assumption, others, such as *Dracula*, fully embrace the idea that those with bodies physically marked as "other" are to be feared because these visible markers are indications of spiritual and moral failings.

Southern Gothic thrives on the theme of deformity. Critic Peggy Bailey suggests that such grotesque characters "may be the most visible signs of the Southern Gothic" ("Coming Home" 426). Characters with severe physical disfigurements appear throughout the oeuvre, particularly in the work of Flannery O'Connor, who, as Alan Lloyd-Smith claims "created grotesque people and situations born of—but in excess of—their southern context" (121–22). While later Southern Gothic fully engages with the vampire tradition, the genre more broadly embraces the notion of physical "othering" to indicate problematic characters. To be clear, though, the monstrous dwarfs of Poe's "Hop Frog" (1849) and other characters with physical deformities are not simply evil. Indeed, Southern Gothic frequently upends or, at the very least, complicates such biased assumptions, as with the dwarf of Poe's Hop Frog, who commits murder not only because he himself was mal-treated, but also as revenge for violence done to his beloved. While scenes of violence committed by the crippled, maimed, or otherwise disabled characters add further to the grotesque, such scenes are typi-cally portrayed as the reasonable result of the mistreatment borne by the disabled characters at the hands of the "normal" characters.

Realism versus Supernaturalism and the Gothic

Not all Gothic features the supernatural, and neither does all Southern Gothic. When the supernatural appears, it is sometimes equivocally so, with a possibility that it may be the result of an overactive imagination, a drug-induced altered state, or some manner of mental illness. While the genres of realism and the Gothic might seem to be wholly unre-lated, the two actually flourished simultaneously, and many authors wrote in both genres. Southern Gothic in particular frequently engages with real historical events and people; the American Civil War looms large in Southern Gothic. Ambrose Bierce, author of several Gothic tales, fought in battles at Shiloh, and many of his stories, though per-haps embellished, also provide faithful renderings of the real horrors of battle. His particularly Gothic tales of the Civil War include "Oc-currence at Owl Creek Bridge" (1890), in which Peyton Farquhar, a Confederate sympathizer, is executed in Alabama; "Killed at Resaca" (1877), in which Lieutenant Herman Brayle dies quite graphically on the battlefield; and "Chickamauga" (1889), in which a deaf-mute child encounters the gruesomely wounded bodies of soldiers retreating from battle. Even Mark Twain, though mostly known for his realism and humor, also dabbled in the Gothic, perhaps most notably in *The Trag-edy of Pudd'nhead Wilson* (1894), *A Connecticut Yankee in King Ar-thur's Court* (1889), and many of the stories and fragments that were later collected in *The Devil's Racetrack: Mark Twain's "Great Dark" Writings* (Salomon 333). A survey of Southern Gothic literature—particularly looking at key figures such as William Faulkner, Flannery O'Connor, and Carson McCullers—immediately shows that the line between the horrors of the fantastic and the realism of the mundane are deeply intertwined in this genre, or what critic Peggy Bailey refers to as "the realistic tradition of the Southern Gothic" ("Coming Home" 424). As Dana Luciano explains, the Gothic "consistently engages, using gothic tropes and sensational techniques, the agonizing realities of everyday American life—the harsh pressures of market capitalism and the melancholy failures of the democratic ideal—as they etch themselves into the vulnerable bodies caught in narrative webs of seduction, deception, and betrayal" (315). While twenty-first-century Southern Gothic seems to be filled with the vampires of Anne Rice and Charlaine Harris, such supernatural beings are not entirely necessary to create a true Southern Gothic masterpiece.

Just as the more general genre of the Gothic is one of wide variations and contested definitions, defining "Southern Gothic" often devolves to a claim of "I know it when I see it." Ultimately, most of the standard, traditional Gothic tropes are also found in Southern Gothic: creepy buildings, mysterious landscapes, unhealthy obsessions with the past, revelations of dark secrets, acts of violence, and troubled mental states are all the hallmarks of the Gothic more generally, and these all invariably crop up in Southern Gothic as well. Southern Gothic deploys these tropes (and more) in a setting—whether historical or contemporary—that is physically in (or sometimes imaginatively linked to) the American South. Sometimes this setting is quite specific to a particular city or state; such a text may detail the geography, climate, history, and culture of that area, as with the specificity of New Orleans in Anne Rice's vampire novels. But Southern Gothic need not be entirely geographically specific; it can also be deployed through portrayals of more general Southern cultural anxieties: apprehension about race, denial and recovery of historical horrors and disgrace, and grief over cultural or personal loss, as in Cormac McCarthy's postapocalyptic version of the Southern Gothic in *The Road* (2006). Southern Gothic has a profound tie to an often uncanny geographic and cultural place (the American South), but that place is also constantly changing; this provides fertile ground for the writers and readers who engage with this genre.

Notes

1. For more information on Glasgow's article, see Louis Palmer's "Bourgeois Blues" (120–21) and Peggy Dunn Bailey's "Female Gothic Fiction" (270).

2. While Victorian Gothic, American Gothic, postcolonial Gothic, and a host of other subgenres of the Gothic have been the subject of numerous monographs and articles (particularly in the past twenty years), Southern Gothic continues to be a somewhat enigmatic genre: known to exist and to be quite popular, but rarely receiving extensive scholarly attention. The few articles of literary criticism that foreground "Southern Gothic" specifically mention the relative lack of scholarship in this area. See Meredith Miller's "'I Don't Want to be a [White] Girl'" (134) and Margie Burns's "A Good Rose is Hard to Find" (121 n4) in particular.

3. These are the dates proposed by Maggie Kilgour in The Rise of the Gothic Novel (3); many other scholars also refer to these dates as the primary rise.

4. In Gothic Passages, Justin Edwards uses the term "Gothic Slave Narratives" to refer to texts such as William and Ellen Crafts's Running a Thousand Miles for Freedom (35).

5. As Terence Whalen explains in Poe and the Masses, Poe was well aware of Matthew Lewis's works (144).

Works Cited

Bailey, Peggy Dunn. "Coming Home to Scrabble Creek: Saving Grace, Serpent Handling, and the Realistic Southern Gothic." *Appalachian Journal* 38.4 (2011): 424–39. Print.

___. "Female Gothic Fiction, Grotesque Realities, and *Bastard Out of Carolina*: Dorothy Allison Revises the Southern Gothic." *Mississippi Quarterly* 63.1 (2010): 269–90. Print.

Bierce, Ambrose. *The Civil War Short Stories of Ambrose Bierce*. Lincoln: U of Nebraska P, 1988. Print.

Brown, Charles Brockden. *Edgar Huntly; or, Memoirs of a Sleep-Walker*. 1799. New York: Penguin, 1988. Print.

___. *Wieland; or, The Transformation*. 1798. New York: Penguin, 1991. Print.

Burns, Margie. "A Good Rose is Hard to Find: Southern Gothic as Signs of Social Dislocation in Faulkner and O'Connor." *Image and Ideology in Modern/Postmod-*

ern Discourse. Ed. David Downing and Susan Bazargan. Albany: State U of New York P, 1991. Print.

Crafts, William, and Ellen Crafts. *Running a Thousand Miles for Freedom*. 1860. Baton Rouge: Louisiana State UP, 1995. Print.

Donaldson, Susan V. "Making a Spectacle: Welty, Faulkner, and Southern Gothic." *Mississippi Quarterly* 50.4 (1997): 567–84. Print.

Edwards, Justin D. *Gothic Passages: Racial Ambiguity and the American Gothic*. Iowa City: U of Iowa P, 2003. Print.

Ellis, Kate Ferguson. *The Contested Castle: Gothic Novels and the Subversion of Domestic Ideology*. Chicago: U of Illinois P, 1989. Print.

Faulkner, William. "A Rose for Emily." *William Faulkner: Selected Short Stories*. New York: Modern Lib., 2012. 47–59. Print.

___. *Absalom, Absalom!* 1936. New York: Vintage, 1991. Print.

Ginsberg, Lesley. "Slavery and the Gothic Horror of Poe's 'The Black Cat.'" *American Gothic: New Interventions in a National Narrative*. Ed. Robert K. Martin and Eric Savoy. Iowa City: U of Iowa P, 1998. 99–128. Print.

Glasgow, Ellen. "Heroes and Monsters." 1935. *Defining Southern Literature: Perspectives and Assessments, 1831–1952*. Ed. John E. Bassett. Madison: Fairleigh Dickinson UP, 1997. 357–60. Print.

Goddu, Teresa A. *Gothic America: Narrative, History, and Nation*. New York: Columbia UP, 1997. Print.

Hawthorne, Nathaniel. *The House of the Seven Gables*. 1851. New York: Norton, 2005. Print.

Kilgour, Maggie. *The Rise of the Gothic Novel*. London: Routledge, 1995. Print.

Lloyd-Smith, Alan. *American Gothic Fiction: An Introduction*. New York: Continuum, 2004. Print.

Lewis, Matthew. *The Monk*. 1794. Oxford: Oxford UP, 1992. Print.

Luciano, Dana. "The Gothic Meets Sensation: Charles Brockden Brown, Edgar Allan Poe, George Lippard, and E. D. E. N. Southworth." *A Companion to American Fiction 1780–1865*. Ed. Shirley Samuels. Hoboken: Wiley, 2008. 332–48. Print.

Martin, Robert K. "Haunted by Jim Crow: Gothic Fictions by Hawthorne and Faulkner." *American Gothic: New Interventions in a National Narrative*. Ed. Robert K. Martin and Eric Savoy. Iowa City: U of Iowa P, 1998. 129–42. Print.

Maturin, Charles Robert. *Melmoth the Wanderer*. 1820. New York: Penguin, 2001. Print.

McCullers, Carson. *The Heart is a Lonely Hunter*. 1940. New York: Houghton, 2010. Print.

Miller, Meredith. "'I Don't Want to be a [White] Girl': Gender, Race and Resistance in the Southern Gothic." *The Female Gothic: New Directions*. Ed. Diana Wallace and Andrew Smith. New York: Palgrave, 2009. 133–51. Print.

O'Connor, Flannery. *A Good Man is Hard to Find and Other Stories*. 1955. New York: Houghton, 1992. Print.

Palmer, Louis. "Bourgeois Blues: Class, Whiteness, and Southern Gothic in Early Faulkner and Caldwell." *Faulkner Journal* 22.1 (2006): 120–39. Print.

Poe, Edgar Allan. *The Selected Writings of Edgar Allan Poe*. Ed. G. R. Thompson. New York: Norton, 2004. Print.

Punter, David, and Glennis Byron. *The Gothic*. Blackwell, 2004. Print.

Radcliffe, Ann. *The Italian*. 1797. Oxford: Oxford UP, 1986. Print.

___. *The Mysteries of Udolpho*. 1794. Oxford: Oxford UP, 1984. Print.

Salomon, Roger B. "Gothic." *Mark Twain Encyclopedia*. Ed. J. R. LeMaster and James D. Wilson. New York: Garland, 1993. 332–34. Print.

Shelley, Mary. *Frankenstein; or, The Modern Prometheus: The 1818 Text*. Ed. Marilyn Butler. Oxford: Oxford UP, 1998. Print.

Simms, William Gilmore. *Castle Dismal; or, The Bachelor's Christmas*. New York: Burgess, 1844. Print.

___. *Matilda; or, The Spectre of the Castle, an Imaginative Story*. Boston: Gleason, 1846. Print.

Southworth, Emma Dorothy Eliza Nevitte (E. D. E. N.). *The Hidden Hand*. 1859. New York: Oxford UP, 1997. Print.

Stevenson, Robert Louis. *The Strange Case of Dr Jekyll and Mr Hyde*. 1886. New York: Signet, 1987. Print.

Stoker, Bram. *Dracula*. 1897. Ed. Nina Auerbach. New York: Norton, 1997. Print.

Stowe, Harriet Beecher. *Uncle Tom's Cabin*. 1852. Oxford: Oxford UP, 2002. Print.

"Terrorist Novel Writing." 1798. *Gothic Documents: A Sourcebook 1700–1820*. Ed. E. J. Clery and Robert Miles. Manchester: Manchester UP, 2000. 182–84. Print.

Tuckey, John S., ed. *The Devil's Racetrack: Mark Twain's "Great Dark" Writings*. Berkeley: U of California P, 1980. Print.

Twain, Mark. *A Connecticut Yankee in King Arthur's Court*. 1889. Berkeley: U of California P, 1979. Print.

___. *The Tragedy of Pudd'nhead Wilson*. 1894. New York: Penguin, 1969. Print.

Walpole, Horace. *The Castle of Otranto*. *"The Castle of Otranto" and "The Mysterious Mother."* Ed. Frederick S. Frank. Peterboro: Broadview, 2003. Print.

Whalen, Terence. *Poe and the Masses: The Political Economy of Literature in Antebellum America*. Princeton: Princeton UP, 1999. Print.

Wilde, Oscar. *The Picture of Dorian Gray*. 1890. Oxford: Oxford UP, 1990. Print.

"Dark Legacy": Gothic Ruptures in Southern Literature

Christopher J. Walsh

This essay will attempt to answer why the Gothic has been such a durable—and ambiguous—feature in critical discussions of the Southern literary tradition. It will do this by initially (and briefly) sketching some historical and contextual reasons as to why the Gothic plays such an important role in the nation's, but more specifically the region's, critical literary practices. It will then look at the critical discussions surrounding some of its chief practitioners (Edgar Allan Poe, William Faulkner, Flannery O'Connor) and analyze what is arguably the chief critical reason for its continued relevance, namely how it engages with and articulates the South's shameful legacy of slavery and racial segregation. It will conclude by briefly contemporizing the debate and ask if—in a supposedly post-racial, post-regional and most definitely post-Agrarian South—the Gothic has continued relevance to how critical discussions about the region's literature are conducted.

There is no doubt that the Gothic as a mode or genre, much like many of its representative texts, engenders feelings of dread and confusion among readers due to its inherent ambiguity; as the respected Gothic critic David Punter has rightly observed, the Gothic is a term which has "a wide variety of meanings" (1). This is compounded by the fact that literary Gothic is so often associated with locales imbued with a mysterious antiquity. So how can a nation and a region which is supposedly "historyless," which lacks ruins, which stresses rationality, progress , optimism and a belief in the future be said to have a Gothic literary tradition? This paradoxical ambiguity has been observed by Donald Ringe who in his study *American Gothic* acknowledges the following about the nation's founding fathers:

Americans were thoroughly imbued with eighteenth-century thought. They shared a common belief in the primary value of reason, the absur-

---

dity of mythology, and the danger of superstition. They dismissed ghosts, goblins and witches as the relics of a more credulous age and were proud of the fact that American society had been formed when such phenomena were no longer credited and tales of superstition had been relegated to the nursery...If their writing was to reflect the national experience, it would have to be based on a fundamental rationalism and to depict realistically the actualities of American life. (2–3)

Ringe's study explores the contradictory reasons why the Gothic flourished in a nation that placed such a heavy emphasis on Enlightenment values based around the empirical and the rational. We should note that the politically independent nation is almost as old as the genre itself, especially if we accept the common critical assumption that the literary Gothic came into being with the publication of Horace Walpole's novel *The Castle of Otranto* in 1764. So we encounter our first significant paradox here; the nation that espoused equality and freedom also initiated a Gothic tradition that articulated cultural anxieties about denial and marginalization that was a direct result of the culturally enshrined narratives that were meant to have the opposite effect.

The paradoxes keep revealing themselves if we turn our attention to the South. From its very inception the South created a mythology for itself (one thinks of Jefferson's *Notes on the State of Virginia* here with its utopian vision of independent yeoman farmers striving for perfectibility) that was predicated on the vision of a settled, stable and unchanging region based upon agrarian values. The South has always been engaged in its own historical process of mythological construction which counters Ringe's claim in the quote cited above. The old antebellum South was nothing but myth, and its narrative of a supposedly halcyon past concealed all manner of social, familial and of course racial denials and suppressions. All of these progressive cultural narratives naturally have their flipside and the Southern Gothic set to work by exposing their abuses and silences. As Allan Lloyd-Smith has insightfully acknowledged, the Gothic "is about the *return* of the past, of the repressed and denied, the buried secret that subverts and corrodes the present, whatever the culture does not want to know or admit, will not or dare not tell itself," and that Southern (and American Gothic for that matter) subsequently "explores the tensions between a culturally sanctioned progressive optimism and an actual dark legacy" (Lloyd-Smith 1,118).

The final two words from Lloyd-Smith's second quotation ("dark legacy") are obviously loaded with significance for our purposes here. The "dark legacy" explored by Southern Gothicists primarily had to (and still does) engage with the legacy of slavery which stood as the most obvious rebuke to the nation's cultural narratives of equality and rationality. The 'dark legacy' which still informs the Southern Gothic is therefore racial, political, moral, religious, spatial and even environmental in nature. It is ironic that narratives of liberty (be they political, spiritual or spatial) turn out to be narratives that imprison, and this critical debate continues to frame discussions of the region's literature. Reason stifles rather than liberates; "darkness" is racial as much is it moral, and it results in a culturally sanctioned violence; the region's fabled agrarian idyll provide a palimpsest for Gothic settings but they eventually exhaust themselves which results in dispossession and alienation, and what one critic has referred to as the "God-intoxicated atmosphere" of the South has generated a healthy amount of critical attention as practitioners of Southern Gothic subject their characters to often macabre searches for spiritual salvation (Gray 279).

So whilst Southern Gothic may not have had the ruined castles, mysterious Catholic practices or decaying aristocratic dynasties that were utilized by early European literary Gothicists such as Horace Walpole, Anne Radcliffe or Matthew Lewis it did have its own source of blackness, which was "not simply [identified] with evil but with *racial* blackness" (Lloyd-Smith 45).As an imaginative category "blackness" is therefore the central concern in many of the critical discourses about Southern Gothic. In her analysis of the "recovered" text *The Bondswoman's Narrative* Teresa Goddu has claimed that the mode "tells stories of racial desire and dread" and that the Gothic becomes the "mode through which to speak what often remains unspeakable within the American national narrative—the crime of slavery" (63). Goddu continues to make the crucial point that the primary cultural and political anxiety that Southern Gothic seeks to articulate and re- dress is of course slavery, arguing that "the ghostly origins of the na- tion" arise from the "oppressive social structure of slavery" and that a foundational theme of Southern Gothic is the revelation that the nation is "built on economic exploitation and racial terror" (63).

Critical consensus reveals that the novel through which these themes—the terrors of racial subjugation, the legacy of slavery, the persistence of historical memory, the ability of a dark past to rupture contemporary reality and distort reconstituted subjectivities—receives its most sophisticated treatment in Toni Morrison's *Beloved*. We should acknowledge that although large parts of the novel are set in Cincinnati the location of the acute psychological trauma experienced by Sethe and other significant characters is Kentucky and Georgia. The ghostly personification of Beloved, the daughter of Sethe, who chose to kill her rather than expose her to the horrors of slavery, returns to haunt Sethe and her new family where they are supposedly living as "free" citizens. The reappearance of Beloved of course reminds us of the ideological function of the supernatural and ghosts as they "are never just ghosts; they provide us with an insight into what haunts our culture," and it allows Morrison to investigate the legacy of slavery by critiquing bi- narisms such as salve and free, past and present, corporeal and spectral and so on (Smith 153).

Critics have also observed how *Beloved* has made another notable contribution to the Southern Gothic as it shows "American history as a haunted house" (Goddu 63). This achieves two things; Morrison is able to demonstrate through a fragmented and polyphonic narrative structure how the pain of a regional and indeed national trauma can still impede upon individual lives, and it can do that by invading the site (the domestic) that is held up to be an impregnable refuge against such horrors. For Fred Botting this fact accounts for the novel's enduring appeal; "The haunted house, and the ghostly reminder of transgression which inhabits it, provides the scene for a narrative that moves between the past and the present to uncover, in the interweaving of a repressed individual history with a suppressed cultural history, the external and internal effects of racial oppression" (161).

Beloved is also significant in terms of how it contemporized the critical and theoretical approaches to Gothic. This is most evident in how the novel is ripe for what are quite often sophisticated psychoanalytical and postmodernist or poststructuralist readings which focus on the treatment of fragmented subjectivities and how language strains to record (and is perhaps incapable) of documenting the horrors at the heart of the novel. Two ideas from two theorists come to mind here, namely Julia Kristeva's theory of the "abject" and Jacques Lacan's concept of the "Real." For Kristeva the abject can be read as something that "from its place of banishment . . . does not stop challenging its master," and Morrison's novel succeeds in challenging the South's dark "master" narrative of racial subjugation, violence and exclusion (Kristeva 2). Lacan's concept of the Real is arguably more challenging but it allows us to see how the subject matter of *Beloved* demands but also resists representation. Eric Savoy articulates the applicability of the "Real" as follows: "The historical dimension of American Gothic is entirely congruent with the notion of the Real—of the myriad things and amorphous physicality beyond representation that haunt our subjectivity and demand our attention that compel us to explanatory language but resist the strategies of that language" (169). Whilst undoubtedly complex and harrowing the overview of responses to *Beloved* allows us to see how Southern Gothic is able to maintain an engaging historicist interest through its articulation of a deep-rooted cultural anxiety; it also demonstrates Gothic's continued relevance to contemporary critical debates.

We will now jump back in historical terms to consider the critical reception of Edgar Allan Poe. Poe's work demonstrates how the Gothic mode was ideally suited to the emerging artistic and political consciousness of the region, and he left an indelible mark on the development of the genre in a manner that would reach far beyond the geographical confines of the South. Poe's biography reveals him to be something of a doomed Gothic character, a figure had his own demons and hauntings and whose own relation to the South was somewhat mysterious. In *Southern Aberrations: Writers of the American South and the Problems of Regionalism* Richard Gray claims that Poe was "someone who was not even born in the South but chose nevertheless to perceive himself in Southern terms" and that Poe "played many parts over the course of just over forty years: but the part to which he was most fiercely and consistently attached was that of the Southern gentleman" (2–3). This is significant because [Southern] Gothic is a mode known for its constructedness, if you will, for its very knowing ability to play with its identity and conventions, to undermine hierarchies and subjectivities, and Poe engaged in exactly the same performative way when creating his own "Southern" identity. Despite this, Poe successfully and repeatedly managed to tap into "many of the secret fears and guilts of his region" (15).

One of the central thematic tensions at the heart of the rise of Southern (and indeed American Gothic) is how it deconstructs cultural narratives which promote an unassailable belief in rational, progressive values. This has been remarked upon by many commentators of the Gothic but it is most succinctly expressed by Alan Lloyd-Smith who claimed that for Poe "the interplay between reason and horror released the energies of his most powerful work," and that the "crisis or breakdown of reason gave Poe his great themes" (67–8). This can be seen repeatedly in his work but it his short stories including The Fall of the House of Usher, William Wilson and The Black Cat that have perhaps attracted the most attention in this regard.

Of course what also cements Poe's place as one of the leading practitioners of Southern Gothic is his treatment of race, of the region's "dark legacy." Eric Savoy is a critic who has offered insightful analysis on this aspect of Poe's aesthetic and he observes that:

. . . several of his most celebrated texts are rightly understood now as a profound meditation upon the cultural significance of 'blackness' in the white American mind. A surprising amount of Poe's work may be said to Gothicize the deep oppression and violence inherent in his culture's whiteness and thus to transform America's normative race into the most monstrous of them all. (182)

For Savoy this process is particularly apparent in a story such as "The Black Cat" in which "blackness allegorizes not merely a personal (or even cultural) melancholia, as it does in 'The Raven,' but the abject underside of a national 'normality'" (Savoy 182). Poe's value to the development of the Southern Gothic can therefore be attributed to his ability to destabilize hierarchies of order and to critique the South's prevailing mythology and narrative. It is perhaps somewhat ironic that Poe was apparently so easily seduced by the myth of the aristocratic South that he adopted its mores and yet his fiction seeks to continually subvert the Gothic practices that this mythology sought to reinforce.

Poe also made significant contributions to the stylistic development of the Gothic as a mode or a genre, innovations that were perhaps initiated by his fascination with the South but which would ultimately have a far greater geographical influence. This has been acknowledged by David Punter who claims that Poe's "greatest contribution was in terms not of themes but of structure and tone in which he has never been surpassed" (202). These elements of structural and tonal innovation are elaborated upon by Botting who claims the following for Poe's legacy:

The various devices, styles and subjects that Poe uses and transforms influence all subsequent Gothic writing: the doubles, mirrors and the concern with modes of representation; the scientific transgressions of accepted limits; the play of internal and external narrations, of uncertain psychological states and uncanny events; and the location of mysteries in a criminal world to be penetrated by the incisive reason a new hero, the detective, have become staples of the Gothic. (122–23)

This leads us onto the figure who stalks the imaginative and critical landscapes of the Southern Gothic, monstrously haunting the creative process and the manner in which we try and talk about the region's literature. We are of course referring to William Faulkner here, the Nobel Prize winning author of such novels as *The Sound and the Fury*, *As I Lay Dying*, *Light in August* and *Absalom! Absalom!* and short stories such as "A Rose for Emily" which is so frequently held up as an exemplar of the Southern Gothic tradition. As the Southernist Martyn Bone quite rightly identifies, authors and critics always have to be aware of the "looming presence of Faulkner" (155).

It is perhaps with the creation of Yoknapatawpha County and the series of novels beginning with *The Sound and the Fury* that marks Faulkner's greatest contribution to the development of the Southern Gothic. There is a vast amount of critical material available about his work but our (admittedly extremely brief) focus here will acknowledge two main aspects to this critical practice; his use of geographical representations to develop a usable spatial imaginative repository for the Southern Gothic mode and his highly modernistic use of language which creates the impression that "there is no exit from the darkly illuminating labyrinth of language" (Botting 14.).

Faulkner did set some of his work in locations other than Yoknapatawpha County (novels such as *Soldiers' Pay* and *Mosquitoes* are located in Virginia and New Orleans, for example) but it is the novels set in his postage stamp of soil that do so much to develop the Southern Gothic. Indeed of his nineteen novels "all but five are set, in large part, in a notional county" (Godden 436). The continued importance of this "notional county" to Faulkner's aesthetic allowed him to create a palimpsest of "haunted swamps, lost plantations, and defeated southern towns [that] offer a Gothic landscape comparable to the ruins of feudalism in English Gothic" (Lloyd-Smith 117). Faulkner's fiction charts the progression from pre– to post–Civil War territories, from premodern to modernized, and one of the great "terrors" of his work—aside from the spectral spatial locales highlighted above—is generated by the economic transformation of the South. Whilst this process may not sound particularly Gothic it resulted in his characters being subjected to phenomena such as alienation, fragmentation and uprootedness which are nonetheless familiar to many Gothic protagonists. This rupture between the past and the present, between a past that was naively imagined and mythologized and a present that is subject to painful social, racial and economic transformations, is an archetypal moment for Southern Gothic where the "dark legacy" of the past clashes with psychological and geographical concerns of the present. Faulkner's fiction therefore attests to how the Gothic can engage in unfolding cultural debates, as acknowledged by Richard Godden; "Faulkner turns to the painfully protracted creation of a global allegory at the historical moment when *his* South, held together by issues of dependency, comes apart; when its inherently cohering center, a regime of accumulation founded on coerced labor, is abruptly modernized by a regional shift towards a waged economy" (450).

One of the most celebrated and critically discussed aspects of Faulkner's aesthetic is his use of language. His linguistic innovations and use of highly modernistic tropes such as stream of consciousness and narratives in which events unfold via the perspectives of multiple narrators (the disparity between the cognitive and linguistic ability of such narrators is often striking) does much to add to the Gothic atmosphere of his works. Indeed this can frequently pose a significant challenge for students and first time readers as chronology, genealogy, focalization and setting seem to be enveloped in their very own Gothic-like maze that is impenetrable and disorienting. This linguistic effect is most apparent in *Absalom! Absalom!*, generally acknowledged as his most Gothic text, as skillfully delineated by Richard Gray in the passage below:

> Convoluted sentences and a cumulative syntactical pattern create the effect of thought flow, of a consciousness ranging free over the myriad possibilities latent in each moment's experience, while a disruptive use of

parentheses and grammatical forms, and the continual juxtaposition of contradictory images and suggestions, prevent the reader from absorbing that experience into any preconceived framework of value. . . . Sentences seem to have no end, possibilities of no definite conclusions, and the pervasive effect is one of hallucination or nightmare. . . . This is a language that creates a sense of mystery. It encourages confusion and seems therefore eminently suited to a narrative in which events are divested of logical explanation. (Gray 246–47)

The publication of Faulkner's *The Sound and the Fury* in 1929 is generally regarded to be the start of the Southern Renaissance, a flowering of imaginative and critical intellectual activity concerning Southern literature that would last until the late 1940s. Alongside Faulkner other key members of the Renaissance included Katherine Anne Porter, Tennessee Williams, Robert Penn Warren and Allen Tate. All of these figures produced prose, poetry and dramatic texts of great merit, but the last two writers listed above are particularly significant because, as members of the Agrarian and Fugitive groups, they had dual roles as author/poets *and* critics and therefore did much to set the terms of what Southern literature subsequently could and could not be. In many ways such groups were reacting to the "abjecting" of Southern society as it was dismissed culturally and ruptured economically (especially the way in which traditional agricultural practices and centers were rendered obsolete) by the developing trends in what was becoming an increasingly corporate America, all of which also seemed to them to be originating out of the North of the country. Groups such as the Agrarians wanted, as their name suggests, to return to fundamentally simple agrarian economic practices which were anti-accumulative; they also wanted a Southern literature that was structured around the key principles of place, community and history.

However, Southern writers who were in the generation immediately following the Renaissance found much to quibble with these formulations, and the critique is carried out most strenuously in the work of

Walker Percy and Flannery O'Connor, with the latter being the main focus of our attention here. Her slim body of work, which included the seminal novels *Wise Blood* and *The Violent Bear it Away* along with a number of short stories, attempts to engage with regional *and* national narratives, and it offers—in a world of deterioration, decay and dislocation—an insight to the potential for spiritual salvation in a Southern landscape that was "God intoxicated" and, especially during the period of her major work, perpetually on the brink of nuclear apocalypse.

Like Poe, O'Connor led a brief (she died in August 1964 at the age of 39 from lupus) but aesthetically accomplished life. Her gender and illness made her something of an outsider, a marginalized condition that was compounded by her faith as a Roman Catholic in a predominantly protestant region. However her faith, and the way it influenced her aesthetic, arguably made the most important contribution to the way in which she contemporized the Southern Gothic. Her emphasis on the potential for spiritual salvation in her cast of grotesque characters ensures that her work transcends any accusation of local color as she repeatedly "signals the potential for spiritual progress" in rapidly changing pastoral and indeed racial landscapes (Watson 217).

The Gothicism of her work can be attributed in large part to the willingness she displayed to engage with regional and national cultural anxieties in a social milieu that was both revolutionary and reactionary, rural and urban and increasingly unstable. She lived in a highly Gothic moment where the dialectic between reason and chaos—perhaps the ultimate catalyst for American and Southern Gothic—was especially pronounced, a point intelligently observed by Jay Watson below:

The paradigmatic O'Connor narrative sets these self-absorbed, self-deceiving figures down in a realistically rendered social landscape, a postwar South characterized by dynamic transformation: new forms of movement and tension between country and city, accelerating class mobility and racial activism, and the breakdown of traditional hierarchies and codes. In this fluid, unpredictable, rapidly modernizing environment, O'Connor's

secular intellectuals and complacent class snobs experience unsettling encounters with a rogue's gallery of subaltern figures no longer content to
dwell silently on the periphery of Southern social existence. (209)

These themes are particularly apparent in her debut novel *Wise
Blood*, published in 1952, whose principal character Hazel Motes,
a "social type O'Connor returned to throughout her career; the rural
southerner whose traditional world has collapsed and who is destined
for a deracinated life in the postwar—and emergently postmodern—
city" (O'Gorman 167). As we have seen sites where meaning and borders collapse are perhaps the archetypal setting for [Southern] Gothic
texts, and such implosion is even more pronounced in a society that
sought to demarcate itself on strictly formulated mythical, social, racial and economic lines. Susan Castillo is another critic who sees this
as the key aspect of O'Connor's contribution to the Southern Gothic,
or grotesque as she terms it. For Castillo *Wise Blood* is "characterized
by an aesthetic of liminality," whose characters "inhabit a fluid realm
in which conventional borders are effaced or erased or shrouded in
mystery, in which ontological or epistemological certainties no longer
exist." This assessment allows us to see *Wise Blood* as another "abject"
text in which sites of meaning are collapsed and cultural hierarchies
are inverted, a point also acknowledged by Castillo who claims that
the "usual boundaries between human beings, animals, plants and even
objects are seen as tenuous" (Castillo 494).

Like many Southern Gothic texts her work seems somewhat anachronistic as O'Connor again and again returns to the potential for spiritual salvation in a world that was increasingly dominated by secularism
and scientific rationalism. According to Farrell O'Gorman her faith,
like Walker Percy, a fellow Catholic writer from the South, allowed
her to "seek out the depths of the immediate world around" her, and it
never became a subject for pastiche as it would do as Southern writing
took an increasingly postmodern turn in the generations to follow (13).
This is not to suggest that her faith resulted in her aesthetic taking on

overly didactic or instructive turn. In fact quite the opposite is true, as evidenced in her short stories such as "The Artificial Nigger" where "the South's repressed nightmare resurface in gothic forms," and the reader is "confronted with the instability of racial categories and racialized identities in the South" (Castillo 496). In her novels and short stories O'Connor comes back again and again to metaphors associated with sight, with how mainstream culture sees the South and how her cast of grotesque characters see their region and their changing spiritual and social position within it. This challenge to official narratives by "monstrous" or abject characters is one of her key contributions to the development of the Southern Gothic. She is joined in this project by Eudora Welty whose short fiction especially raises "the possibility of alternative gazes, alternative perspectives" where the possibility for "alternative narratives is raised repeatedly" (Donaldson). In many respects O'Connor and Welty realigned the gaze of Southern Gothic and expanded its parameters.

O'Connor and Welty can be seen as transitional figures in the history of Southern Gothic. The past does of course still inform the present, but Southern authors have increasingly found that they are unable to retreat into a "mythic southern past" (Bone 156). The sacrosanct principles formulated and strictly adhered to by major Renaissance figures (those being community, history and place) are no longer workable, and Bone observes that "few novelists writing about the South feel compelled to glance backward—longingly or anxiously—at the receding shadow of the Dixie Limited" (Bone 164).

This is not to say that Southern Gothic has ceased to exist as a viable mode with which to critique and interrogate cultural anxieties. A brief comparison of the function of the Gothic in the work of O'Connor and Harry Crews reveals how it remains relevant and incredibly flexible, as identified by Bone; "whereas the grotesque in O'Connor's fiction was bound up with spiritual matters, the corporeal concerns in Crews's writing are tied to class and poverty" (162). So whilst the Gothicized focus has shifted from the spiritual to the social it is, in the works of Crews,

Barry Hannah, William Gay, Dorothy Allison and Jayne Anne Phillips, to name a few examples, still there, even if the anxieties expressed are now transnational rather than strictly regional. Bone's choice of the adjective 'corporeal' is also significant as it confirms how Southern Gothic fiction is still concerned with the abject, of the physical manifestations of deeper cultural fears about monstrosity and change.

Louisiana, and New Orleans in particular, remain sites which continue to play an important role in the Southern Gothic tradition. Robert Mighall claims that "New Orleans' allegiances make it a temporal and cultural anomaly, a breach in the fabric of time and space" and that, thanks primarily to the vampire-filled work of Anne Rice, it is "probably the place most readily associated with vampires," due primarily to its status as a "repository of pastness" (59–60). Perhaps more than any other American city it has resisted the imposition of rationality and, with via oppositional subcultures such as voodoo, it's still a site where the dialectic between terror and unreason is evident in its cultural artifacts. This is borne out when we consider the popularity of Charlaine Harris's Sookie Stackhouse novels (and the popular *True Blood* television series on which they are based), a series of texts which distort hierarchies in familiar Gothic fashion. For those who prefer the more empirical concerns of the Gothic then James Lee Burke's fiction that is set in post–Katrina New Orleans—specifically *The Tin Roof Blowdown*—reveals how the "dark legacy" still functions in Southern society, especially when the veneer of rationality slips in a community forsaken by the authorities and the city turns into an abject nightmare, where inescapable physical death and decay personify a deeper moral degeneration. As Harris's and Burkes' work confirms, "the Gothic is a natural form of reference here, as guilts and fears deeply lodged in the national psyche erupt from this city on the edges of that brave New World and those united states" (Mighall 62).

As the case of New Orleans demonstrates Southern Gothic may no longer have to automatically look back to sustain itself. The region's defeat in the Civil War obviously lent itself to melancholic introspections and mythologizing tendencies, and whilst the agonized memories which caused that conflict still linger they are now joined with other cultural anxieties and abject spaces that ensures that the genre will continue to thrive in the region. Southern Gothic "is not simply an aesthetic or psychoanalytic category but an unofficial political history and a methodology for hearing the voices of dissent that interrupt narratives of national [and regional] consciousness" and as long as those narratives need disrupting, as long as abject spaces exist which are still able to collapse meaning and articulate the ever present but modified versions of the South's "dark legacy," then Southern Gothic will continue to maintain its relevance and importance (Idiart and Schulz 138).

Works Cited

Bone, Martyn. "Southern Fiction." *The Cambridge Companion to American Fiction after 1945*. Ed. John N. Duvall. Cambridge: Cambridge UP, 2011. 154–166. Print.

Botting, Fred. *Gothic*. Oxford: Routledge, 1995. Print.

Byron, Glennis, and David Punter, eds. *Spectral Readings: Towards A Gothic Geography*. Basingstoke: MacMillan, 1999. Print.

Castillo, Susan. "Flannery O'Connor." *A Companion to the Literature and Culture of the American South*. Ed. Richard J. Gray and Owen Robinson. Oxford: Blackwell, 2007. 486–501. Print.

Donaldson, Suzanne V. "Making a Spectacle: Welty, Faulkner, and Southern Gothic." *Mississippi Quarterly* 59.4 (1997): 567–583. *Academic Search Complete*. Web. 2 Nov. 2012.

Duvall, John N. *The Cambridge Companion to American Fiction after 1945*. Cambridge: Cambridge UP, 2011. Print.

Godden, Richard. "William Faulkner." *A Companion to the Literature and Culture of the American South*. Ed. Richard J. Gray and Owen Robinson. Oxford: Blackwell, 2007. 436–453. Print.

Goddu, Teresa A. "American Gothic." *The Routledge Companion to Gothic*. Ed. Catherine Spooner and Emma McEvoy. London: Routledge, 2007. 63–72. Print.

Gray, Richard J., and Owen Robinson, eds. *A Companion to the Literature and Culture of the American South*. Oxford: Blackwell, 2007. Print.

Gray, Richard J. *The Literature of Memory: Modern Writers of the American South*. London: Edward Arnold. 1977. Print.

___. *Southern Aberrations: Writers of the American South and the Problems of Regionalism*. Baton Rouge: Louisiana State UP. 2000. Print.

Hogle, Jerrold E., ed. *The Cambridge Companion to Gothic Fiction*. Cambridge: Cambridge UP, 2002. Print.

Idiart, Jeanette, and Jennifer Schulz. "American Gothic Landscapes: The New World to Vietnam." *Spectral Readings: Towards A Gothic Geography*. Ed. Glennis Byron and David Punter. Basingstoke: MacMillan, 1999. 127–139. Print.

Kristeva, Julia. *Powers of Horror: An Essay on Abjection*. Trans. Leon S. Roudiez. New York: Columbia UP, 1982. Print.

Lloyd-Smith, Allan. *American Gothic Fiction: An Introduction*. London: Continuum, 2004. Print.

Mighall, Robert. "Gothic Cities." *The Routledge Companion to Gothic*. Ed. Catherine Spooner and Emma McEvoy. London: Routledge, 2007. 54–62. Print.

O'Gorman, Farrell. *Peculiar Crossroads: Flannery O'Connor, Walker Percy, and Catholic Vision in Postwar Southern Fiction*. Baton Rouge: Louisiana State UP, 2004. Print.

Punter, David. *The Literature of Terror: A History of Gothic Fictions from 1765 to the Present Day*. London: Longman, 1980. Print.

Ringe, Donald A. *American Gothic: Imagination and Reason in Nineteenth-Century Fiction*. Lexington: UP of Kentucky, 1982. Print.

Savoy, Eric. "The Rise of American Gothic." *The Cambridge Companion to Gothic Fiction*. Ed. Jerrold E. Hogle. Cambridge: Cambridge UP, 2002. 167–188. Print.

Spooner, Catherine, and Emma McEvoy, eds. *The Routledge Companion to Gothic*. London: Routledge, 2007. Print.

Watson, Jay. "Flannery O'Connor." *The Cambridge Companion to American Fiction after 1945*. Ed. John N. Duvall. Cambridge: Cambridge UP, 2011. 207–219. Print.

Flannery O'Connor and Harry Crews Get Naked _____

Henry Lowell Carrigan, Jr.

Harry Crews (1935–2012) and Flannery O'Connor (1925–1964) each grew up deep in the piney woods, swamps, and rural backwaters of south Georgia. Born on the northern edge of the Okefenokee Swamp, Crews grew up in a life of poverty where he, as he narrates in *A Childhood* (1978), the memoir of his first six years, would fish for chickens through the loose floorboards of his front porch. Stories animated Crews's early life, and he grew up surrounded by good storytellers whose tales were like magic to him and transformed his world. One of his favorite childhood memories involves looking at one of the few books in the sharecropper's shack where he lived—the Sears Roebuck catalog—and making up stories for the people pictured in its pages. This first brush with storytelling embedded itself within him, and when he eventually joined the Marines, left the South and saw and experienced other parts of the world, and signed up to study with Andrew Lytle at the University of Florida, the powerful embrace of storytelling would not let him go. Yet he struggled to slip into the life of a writer, publishing his first novel, *The Gospel Singer*, in 1968. On the strength of this novel, Crews began an almost thirty-year teaching career at the University of Florida, from which he retired in 1997, and he continued to publish fiction that sometimes received high praise and other times drew mixed reactions from reviewers. During these years, Crews also wrote gritty and highly respected journalism for *Playboy* and *Esquire*, where he used his uncanny ability to take on the persona of his subjects as he often profiled carnival workers, alligator poachers, and evangelists. Well known for his rough living and his punch-drunk and brutal honesty, Crews drew a cultish following for his often violent, but always humorous and dead-on, novels filled with freakish denizens of the New South trying to find their way with Old South rural canniness. A short-lived punk band honored his work by naming themselves after him, and his role in the Southern cult film *Searching for the*

Wrong-Eyed Jesus (2003) bolstered his reputation as a kindhearted but ornery guide to the dark heart and the deep secrets of the South. When Crews died in 2012, the Southern Gothic tradition lost a pugnacious and audacious novelist with a deep affinity for looking at the world with all its blemishes, seeing through the masks behind which most people hide, and using humor, however sarcastic, to reveal the truth beneath the lies behind which we often hide.

Fellow Georgian Flannery O'Connor made her mark early in life and her own writings left an indelible impression on later Southern writers like Crews, as well as a deep and lasting impact on writers and readers around the world. Raised as an only child in Milledgeville, Georgia, O'Connor first saw the light of fame not by fishing for chickens through loose porch boards, like Crews, but by teaching a chicken to walk backward for a newsreel in which she appeared along with the chicken. In her witty way, O'Connor declared that the rest of her life had been an anticlimax. O'Connor's Roman Catholic faith influenced her life and writing, and her thirty-two stories and two novels are filled with veiled or explicit references to her faith. In addition, she often spoke at invited lectures about the relationship between faith and fiction. She attended and graduated from the Georgia State College for Women and then attended the famous University of Iowa Writers' Workshop, eventually publishing her first novel, *Wise Blood*, in 1952. A prolific letter writer, O'Connor faithfully addressed questions from friends and fans alike regarding the meaning of her stories, the relevance of her faith to her writing, and the theological questions that puzzled and motivated her struggles. Although she cut back on her travel after she was diagnosed with lupus and stayed closer to Andalusia, the family home in Milledgeville, she continued to write steadily until her death in 1964.

The region in which Crews and O'Connor grew up and that defined them is largely Evangelical Protestant, with, as O'Connor once wrote, a ragged Christ moving from tree to tree. In different ways, this Christ-haunted South deeply marks their approaches and attitudes toward writing fiction, for each writer's stories and novels portray characters getting naked and baring their souls not only in an effort to find themselves, but also characters who are lost, unable to find wholeness or self-identity in a broken world, or who are seduced by the glitter and shine of the modern world and must be shocked or startled into seeing a way toward wholeness and redemption. Crews depicts freakishly grotesque men and women caught in a world where old values have been replaced by new ones, country replaced by city, and where the struggle to know and to hold onto the truth is a violent one. Born on the shores of the Okefenokee Swamp, the stories and novels of Crews and O'Connor introduce readers to a wide range of such startling figures, from the angry misfit preacher Haze Motes to a variety of grotesque country folks caught between the certainty and illusion of a changing landscape.

In an interview about the role of the novelist, Harry Crews once declared: "If you're gonna write, for God in heaven's sake, try to get naked. Try to write the truth. Try to get underneath all the sham, all the excuses, all the lies that you've been told" (*Getting Naked* 288). Over thirty years earlier, Flannery O'Connor made a similar proclamation:

> When you can assume that your audience holds the same beliefs you do, you can relax a little and use more normal means of talking to it; when you have to assume that it does not know, then you have to make your vision apparent by shock—to the hard of hearing you shout, and for the almost-blind, you draw large and startling figures. (*Mystery and Manners* 34)

Although Crews and O'Connor might never agree on the role that religion plays in the writing of fiction, they nevertheless agree that the central act of the novel is revelation—disclosing the truth of one's relationship to oneself, to others, to creation or nature, and to God. For Crews, baring one's body and soul to the elements and to the hypocrisies of everyday life serves as the means to revelatory activity; that is, when you are getting naked, you are revealing your vulnerabilities and your openness to truth to a world that makes sport of attacking an individual's weak points and handing him or her a false sense of self with which to go through life. Crews's novels are chock-full of characters that the rest of the world considers freaks precisely because these individuals do not accept the false identities that the world has created for them; they have gotten naked to reveal to themselves and others the truths they recognize about the corruption of the world and about their own selves. Only a marginal religious believer, Crews illustrates in his novels that revelation occurs through the body, when an individual "gets naked."

O'Connor, in contrast, views the cosmos and nature, as full of mystery and grace that allow individuals to understand, if they can only see and recognize it, their wholeness in a broken world, their inextricable bond to others struggling with the same questions about truth, and their relationship to God. A lifelong Catholic, O'Connor wrote several essays probing the relationship between fiction and faith and approaches her writing from the standpoint of belief. Her fiction often focuses on an individual's blindness—his or her inability to see the truth and grace around them—and she often sends in characters that might seem at first less than human (startling figures) to help these individuals see the light. Even so, the revelatory acts in O'Connor's novels and stories occur, as they do in Crews's fiction, in and through the physical and very seldom through the vehicle of the spiritual or the explicitly religious.

Indeed, the strongest thematic similarity between Crews and O'Connor is seeing, vision, and the shattering of blindness. Revelation functions primarily as an act of vision, and the great medieval mystics of the Christian traditions often told stories of visions they experienced of the love of God, of God's messages to them about community, or of God's punishment. The biblical book of Revelation takes its name from a series of visions that its author, John, records while in exile in a strange country. In fact, the Greek word *apocalupsis*, from which the English word "apocalypse" derives, means "to unveil" and thus to see clearly the truth beyond the shades behind which it has been hidden. Revelation is always an act of knowing, and an individual must somehow respond to this new knowledge either with wonder or skepticism. At any rate, the new knowledge changes an individual's perspective on life, either for better or worse. In traditional terms, the response to revelation is faith; the fiction of both Crews and O'Connor does not operate so explicitly in this fashion. Even in O'Connor, whose Catholic perspective might have forced her to portray one-dimensional characters whose lives change immediately and irrevocably when new knowledge is revealed to them, individuals struggle to sort out what this new knowledge means for their often limited lives. For both Crews and O'Connor, the moment of seeing, the removal of blindness—or in the case of O'Connor, blinding for the sake of seeing in her novel *Wise Blood*—is fundamental; the response is not always fully developed. Moreover, for each writer, the body is the location on which revelatory activity is inscribed, and thus the twisted and broken bodies of freak show freaks, bodybuilders and karate champs, disabled country girls, and gorilla-suited country boys are the sites where revelation occurs in these writers' works, illustrating the inextricable connection between physical vision and intellectual knowing.

One of the most enduring themes of Gothic literature that the Southern Gothic tradition picks up is house as the site of revelatory activity. In novels as diverse as Ann Radcliffe's *Mysteries of Udolpho* (1794), Jane Austen's *Northanger Abbey* (1817), Horace Walpole's *The Castle of Otranto* (1764), Nathaniel Hawthorne's *The House of the Seven Gables* (1851), and Charlotte Brontë's *Jane Eyre* (1847), the older manse with its secret passageways or haunted halls—or in *Jane Eyre*'s case, a mysterious creature in the attic—is a living creature, a mysterious body, that reveals slowly to its inhabitants and its visitors its long-held secrets. Edgar Allan Poe's "The Fall of the House of Usher" and "The Tell-Tale Heart," among others of his Southern Gothic tales, feature houses that seem to have come alive, revealing their grotesque secrets to those who have the ears to hear and the eyes to see. Crews and O'Connor shift this emphasis on the living house slightly in their fiction as the body becomes the building, "temple of the holy ghost," that either through extreme religious ascetic practices, such as self-flagellation and blinding, or through the athletic asceticism of body-building yields up new insights into the nature of humankind, self, and world.

As many critics have pointed out, grotesque characters—often described as freaks—populate the novels and stories of Crews and O'Connor, and these sometimes physically repulsive individuals function as the vehicle through which others see the world in new ways. In her typical tongue-in-cheek manner, O'Connor once remarked that she had found that "anything that comes out of the South is going to be called grotesque by the Northern reader, unless it is grotesque, in which case it's going to be called realistic" (*Mystery and Manners* 40). Yet, the grotesque, the out of the ordinary, the creature or object that might be so repulsive that it takes us out of ourselves to see the world differently, functions as a vehicle of revelation both for Crews and O'Connor. O'Connor expresses the function of the grotesque as a means of revelation quite powerfully: "The writer of grotesque fiction is looking for one image that will connect or combine or embody two points; one is a point in the concrete, and the other is a point not visible to the naked eye, but believed in by him firmly, just as real to him, really, as the one that everybody sees" (42). Just as in Mary Shelley's *Frankenstein* (1818), the abhorred creature composed of the flesh and organs from cadavers reveals forcefully to Victor what it means to be human, the deformed denizens of Crews and O'Connor's fiction reveals powerful truths about the nature of humanity and its place in a distorted and confused world.

Almost all of O'Connor's stories and novels involve the revelation of mystery and grace through nature, especially with the body as the site of such disclosing activity. In one of her later stories, "Parker's Back," O. E. Parker's back literally becomes the site—and the sight—of a revelation that alters his vision of himself and the world and that changes and challenges the views of those around him about the nature of beauty and grace. When the young Parker goes to the carnival side-show and sees the tattooed man, he experiences a kind of conversion: "It was as if a blind boy had been turned so gently in a different direction that he did not know his destination had been changed" (*Everything That Rises* 219). Although his body is already covered with tattoos, Parker decides in this moment of turning that he will get a special tattoo on his back in order to get the attention of his wife, Sarah Ruth, a conservative religious woman who is "forever sniffing up sin" (220). Parker is already on something of a religious journey before he decides to get the tattoo of God on his back; his name, Obadiah Elihue, means "prophet of God," and his encounter with the tattooed man nudges him to consider the wonder and beauty of creation in a way that he had tried to express though his previous tattoos of animals and plants. Parker spends two days having his back adorned with this new tattoo. Once he finishes the eyes in the tattoo, the tattoo artist forces Parker to look at his back, and in that moment, his conversion is complete: "Parker sat for a long time . . . examining his soul. He saw it as a spider web of facts and lies that was not at all important to him. . . . The eyes that were now forever on his back were eyes to be obeyed. He was as certain of it as he had ever been of anything" (241). Looking for guidance, Parker returns to Sarah Ruth, who refuses to look at the tattoo, calling it an idolatry and beating Parker on his back with a broom, driving him from his house and out into the wilderness to find his own way. "Parker's Back" reveals a protagonist who loves the world and strives to find an enduring connection to it by means of his aesthetic—and ascetic—marking on his back. His acceptance of the need to be obedient means that he, like Haze Motes in O'Connor's *Wise Blood* who blinds himself, will carry the marks of his new way of life with him forever.

Perhaps one of O'Connor's most humorous stories, "Good Country People" also illustrates the role of the body and the bodily as the site of revelation. Every morning, Mrs. Hopewell rises early at seven o'clock and lights the gas heaters in her and her daughter's room. Joy, her daughter, is a large blond girl with an artificial leg. Soon after, Mrs.

Freeman arrives for breakfast and hollow chatter about the news of the day. Joy is thirty-two with a PhD in philosophy that she holds over her mother and Mrs. Freeman like a sword. At the table, the "large hulking Joy, whose constant outrage had obliterated every expression from her face, would stare just a little to the side of her, her eyes icy blue, with the look of someone who has achieved blindness by an act of will and means to keep it" (*Good Man* 244). In fact, Joy so dislikes her name that, in order to spite her mother, she changes it to Hulga. One morning a young man, Manley Pointer, arrives at the farm selling Bibles, and he and Hulga agree to meet a few days after for a picnic. During the night, Hulga imagines that she seduces young Pointer: "she very easily seduced him and . . . had to reckon with his remorse. True genius can get an idea across even to an inferior mind. She imagined that she took his remorse in hand and changed it into a deeper understanding of life. She took all his shame away and turned it into something useful" (255).

In typical O'Connor fashion, the tables turn and Pointer, who presents himself as "good country people" at the opening of the story now reveals himself as simply a man who is out for himself, a collector of sorts who is more interested in Hulga's wooden leg than in her. As the seduction scene unfolds, Pointer convinces Hulga to demonstrate her love for him by revealing the point at which her artificial limb connects to her leg; when she does so, he removes the limb and does not rejoin it, holding onto it away from Hulga. Panicking, Hulga cries for him to give her back her leg, calling Pointer a good Christian. In the climactic moment of the story, Pointer responds: "I may sell Bibles but I know which end is up and I wasn't born yesterday and I know where I'm going. . . .You ain't so smart; I been believing in nothing ever since I was born" (261). Through this ironic reversal, played out on the site of Hulga's body, Pointer, who does not approach life intellectually but who lives out his life collecting whatever physical objects he can carry in his briefcase, demonstrates to Hulga the ineffectuality of living the life of the mind. He has believed nothing all his life, and he has been able to see through people and their needs, desires, and wants quite well. He points out—his name is of course significant—to Hulga that neither desire nor intellect alone provides the key to understanding life; just when you think you have found the "pointer" to life's meaning, he observes, you discover otherwise. As Pointer leaves Hulga alone in the desolate barn without her glasses or her wooden leg, she is physically and mentally stranded, bereft of the knowledge that might have saved her but wiser—whether she will be able to embrace such knowledge is unclear—to the ways of the world.

Just as O'Connor's stories and novels locate the body as the site of revelation, so do Harry Crews's novels. Many critics have called attention to the number of grotesque characters and freaks. Some critics have likened Crews to Flannery O'Connor and Carson McCullers strapped side by side on a roller coaster. His second novel, *Naked in Garden Hills* (1969), features a six-hundred-pound homosexual Metrecal addict, a failed jockey who rides a chair as he watches the races on television, and a man given to romping naked though an old mine. Another novel, *A Feast of Snakes* (1976), set in the small south Georgia town of Mystic, features sodden dirt farmers, peg-legged deputy sheriffs, and languishing football players-turned-liquor runners all gathered for the town's annual rattlesnake hunt. Many of his novels feature midgets, and in *The Gospel Singer*, Foot, named for his twenty-seven-inch foot, owns and operates a traveling freak show of which he is the star attraction. In *Car* (1972), auto mechanic Herman Mack devours a Ford Maverick piece by piece.

Whereas O'Connor's characters practice a religious asceticism, often reducing the body in hopes of attaining spiritual unity, Crews's characters practice an athletic aestheticism. Given Crews's own days as a boxer and blood sports fanatic—he never backed down from a fight and loved a good cockfight—his emphasis on the benefits of sports and their capacity for honing the body to prepare it for receiving wisdom makes sense. Crews observes that "ultimately, sports are just about as close to what one could call the truth as it is possible to get in this world" (*Getting Naked* 249). Several of his novels focus on the discipline involved in various sports that force individuals to pare down their bodies as both a preparation for a struggle toward a certain goal and as an enhancement of their knowledge of the world and themselves. *Karate is a Thing of the Spirit* (1971), *Body* (1990), and *The Knockout Artist* (1988) all feature contests of the will and competitions of the body that require participants to test themselves against others and against themselves as they try to find truth. Participation in sports offers the ultimate chance to get naked and to get close to the truth about self-identity; preparation for a competition requires the accumulation of knowledge about another and his or her identity, as well as an accumulation of knowledge about practices that enable further success in a competition. Even in defeat, athletes gain knowledge of themselves and others that enables them to continue to develop their skills and understanding.

In the epigraph to *Body*, Crews quotes the great high-wire walker Karl Wallenda: "Walking the wire is living. The rest is just waiting." Uttered just a few weeks before Wallenda fell to his death, his words capture the intensity and the utter self-absorption with which he viewed his job. Like every athlete, Wallenda trained for the moment of the event, and his words serve as a perfect introduction to Crews's novel of bodybuilding in which body, soul, and mind spend every waking minute in training for the competition. In *Body*, bodybuilder and trainer Russell "Muscle" Morgan transforms Dorothy Turnipseed, a secretary from Waycross, Georgia, into Shereel Dupont, a model of physical perfection and a leading contender in the Ms. Cosmos contest. Once Dupont begins her regime of training, she is focused and engaged, and winning becomes everything for her.

When Shereel walks into this new world, it appears to her—and to Russell, who believes he has indeed discovered a woman from a great gene pool whom he can train to reign as the queen of the world—that this is a perfect world: "Everybody seemed perfect of his kind . . . with a kind of mindless confidence, as though the world would never die, could never die. Age and death seemed defeated here. . . . Their skins circumscribed their worlds, worlds they inhabited with obvious joy, contentment, and pride" (*Body* 17). In this moment, Shereel undergoes a kind of conversion experience: Here she can turn her life around; here she can become a new person; here she need be nothing other than what she can make herself to present to others in this contest, to her family, and to the world (cosmos). Shereel's body, sculpted with Russell's training, reveals to her endless possibilities of creation: "He'd made her somebody, made her hear thundering applause and shouts of approval, even love. He'd given her a cause in the world, a cause such as she had not known existed for anybody. And for that, she had done everything he had asked of her. And she was glad to do it, even to having her name changed" (23–24). She is a new person, and her discipline, along with Russell's training, gives Shereel purpose and direction in life; she gives up her old life and prepares to enter this new domain in search of new revelations about herself and others.

Winning the competition does have its benefits and its risks. Shereel cannot ultimately control the outcome of the contest, but she can control her own preparedness for the competition, and she strives mightily to do this. Her family disrupts these best-laid plans when they arrive in town ready to cheer her on to victory; the Turnipseeds offer just the opposite picture of control. Earnestine and her daughter, Earline, Shereel's sister, arrive "sharing a bag of pork skins, both of them patiently chewing and shifting from foot to foot, causing the shiny red bows [on their dresses] to undulate over their massive hips" (27). Indeed, the men in Shereel's family have "substantial bellies. . . . and their arms and legs [are] roped with heavy, ill-defined muscles" (37). Shereel, steeled against any such disruptions, does not allow her family to control her, and in the end, she sheds them as she has previously shed pounds to sculpt her body. Her body teaches Shereel all she needs to know about herself.

As she enters the competition, Shereel begins to recognize that the glittering world of bodybuilding she first encountered is not so perfect after all. It has benefits and costs: "On one side of the ledger was winning and its consequences . . . Shereel Dupont, Ms. Cosmos, was somebody, somebody to reckon with. . . . On the other side of the ledger was the alternative to winning. And she did not know, could not imagine, the consequences of not winning. That side of the ledger was not only blank, it was dark" (228–29).Thus, in Shereel's case, the perfect body allows her to maintain perfect control, unless she loses the competition. Since she has defined herself solely and purely through her body, Shereel will cease to exist if she loses the competition, but she will rule the world if she wins it. Indeed, *Body* illustrates one of Crews's observations about the nature of fiction: "Fiction always deals with extremes. Fiction is always about someone whose ass in on the line. . . it is in a crisis, conflicts, in what I think of as 'blood moments,' that you find out who the hell you are, what you really are, what you really believe, what you're really capable of" (*Getting Naked* 242).

In his or her own way, both Crews and O'Connor offer portraits of a world falling apart, a world with few certainties—the power of discipline, either physical or spiritual—and a world where individuals can look into their own hearts, minds, and bodies and find there revealed the clues to self-identity and relationship to others. O'Connor was fond of writing about and lecturing on the power of fiction to reveal mystery to us. She famously declared that "the fiction writer presents mystery through manners, grace through nature, but when he finishes there always has to be left over that sense of Mystery which cannot be accounted for by any human formula" (*Mystery and Manners* 153). O'Connor's stories and novels portray characters for whom revelatory activity is located at the site of the body; they undergo physical trauma or physical dislocation in order that they may be jarred, startled, and shocked into seeing their lives and the world around them anew.

Harry Crews once said that if he had done his job right when he was writing, he would "really get you turned back on yourself, and on your own code of ethics or morality or vision of the world or sense of self or whatever. If I get you turned back on yourself, then I done my job. I've done what I set out to do" (*Getting Naked* 290). Pick up any of Crews's novels, from his first widely acclaimed *The Gospel Singer* to his later novels, such as his less widely praised *Celebration* (1998), and you will find a writer baring his soul and trying to get readers to turn back on themselves and search their hearts.

Harry Crews's and Flannery O'Connor's fiction may sometimes be hard to read because their works are filled with violence, blood sport, and grotesque characters. Nonetheless, they demand to be read, for they drive us to confront our often grotesque sense of selves, the lies we tell ourselves to protect ourselves from harsh truths, and the destruction of our society and the world around us under the banner of illusory values.

Works Cited

Asals, Frederick. *Flannery O'Connor: The Imagination of Extremity*. Athens: U of Georgia P, 1982. Print.

Bledsoe, Erik, ed. *Perspectives on Harry Crews*. Jackson: UP of Mississippi, 2001. Print.

Brinkmeyer, Robert H. *The Art and Vision of Flannery O'Connor*. Baton Rouge: Louisiana State UP, 1989. Print.

Cash, Jean. *Flannery O'Connor: A Life*. Knoxville: U of Tennessee P, 2002. Print.

Crews, Harry. *All We Need of Hell*. New York: Harper, 1987. Print.

___. *Blood and Grits*. New York: Harper, 1979. Print.

___. *Car*. New York: Morrow, 1972. Print.

___. *A Feast of Snakes*. New York: Atheneum, 1976. Print.

___. *Getting Naked With Harry Crews: Interviews*. Ed. Erik Bledsoe. Gainesville: UP of Florida, 1999. Print.

___. *Naked in Garden Hills*. New York: Morrow, 1969. Print.

___. *Scar Lover*. New York: Poseidon, 1992. Print.

Gentry, Marshall Bruce. *Flannery O'Connor's Religion of the Grotesque*. Jackson: UP of Mississippi, 1986. Print.

Gooch, Brad. *Flannery: A Life of Flannery O'Connor*. New York: Little, 2009. Print.

Gordon, Sarah. *Flannery O'Connor: The Obedient Imagination*. Athens: U of Georgia P, 2000. Print.

Gretlund, Jan Nordby, and Karl-Heinz Westarp, eds. *Flannery O'Connor's Radical Reality*. Columbia: U of South Carolina P, 2006. Print.

Hewitt, Avis, and Robert Donahoo, eds. *Flannery O'Connor in the Age of Terrorism: Essays on Violence and Grace*. Knoxville: U of Tennessee P, 2011. Print.

Hobson, Fred. *The Southern Writer in the Postmodern World*. Athens: U of Georgia P, 1991. Print.

Magee, Rosemary, ed. *Conversations with Flannery O'Connor*. Jackson: UP of Mississippi, 1986. Print.

O'Connor, Flannery. *The Complete Stories*. New York: Farrar, 1971. Print.

___. *Collected Works*. New York: Lib. of Amer., 1988. Print.

___. *Everything That Rises Must Converge*. New York: Farrar, 1965. Print.

___. *The Habit of Being: Letters*. Ed. Sally Fitzgerald. New York: Farrar, 1979. Print.

___. *Mystery and Manners: Occasional Prose*. Ed. Sally Fitzgerald and Robert Fitzgerald. New York: Farrar, 1969. Print.

___. *3: Wise Blood, A Good Man is Hard to Find, The Violent Bear It Away*. New York: Signet, 1960. Print.

O'Gorman, Farrell. *Peculiar Crossroads: Flannery O'Connor, Walker Percy, and Catholic Vision in Postwar Southern Fiction*. Baton Rouge: Louisiana State UP, 2004. Print.

Westling, Louise. *Sacred Groves and Ravaged Gardens: The Fiction of Eudora Welty, Carson McCullers and Flannery O'Connor*. Athens: U of Georgia P, 1985. Print.

Wood, Ralph C. *Flannery O'Connor and the Christ-Haunted South*. Grand Rapids: Eerdmans, 2004. Print.

The Road beyond Zombies of the New South_____
Jay Ellis

I've seen the meanness of humans till I don't know why God ain't put out the sun and gone away.

(Cormac McCarthy, *Outer Dark* 192)

We wouldnt ever eat anybody, would we?
No. Of course not.

(The Road 108)

In Cormac McCarthy's *The Road* (2006), a man and his son travel through a postapocalyptic South. Virtually no animal or plant life remains for sustenance in this charred world. Whatever calamity has struck, the earth spins in a clouded void, the sun struck by "some cold glaucoma dimming away the world" (*Road* 3).[1] Danger is everywhere, walking the road itself, in the often-burning dark woods alongside it, and certainly within some indoor spaces, in the form of those remaining humans who have become cannibals. For those who will not practice cannibalism, finding food means venturing indoors, looking for hidden or otherwise overlooked canned goods.

Like many of the homeless on our everyday streets, the man and boy travel with a shopping cart. This ironic conveyance helps them carry not only whatever food they might find, but also the vestiges of civilization, such as a different tarp to sleep under from the one on which the man spreads their meager meals (*Road* 4–5). They refer regularly, figuratively, to "carrying the fire" (70, 109, 182, 238), as if it is their duty somehow to preserve the fragile distinctions between conscious humanity and an older, more rudimentary and atavistic form of bipedal life—their calling to weave a moral thread through an otherwise indifferent universe.

McCarthy had already hinted at the literal disappearance of the sun from the world, as in the epigraph above. *Outer Dark* was published in 1968, nearly forty years earlier, and was McCarthy's second book. The man wondering why "God ain't put out the sun" (*Outer Dark* 192) had earlier found a baby abandoned by its own father to die in the woods, not long after the father dreams of an eclipse that stalls at full darkness. By the end of the book, the father sees that son cannibalized (*Outer Dark* 236). Eschatological concerns recur in all nine of the novels leading up to *The Road*; they also regularly accompany individual acts of cannibalism, or a fear of this as an end worse than death alone. As McCarthy's characters see the world end, or feel as if it is ending, they often fear or witness or succumb to cannibalism.[2] The qualified identity of cannibals in *The Road* will lead this chapter to a consideration of zombies in three groups: those traveling with a truck, an army with slaves pulling carts, and those controlling an abattoir cellar in the "once grand house" of a former plantation (89). We will therefore explore a Gothic haunted both by Old Southern slavery guilt, and by anxiety over New Southern consumption.

The Fire of Consciousness

In McCarthy's *Suttree* (1979), discussed at length by Chris Walsh here in a later chapter, apocalypse repeatedly imbues the sense experience and reflections of the characters. When the poor homeless Harrogate nearly freezes to death in a concrete pillbox under a viaduct, he generalizes his predicament: "I believe it's the end of the world" (*Suttree* 173). Suttree sets him straight:

> You're funny, you squirrely son of a bitch. Do you think the world will end just because you're cold?
> It aint just me. It's cold all over.
> It's not cold by Rufus's stove. Now get your ass up there. I'll see you later. (173)

Humor pulls the characters back from the brink in this scene. But *The Road* extends this fear, and many others, into a fully realized, often realistic, and yet subtly allegorical story of a father trying to stay alive long enough to see his son safely through a fallen world. Instead of Suttree looking after the grown—if comically incompetent—"city rat" Harrogate (115) and others down on their luck in Knoxville's urban squalor, the main character of *The Road* stands to lose his son. Any parent worries about the safety of his or her child, particularly away from the protection of that parent. *The Road* presents the father with the ultimate nightmare in these terms.

In another anticipation of this threat in *The Road*, the father in *Suttree* loses his son twice: first by leaving him and his mother, and again when the boy dies. Death haunts *Suttree*. We only learn that Suttree has a son when he learns that he has died (*Suttree* 148). Less seriously abandoned than the son in *Outer Dark*, but "abandoned" nonetheless (150), the boy seems forever lost to him even before Suttree can insist on burying the boy himself. He wanders the graveyard first, musing on the difference between his son and him, the threshold of death between them: "How surely are the dead beyond death. Death is what the living carry with them. A state of dread, like some uncanny foretaste of a bitter memory" (*Suttree* 153). This points to the time problem of death (writ large, of apocalypse): beyond that ultimate ending we can know nothing.

It also points, however, to ambiguities around death in McCarthy's later work. In *The Road*, death is neither the last thing to fear nor the worst. And the persistence of figures in dreams in the novel, as well as the nature of the cannibals, calls into question even the temporal force of death. Indeed, the cannibals of *The Road* turn Suttree's Shakespearean observation into a question: "How surely are the dead beyond death"? That "beyond" may be true for the dead, but not to us in relation to death or the dead. The dead who are somehow not dead, or the living who remind us too much of the dead—these are definitions for the figures we call zombies.

The fear that leads the mother in *The Road* to walk away to her suicide is not of death, but of rape and cannibalism; she argues that death is already "here," so there is "nothing left to talk about" (48). Death then becomes personified for her—a familiar personification in the Gothic—as "a new lover" who can give her what the man cannot, an end to things more noble than being raped, murdered, and cannibalized (*Road* 48). The dead, however, unlike "death," become conflated with the living cannibals in *The Road*, and they even become conflated with the soon-to-be dead; the result is a New Southern zombie, the consumer and the consumed differentiated only by power, and by an unstable threshold of death. We will see the lack of consciousness, of a soul, in the book's cannibals; this threat—that one could become a soulless zombie—outruns the fear of death in *The Road*.

The soul of Suttree's son was never known to him; the reader struggles to see more than a conceit buried, which suggests that not only to the son is death final, but to this father, because he knows nothing of what he lost. By contrast, *The Road* on any given page has more lively, tender, and convincing interplay between a father and son than one can find between any two such characters in all the rest of McCarthy. Well before its ending *The Road* convinces us that the risk the father is willing to take (that the mother is not) provides more than the possibility of mere survival with the boy. Each day with the boy, the father sees his son grow more likely to carry the fire of consciousness alone. He will have a soul. Where Suttree remembers nothing but his son's "tiny hand" at a carnival (*Suttree* 150), the father in *The Road* knows his son so well as to hold him in reverence. He believes in God only enough to reproach him, yet the boy is the father's "warrant." "If he is not the word of God God never spoke" (*Road* 4).

The boy's holiness resides in two agreements, one figurative, and the other literal: they are carrying the fire, and they will not eat people. Ultimately, these two are revealed as connected. No exceptions are allowed by this covenant against cannibalism, not even what anthropologists call "survival cannibalism," as in McCarthy, personhood depends on strict refusal of cannibalism regardless of circumstances, and we will see how those involved in any form of it in *The Road* are portrayed either as more rudimentary humans, or less than fully human—as zombies. Whether or not the father's motivations are selfish, as the mother argues, what is at stake for the reader is whether or not anyone with a soul survives *The Road*, keeping that soul intact. When McCarthy presents cannibals to the reader, we see the importance of this in negative, Gothic terms. The first we see, the zombies of the truck people, seem organized for collective movement as they struggle to start up their stalled truck. In this, they share what Barnard Turner finds in all "zombies of the Gothic a sense of indifference to the human need of having a home" (212). These zombies represent an evolved type of the zombie figure, of course; rather than reanimated dead or deadened living human beings controlled by another, the cannibals of the truck people and the once grand house are zombies because they share what Peter Dendle identifies as essential for all zombies "at the most abstract level," an "effaced consciousness" (47).

We may note that while the word "consciousness" never appears in *The Road*, the word "soul" appears twice: first, when the man wonders if God has a soul, and second, when he refers to the boy's soul; again, the boy remains more holy than God in this sense. His father wonders whether or not he can kill him to save him from what his mother warns will happen. He worries that the pistol might fail. "Could you crush that beloved skull with a rock? Is there such a being within you of which you know nothing? Can there be? Hold him in your arms. Just so. The soul is quick. Pull him toward you. Kiss him. Quickly" (*Road* 96).

The man's thoughts race here because they have just escaped their closest brush with cannibals, having gone into the wrong house and, worse, down into its abattoir cellar. They are hiding from cannibals, but also worse, because the cannibals in *The Road* clearly present us with a Gothic life-form liminal to death, and one of whom our fear arises from the realization that they are alive and not at the same time—because they lack souls. In this sense and more, as we get closer looks at them, they are zombies.

Cannibals of the Old South

Early on, the man in *The Road* thinks "the bloodcults must have all consumed one another" (14). We find that they have not, and their cannibalism seems to run beyond survival and to include ritual, a practice abhorrent to readers and yet one familiar to anthropologists. Encounters with the living cannibals prowling the book, however, hardly echo other references to a ritual cannibalism that—however much we reject such an idea—has been practiced by peoples with rich systems of symbol, belief, and, for that matter, empathy and tender feeling for others. In other words, McCarthy presents us with evidence of atavistic ritual cannibalism, but only indirectly.

In one such example, the man and boy encounter first the evidence of a slaughter, then from a safe enough distance, the "army" that must have committed that slaughter. Finding a site of massacre, the man sees a mixture of both symbolism and unadorned practicality in the evidence of cannibalism: "A frieze of human heads, all faced alike" that bear "crude tattoos etched in some homebrewed woad [a blue plant-based dye]" of "spiders, swords, targets. A dragon. Runic slogans, creeds misspelled" (*Road* 76). On the one hand, the scene certainly conforms to what we would expect of what the man calls "bloodcults." On the other hand, however, the same site includes "gray coils of viscera where the slain had been field-dressed and hauled away" (76). What, exactly, occurred at this site? The heads, positioned as they are along a wall, suggest some message left behind. But the description of those "viscera" read more like a hunt ("field-dressed"), and—only vaguely here—a commercial enterprise ("hauled away") that remained focused on survival by predation, rather than any ritual. The victims here bear signs and symbols. Their predators soon appear.

The next day the man and the boy see an "army" of cannibals, "in clothing of every description." They nonetheless wear matching "red scarves at their necks"—or "as close to red as they could find" (*Road* 77). Horrifying as they are, we must note that even this living "army" of primitive warriors so large they make the ground shake seems not to have taken captives for cannibalism. As they pass, we see slaves, who pull wagons full of "goods of war," nearly a dozen women we may assume are also slaves, "some of them pregnant," and "a supplementary consort of catamites . . . in dogcollars and yoked each to each" (77–78). These three groups of people are slaves for labor or sex; the word "catamites" points to the mother's fear that the boy would be raped. But her assumption that he would be eaten is not in evidence in this scene.

While the narration makes clear that this army left behind the few remains found by the man the previous day, McCarthy leaves that to our unavoidable inference. The focus of description, however, remains on a Gothic scene so old as to be irreducible to a single continent, let alone the American South, and yet, that this army uses slaves to pull along "goods of war" does not quite fit the desperate focus on food in the novel. This red scarf army has fallen back to codes of identification and a focus on display of goods won in war (both "goods of war" and the slaves taken). Certainly these are cannibals, and yet they maintain slaves they have at least not yet eaten simply to transport whatever those nonhuman "goods of war" might be (other than food). This enterprise seems doomed by its own attachment to symbols and relations of power—slavery to keep and move what we might infer are somehow commoditized objects in a novel where nothing but food and weapons retain any value. Whatever common enterprise keeps the red scarf army working together for the good of its whole (and no doubt the expense of some individual gains) suggests altruism among its members, but this is already ironically undermined by their common reliance on slaves. This central irony—that of protecting some common cause that meanwhile commoditizes whole groups of people—certainly recalls the Old South.

Following as they do a group of "truck people" (*Road* 59) with more advanced means of movement, they further recall the Confederate Army—a doomed enterprise if ever there was one. The zombie nature of this army furthermore includes that earliest aspect of the zombie as one whose soul has been taken by a larger authority, or as Dendle puts it, "the appropriation of one person's will by that of another" (47). Like any army, they of course move in accord with that central authority, "marching with a swaying gait like wind-up toys" (77). What type of toys would these be? Soldiers, of course. In the South—with slaves encumbering their movements, but also seemingly indifferent to home (or at least lost from it) and forever on the move—this cannibal army, united by its scarves for common conquest, further recalls the Confederate Army of the Civil War.

As Old Southern zombies, the red scarf army simultaneously harkens back to ancient group behavior; they are atavistic. The proximity of our view of the victims' remains and of their predators on the march has narrowed by these scenes. Separated by a day and a space break, the nature of cannibalism seems still human—but atavistically so. As in other McCarthy novels, horror can be found in atavistic reversions to older codes of human behavior. Judge Holden in *Blood Meridian, or The Evening Redness in the West* (1985) lectures on this: "All progressions from a higher to a lower order are marked by ruins and mystery and a residue of nameless rage" (146). The cannibals of the army, then, reach back through the long Gothic past; they are cannibals of old, safely distant in history or fading in dwindling jungle enclaves, according to some anthropological studies as a normative social arrangement (Kantner).

But readers of *Blood Meridian* would know better than to trust the judge, and while the sense of civilization falling backward provides a general backdrop to cannibalism in *The Road*, deeper horror arises from a more modern system of dehumanization we will find. McCarthy's placement of the army and its wake of heads and entrails indeed performs an atavistic reversion that separates the narrative's first zombie predators from the modern destination for living victims, the cellar of the "once grand house" (*Road* 89). Before the atavistic army, that is, we have already seen a more advanced—yet more zombie-like—cannibal, and we see something yet more modern after that army passes.

New Southern Zombies

Considering the truck people, note the details of both a primitive predatory group of hunter-gatherers and of a postindustrial civilization's equipment for protecting the human body against the hazards of reckless chemistry, manufacturing, and factory farming: "They came shuffling through the ash casting their hooded heads from side to side. Some of them wearing canister masks. One in a biohazard suit. Stained and filthy. Slouching along with clubs in their hands, lengths of pipe. Coughing. Then he heard on the road behind them what sounded like a diesel truck" (*Road* 51). In a further conflation of the primitive with the overdeveloped and industrialized, and the natural with the unnatural, even the truck is said to be "running on God knows what" (52). Biodiesel in this scenario may not be a good thing, as "God knows what" hints at perhaps a fuel derived from the grease of cannibalism, its "motor sound[ing] ropy. Missing and puttering" (52).

Why the truck at all? Throughout the novel, objects previously invested with great value are ignored by everyone, including money. The truck allows a greater range of movement for those who ride in it, and yet several people pass before the man and the boy see the truck. Nonetheless, this group is no army. Not even the word "gang" is used by McCarthy for these New Southern zombies, but simply the neutral "people," even as the man and his son correctly identify them as "the bad guys" (*Road* 59, 65). Though less than an army, they certainly seem loosely confederated around the truck in the enterprise of taking victims for food. The truck might provide an edge in combat with an army such as the red scarves who appear a few sections later. But the truck could also provide a means of transport for captives. Whereas the red scarf army needs slaves to pull its carts (thus reducing its use of captives for food), the "truck people" could "haul away" their captives for later consumption. As with the many references in the book to a lost world of commoditized goods now useless, the truck suggests that world already cranking up again.

That confederation of the "truck people," with their vehicle running (however poorly) on "God knows what" fuel, seems less regulated when compared with the red scarves, however. The man later finds the remains of the one he kills to protect the boy, "the bones and the skin piled together with rocks over them. A pool of guts" (*Road* 59). Compared with the "frieze of human heads" left by the red scarf army (76), the mere pile of bones left in the middle of the road by the truck people seems relatively practical—less ritualized—with only the "rocks over them" the slightest gesture at a burial ceremony after they ate one of their own. Who was he?

When the truck first stalls, the man enters the nearby woods where the father and the boy have hidden, discovering them. The first details of this man point to his zombie-like constant hunger and the strong suggestion that—in this world clearly bereft of all other animal life on which to use a knife—he has stayed alive through predatory cannibalism:

> The holes in [his belt] marked the progress of his emaciation and the leather at one side had a lacquered look to it where he was used to stropping the blade of his knife. . . . Eyes collared in cups of grime and deeply sunk. Like an animal inside a skull looking out the eyeholes. He wore a beard that had been cut square across the bottom with shears and he had a tattoo of a bird on his neck done by someone with an illformed notion of their appearance. He was lean, wiry, rachitic. Dressed in a pair of filthy blue coveralls and a black billcap with the logo of some vanished enterprise embroidered across the front of it. (*Road* 53–54)

This man also wears a "dirty crumpled paintmask," "sucking in and out," which heightens our sense of him as half-human, as the same masks worn by the man and his son are not seen so strangely (53). The adjective "rachitic" simply means he has rickets, a disease of malnutrition, but the sound of the word (especially as the word is unusual to most of us reading it for the first time) recalls the word "rat," adding to the animalization of the man. The only way for the narration—consistently through the father's eyes—could infer that he had rickets would be that the long bones of his arms and legs have been softened and warped. Rickets is caused by lack of vitamin D, which we usually create when exposed to the sun; everyone, therefore, in *The Road* must have rickets at this point in the book—particularly the boy. But it is only this zombie-like man who is described in this way; it heightens our sense that he is other than the man and the boy. Of course, he poses a threat, as we soon find when he dives and grabs the boy and holds a knife to his throat. But it is in the book's description of him that we see hints of the zombie type. Indeed, we see the father hunting for vitamin D much later in the book (220–21), so then we know why, perhaps, this man looks more "rachitic" than might the father and son. This modern zombie is hardly alive, but rather described by his outer details of appearance, which include both the unnerving attention to his breathing, but also to practical aspects of his clothing that nonetheless call together stereotypical descriptions of poor Southerners. Along with his "filthy blue coveralls" he wears "a black billcap with the logo of some vanished enterprise embroidered across the front of it" (54). Such caps are called "gimme" caps because large corporations give them away to farmers and ranchers to promote tractors, combines, and other industrial products and means of production in factory farming and animal rearing and slaughtering—such as diesel trucks. This figure represents not only the stereotypical poor white, but also one whose "enterprise" has "vanished."

Before we link that "enterprise" to slavery and the Old South, how do we know we are in the American South at all? Many readers will recognize details in the novel that reveal this, especially when the man and boy reach the ocean. But Wes Morgan has established the path taken in *The Road* to a remarkably precise degree. The house they visit that is the man's home proves to be situated just as was McCarthy's boyhood home south of Knoxville (*Road* 23; Morgan 41). Morgan goes so far as to say that in *The Road*, "McCarthy is fictionally returning once again to his own roots in Knoxville and the southeast," and the scenes in the first third of the book are therefore "described in the most detail" (46). *The Road* has all to do with the South.

But we encounter all of the cannibals in the book (despite references to them earlier) in a less specific landscape, well after the man and boy cross over Newfound Gap and head down out of the Smoky Mountains into the western end of North Carolina. By a few pages later, the rest of the novel must take place in South Carolina. Morgan's identification of scenes with detailed correspondence to sites one could still visit indeed finds these between the first few pages of the novel, when they cross the Cumberland Gap (*Road* 12; Morgan 39) and when they leave that part of the South most familiar to McCarthy from his boyhood, crossing Newfound Gap (*Road* 29; Morgan 42). It is in the relatively amorphous South—identifiable by Morgan only as various possible routes south of Pendleton, South Carolina (45)—that we find the truck people, the red scarf army, and the once grand house. Encountering these, we also glimpse postapocalyptic echoes of the New South, then the Old, and then a conflation of the two.

Enterprise Cannibalism

We know that cannibalism in human history does not preclude consciousness at all, but rather appears with it, and perhaps before it. Anthropologists distinguish, of course, between survival cannibalism of the dead and the killing of others for food, and further separate ritual cannibalism by societies from that which so deviates from surrounding cultural norms that we criminalize it (Kantner). In 1973, a Uruguayan rugby team's plane crashed in the Andes, and sixteen survivors resorted to eating some of the twenty-nine who died in the crash or soon thereafter. One of the fathers of the casualties called those who survived "heroes," and another said at a press conference, "Thank God that the forty-five were there, for sixteen homes have regained their children." This father noted, "As a doctor I understood at once that no one could have survived in such a place and under such conditions without resort to courageous decisions" (Read 314). By contrast, cannibalism among the Donner party in 1846 in the Sierra Nevada has been widely judged as a measure resorted to in a variety of situations that run from understandable survival cannibalism to murder. Some survivors avoided it altogether (Stewart).

There are no such "courageous decisions" in *The Road*, but rather a moral descent, it seems, through a progression that ironically leads not merely back to the atavistic cannibalism of the red scarf army, but forward again, to a cannibalism depending on transportation, communication, and possibly export of surplus food. As we will see when we enter the once grand house, cannibalism in *The Road* cannot be considered outside our historical memory of slavery, but also our awareness of the fragility of human interactions around commerce. If the Old South that gave rise to the once grand house still haunts it, the New Southern economic ironies of consumption, depending on cheap goods manufactured by near-slave labor overseas, and on ubiquitous messages to promote consumption as a means of finding connection, haunt it as well. If cannibalism of any form seems only to exist in *The Road* in connection to slavery and a remembrance of ubiquitous consumption, then the unequivocal injunction against cannibalism becomes more warranted.

Cannibalism cannot be presented directly in *The Road* as something we might condone even from the distance of anthropology, nor from the closeness of understanding it as a "courageous decision" to eat the already dead. As Michel de Montaigne wrote, "[T]here is more Barbarity in eating a Man alive, than when he is dead" (233). We might add that there is more barbarity still, however, if the cannibalism we come closest to seeing is ironically advanced from the "bloodcult" form of the red scarf army. Then cannibalism becomes less the "barbaric" activity of the other, and more the "barbaric" activity of ourselves. We see this in aspects of cannibalism by the New Southern zombies. What the once grand house presents us with is nothing less than an enterprise of collecting and transporting humans, keeping them confined, and eating them in a form of human factory farming. As this is what the man and boy will find, it clarifies the moral equation in the novel: any form of cannibalism whatsoever cannot be practiced by anyone hoping to carry the fire of consciousness into the future. Sympathetic exceptions simply remain outside the book's direct depiction.

Echoes of consumption before the apocalypse meanwhile prefigure the economy of the once grand house before we enter it. McCarthy's novel regularly includes details of a past consumerist culture already adumbrating the horrors of cannibal consumption that follow whatever calamity strikes the planet. Billboards that bear messages "that warned people away" reveal, behind that writing over now-whitewashed backgrounds, the older images of the lost society: "a pale palimpsest of advertisements for goods which no longer existed" (*Road* 108).

In the scene where the father finds a Coke and gives it to the boy, Brian Donnelly finds "a reprieve from a narrative dominated by a bitter struggle to survive while avoiding the marauding bands of cannibals that constitute most of what is left of humanity" (70). Ironically, "this reprieve recalls the ideology that the Coca-Cola brand has worked so assiduously to establish since its inception in 1886" (70). It nonetheless recollects, "in its delineation of the desolate and defunct supermarket, the gross excesses of consumer culture which the novel as a whole seems to critique" (70–71). Indeed, the boy insists that his father share the Coke with him (*Road* 20), and if we ignore the labeling in the scene, it would simply be one of many where the man and the boy commune over what meager food they have. But the label, and the setting, matter.

The supermarket in which they find the Coke is, to Donnelly,

a corporate cannibal that feeds off those weaker entities of the same species and, through the monopoly of supply and demand, drives specialized, individual traders out of business. In this sense the supermarket epitomizes just the sort of self-consuming society McCarthy sends to its demise in the apocalypse that precedes the narrative of *The Road*. Cannibalism as a metaphor for consumption is realized in this novel, and, further, it articulates a relationship between consumption and the horrific, uncanny, and abject. (71)

As Southern literature, aspects of *The Road* suggest the logical results of a more particular culture that collapsed, but that nonetheless retains its habits of production and consumption. Those habits of the red scarf Old Southern zombies revive in Gothic remembering the production and consumption system of slavery. The New Southern zombies, by contrast, have become the masters of a commoditizing system of predation by humans on humans. They even lack industrial sites for this, however, and much like the Old South, rely on the plantation home as a site of both production and consumption, where slavery has become such a literalized form of human commoditization as to make the red scarf army look comparatively humane. Even parsing such distinctions of horror becomes a Gothic exercise, and the full effect of the third group of zombies is to fully conflate distinctions within the metaphorical consumption Donnelly notes in the supermarket.

That the third group operates its enterprise cannibalism from within a house might seem to reverse Turner's observation of indifference by zombies to a home. Not, however, if that home fails to maintain the better distinctions of inside and outside that usually, as Gaston Bachelard noted of the house, "give mankind proofs or illusions of stability"—what he even goes on to call "the soul of the house" (17). Not all houses perform this function, however. Bachelard notes the most Gothic space of the house (without calling it that) is the cellar: "The cellar dreamer knows that the walls of the cellar are buried walls . . . that have the entire earth behind them. . . . The cellar then becomes buried madness, walled-in tragedy" (20). Bachelard goes on to note the regularity of cellars as "criminal" spaces for stories, of course, citing

Edgar Allen Poe's "The Cask of Amontillado" (20). The cellar is "first and foremost the *dark entity* of the house, the one that partakes of subterranean forces. When we dream there, we are in harmony with the irrationality of the depths" (18; italics in orig.).

Plantation Gothic

Reasonably fearful of houses in the upside-down world of *The Road*, the father and son go indoors only when they must, for food. Basements, cellars (finished out or not), the crude root cellars outside a farmhouse—these spaces promise McCarthy's father and son at least the possibility of food. But with the exception of an underground shelter found later on, what food the father and son might find would be the last leftovers, the forgotten and missed canned goods from before an anomic descent into predation reversed the fragile hierarchy of civilized spaces. Inside spaces now also hold the greatest horrors. Despite the boy's fears, however, in most of the houses they enter, they find no one, or at least no one alive, and they often find food. It is in the main house of a plantation, however, the one house in the novel with the deepest history and the darkest cellar, that they find the most Gothic space of *The Road*.

After five days with nothing to eat, they come across a "once grand house sited on a rise above the road" (*Road* 89). It sits not only over that road like a castle, with "southfacing fields," as well as woods; this property includes substantial grounds. It stands "tall and stately with white doric columns across the front. A port cochere at the side" (89). What McCarthy seems to recall from the sound of its pronunciation must be a "porte cochere," a covered path for carriages to deposit guests to a side entrance of the house in bad weather, then to drive on through to an inner courtyard. To clarify the lost grandeur of this house, the man and the boy cross its porch under a "lamp that hung from a *long* chain overhead" (90; italics added), and we are allowed free indirect discourse for his thoughts: "Chattel slaves had once trod those boards bearing food and drink on silver trays" (90). The grandness of this house once relied on slavery; interestingly, their figurative ghosts in this sentence carry food. Including the word "chattel"—which in property law means personal, movable property—particularizes two aspects of slavery here: that each slave was the personal property of his or her legal owner, and that slaves were of course moved. The second definition for the word is merely a slave. This would render this compound noun redundant, except that it reminds us of aspects of these slaves common to the people that the man and boy will soon encounter.

They enter "a broad foyer floored in a domino of black and white marble tiles" (*Road* 90)—even the flooring recalls in blatant fashion a distillation of the color of owners and slaves, as a "domino" of such tiles suggests more black tiles than white, reflecting the differential of slaves to owners. The man notices "fine Morris paper on the walls" (90). Charlotte Gere's history of designer William Morris notes that the wallpaper designs for which he became famous would have been manufactured in the 1870s and 1880s—well after the Civil War. This house maintained its grandeur, then, through Reconstruction and despite losing entirely free labor. McCarthy's inclusion of this detail for the house's walls, intentionally or not, suggests the house built by those "chattel slaves" was later redecorated during Reconstruction; the house therefore maintained its grandeur despite emancipation. More specific than the indictment of general consumerism that Donnelly rightly finds in the Coca-Cola scene, the details of this house adumbrate the evolution of labor that produced and maintained it—in parallel with the evolution of the zombie figure. Because we find the house more than a hundred years later, the occupants of it further suggest comparisons with the evolved zombie of American horror films.

The zombie figure has evolved through so many contradictory characteristics as to carry with it a virtually synecdochic history of race and labor, particularly in Haiti, where the term found its first publication in a novel, and in the United States, where its appearance in film quickly led to further evolution.[3] Kieren Murphy traces the zombie's transitions from a spirit to undead slave (48, 50), but also notes, citing the story of a former slave who had fought under the Haitian Revolution's great general Toussaint Louverture, that a zombie may merely be any living person who resembles a corpse. This slave returns home only to "reject his mother because she looks like a dead body" (Murphy 50). Here the zombie need not be the literal walking dead, but can create a customary "anxiety surrounding the embodied zombie" merely by looking like one (Murphy 50).

Moving on, the father and son find the house's "great hall . . . with ceilings twice the height of the doors" (*Road* 91). That would be fourteen to sixteen feet high. The house's sheer size recalls the monstrous differential of wealth to slavery, of the unending labor it took to produce such a structure, with its "hand-made brick," "kilned out of the dirt it stood on" (89–90). As if to recall the house's first zombie-victims before we see the more recent ones, however, the man and boy first pause at the doorway to the dining room, and see "a great heap of clothing. Clothes and shoes. Belts. Coats. Blankets and old sleeping bags. He would have ample time later to think about that" (90–91). These piles of the personal effects of victims connect this site of Southern Gothic with the Holocaust. Globalizing the context for both slavery and Reconstruction, McCarthy sets the stage for a Gothic encounter that reverberates not only through Southern history, but also through universal tragedy.

After seeing this pile of clothes, the man finds "blackened pots" in the cold fireplace, and then a cord passed through a window "tied to a brass bell . . . in a wooden jib that had been nailed to the window molding" (*Road* 91). This odd bell serves as a grotesque descendant of the service pull that would have been used in the house to summon servants—or slaves. As the man figures out later, it functions as a communications device for alerting people in the house of the approach of potential victims (97). Every sign suggests that this house belongs now to cannibals. And still the man, with the boy in tow, persists in breaking the hasps off a locked door in the floor of the pantry. "There's a reason this is locked," he says (90).

The reader may wonder how he could possibly fail to guess that the lock is not to keep them out, but to keep people inside the cellar below. But the book has not yet portrayed the house as the site of the darkest evil. Previous descriptions of the zombie cannibals, of "bloodcults," "road-agents," and "marauders" (*Road* 14) and of course of the red scarf army and the man from the truck, all focus on threats outside, on the road and in the open. As in most horror films, the man's unwillingness to leave a place the reader knows to be dangerous places moral judgment on him. Never guilty in relation to the monster lurking nearby, the character in danger carries some other sin with them: sexuality, race, or even the unconscious guilt of society—its collusion, condoning, or even mere ignorance of crimes on a larger scale. This certainly becomes true in many horror films of the late 1960s into the 1970s, when racism, the Vietnam War, and other sins of American society erupt in Gothic horror.[4]

Here, the man's persistence, especially in this "once grand house," suggests the resurfacing of repressed cultural memory. The man does imagine the Old South's system relying on those "chattel slaves," but ironically, the grandeur of the house would suggest greater possibilities of stored food. To imagine the dark reality of this postapocalyptic New South's manner of exploitation remains beyond him. The boy, however, born after the catastrophe leading to this world, swears he is not hungry, and pleads with his father to leave. As if the boy remains untainted by connection to the fallen world of consumerism, slavery, and ubiquitous commoditization, the boy expresses the reader's sense that this is no place to explore—that the reasons for the lock on the door runs deep.

That lock, and the difficulty with which the man finally opens it, evidences not only resistance to outside intrusion, but of course, more pragmatically, prevention of escape from inside. McCarthy takes us through the door that Tobe Hooper keeps largely closed to us. In his original version of *The Texas Chain Saw Massacre* (1974), Kirk, the film's first victim, goes into an apparently empty house, drawn to an odd interior doorway through which we hear the sounds of a pig grunting, half squealing. These sounds clearly come from Leatherface, the cannibal family's main butcher, who appears just as Kirk has tripped through the doorway and is beginning to stand up. A brief close-up puts us in the position of the victim as Leatherface—in butcher's apron and wearing a mask of someone else's skin—raises his arm, but then the camera jumps back to the front door where Kirk had entered. We see the blow of what sounds like a hammer and Kirk falls. So far, we are witness but also victim, yet the point of view then jumps to that of the cannibal, bent over at work in a tedious moment of slaughter: the man is not dead and his legs kick uncontrollably. The editing jumps back to relative distance near the front door, and we see the body hauled inside with the only sound from Leatherface that so far seems human. It is a grunt, but where the film previously had to have used either a recording of a pig or an excellent imitation of one, we now hear something of disgust. Leatherface is at work, and the work did not go smoothly. In what has to be one of the more iconic moments of horror in American cinema, he then pulls shut a metal door. The sound is loud, final, and oddly industrial in this old wooden house.

Cannibalism in *The Road* has so far remained a matter of human violence, not directly referencing animals. But this house is itself a ghost of many spaces: the home of plantation owners and the seat of power over slaves, it has just echoed a building in a concentration camp, and it is about to suggest a slaughterhouse. Like the house in Hooper's film, a site of previous mastery over the cultivation of crops and animal breeding and slaughter becomes industrialized. The door Leatherface slams shut, as well as the apron we see him wearing, point directly to the commercial slaughterhouse. The door the man opens is locked so securely that he has to pry up the hasp. To do this he finds a shovel only after passing "a forty gallon castiron cauldron of the kind once used for rendering hogs" (*Road* 92). As if to keep us close to the man's point of view and yet pull away in witness, the narration tells us, "All these things he saw and did not see" (92).

The door pried open, we descend with the man and his son, who is too afraid to stay out of the cellar without his father. As Bachelard reminds us, cellars are intermediary spaces, the part of a house that is most like a cave (20), and here, the floor is literally of clay and the walls of stone. The man's lighter reveals this:

> Huddled against the back wall were naked people, male and female, all trying to hide, shielding their faces with their hands. On the mattress lay a man with his legs gone to the hip and the stumps of them blackened and burnt. The smell was hideous. . . .
>
> Then one by one they turned and blinked in the pitiful light. Help us, they whispered. Please help us. (*Road* 93)

The man drops the lighter and shoves the boy upstairs and through the hatch. This brief view of the victims of cannibalism yet living reveals them as fully pitiable and yet monstrous: the man not only flees because he knows their captors could trap him and the boy with these naked victims, but because they too seem to pose a threat. Repeatedly through this novel the man thinks quickly and tactically, more efficiently than most readers could manage in the severe circumstances through which we follow him. Here, he might have left the door open in hopes that the escaping victims could draw away their captors—just as the man tells the boy he meant to run away from him to draw their pursuers away (*Road* 96). In this moment, however, they seem to be fleeing the victims as much as the cannibals, especially as we saw the effort it took (including the leverage of the shovel) just to raise the door and yet the man "got hold of the door and swung it over and let it slam down" before they run (94).

Cannibalism here, as in *The Texas Chain Saw Massacre*, has erased distinctions between cannibal and victim; neither remains human. Within this plantation house, the cellar abattoir parallels that second interiority within the house in Hooper's film: slaughter on a nearly industrial scale has entered the domestic space where a family once lived.

But ironically, the house in *The Road* was once the grand home of slave owners, whereas Robin Wood sees the family in the horror film (slaughterhouse workers put out of work by technological advances) as "victims, too—of the slaughterhouse environment, of capitalism" (82). Mark Bernard further reads *The Texas Chain Saw Massacre* through foodways studies, and finds "class difference and class struggle are conceptualized in terms of *food*" (416; italics in orig.)

In *The Road*, class seems to have evaporated except in brief moments, such as when the father intentionally uses medical terms when threatening the cannibal who attacks his son. The man reveals his education as a superior aspect of his former life when all this cannibal can think to say after this is, "Are you a doctor?" (*Road* 55). In the house, we have no reason to assume any prior relation of the cannibals to the house, but this does not matter; whether they are the original owners or squatters, they have taken a position of dominance over their victims by occupying the former site of power within slavery and the extended abuses of Reconstruction. "Coming across the field toward the house were four bearded men and two women" (94). We get no other details of these cannibals.

That leaves us with the image of the people in the abattoir cellar, who themselves are zombies in as much as they are totally abject: naked, undifferentiated by gender, and one of them kept alive for nothing but the practical purposes of using him for food one leg at a time. That detail, and others such as the cauldron "once used for rendering hogs," conflates the animal with the human, just as the man's fear and the appearance of the people in the cellar conflate cannibal with victim. Peter Dendle's definition again deepens our understanding of identity in *The Road*:

> Zombification is the logical conclusion of human reductionism: it is to reduce a person to body, to reduce behavior to basic motor functions, and to reduce social utility to raw labour. . . . the process represents a psychic imperialism: the displacement of one person's right to experience life,

spirit, passion, autonomy, and creativity for another person's exploitative gain. (48)

In *The Road*, everyone is a zombie of the New Southern Gothic, as even the man and the boy are often reduced to nothing but sheer physical survival, fighting cold and starvation. The boy questions the father first when he kills the cannibal in defense of his son: "Are we still the good guys?" (*Road* 65). Later, after the father leaves the thief without his clothes to freeze to death, the boy challenges him fully, implicating even himself: "But we did kill him" (219). Even this Christlike child's hair has been mingled with the "filth" of the brains of the cannibal his father shot (58). Both, as much as they refuse cannibalism, have been touched by it.

In *The Road*, the implicit critique of a New Southern economic cannibalism ultimately conflates consumer and consumed, just as its zombies prove to be hardly more zombie-like in their appearance than their victims, though more zombie-like in their actions and affect. The zombies we meet in *The Road* are us and the Other at the same time, and only the critical choice not to eat other people, to carry the fire even against the exigencies of starvation, promises the continuance of what is beyond zombification, of what is human.

Notes

1. Page numbers here indicate the 241-page hardcover edition. Readers with the 287-page trade paperback edition of *The Road* (and indeed anyone working on McCarthy) may find the McCarthy scholar John Sepich's online concordances helpful.

2. Without giving away the ending of another McCarthy novel above, I can here refer to the end of *Blood Meridian*, where I have previously argued the kid is partially cannibalized, as well as raped and murdered, by judge Holden.

3. See Dendle, as well as Murphy for brief histories of the zombie in Haiti and Boon on its reappearance in American film.

4. See especially George Romero's original *Night of the Living Dead* and Tobe Hooper's first version of *The Texas Chain Saw Massacre*. Much scholarship exists on these films. For an overview of 1970s horror films, see Wood.

Works Cited

Bachelard, Gaston. *The Poetics of Space*. Trans. Maria Jolas. Boston: Beacon, 1994. Print.

Bernard, Mark. "Cannibalism, Class and Power: A Foodways Analysis of *The Texas Chainsaw Massacre* Series." *Food, Culture and Society* 14.3 (2011): 413–32. Print.

Boon, Kevin Alexander. "Ontological Anxiety Made Flesh: The Zombie in Literature, Film, and Culture." *Monsters and the Monstrous: Myths and Metaphors of Enduring Evil*. Ed. Niall Scott. Amsterdam: Rodopi, 2007. 33–43. Print.

Dendle, Peter. "The Zombie as Barometer of Cultural Anxiety." *Monsters and the Monstrous: Myths and Metaphors of Enduring Evil*. Ed. Niall Scott. Amsterdam: Rodopi, 2007. 45–57. Print.

Donnelly, Brian. "'Coke is It!': Placing Coca-Cola in McCarthy's *The Road*." *Explicator* 68.1 (2010): 70–73. Print.

Gere, Charlotte. "Morris and Company, 1861–1939." *Victorian Web: Literature, History, & Culture in the Age of Victoria*. George P. Landow, 5 Nov. 2006. Web. 31 Oct. 2012.

Kantner, John. "Survival Cannibalism or Sociopolitical Intimidation? Explaining Perimortem Multilation in the American Southwest." *Human Nature: An Interdisciplinary Biosocial Perspective* 10.1 (1999): 1–50. Print.

McCarthy, Cormac. *The Road*. New York: Knopf, 2006. Print.

___. *Outer Dark*. New York: Vintage, 1993. Print.

___. *Suttree*. New York: Vintage, 1992. Print.

___. *Blood Meridian, or The Evening Redness in the West*. New York: Vintage, 1992. Print.

Montaigne, Michel de. *Montaigne's Essays: In Three Books with Notes and Quotations*. Trans. Charles Cotton. London, 1743. Print.

Morgan, Wesley G. "The Route and Roots of *The Road*." *Cormac McCarthy Journal* 6.1 (2008): 39–47. Print.

Murphy, Kieran M. "White Zombie." *Contemporary French and Francophone Studies* 15.1 (2011): 47–55. Print.

Night of the Living Dead. Dir. George A. Romero. Screenplay by John Russo and George A. Romero. 1968. Elite, 2001. DVD.

Read, Piers Paul. *Alive: The Story of the Andes Survivors*. New York: Avon, 1974. Print.

Sepich, John, Christopher Forbis, and Wesley G. Morgan. "Cormac McCarthy Resources: All Words, by Book." *johnsepich.com*. Christopher Forbis and John Sepich, 2 July 2007. Web. 31 Oct. 2012.

Stewart, George R. *Ordeal by Hunger: The Story of the Donner Party*. Boston: Houghton, 1960. Print.

The Texas Chain Saw Massacre. Dir. Tobe Hooper. Screenplay by Kim Henkel and Tobe Hooper. 1974. Elite, 1996. DVD.

Turner, Barnard. "Heiner Müller's Medea: Towards a Paradigm for the Contemporary Gothic Anatomy." *Spectral Readings: Towards a Gothic Geography*. Ed. Glennis Byron and David Punter. New York: St. Martin's, 1999. 202–16. Print.

Wood, Robin. "The American Nightmare: Horror in the 70s." *Hollywood from Vietnam to Reagan . . . And Beyond*. Columbia UP, 2003. Print.

CRITICAL
READINGS

Charles W. Chesnutt's Southern Gothic of Guilt _____

Ronja Vieth

Introduction

While Southern Gothic literature is known to utilize Gothic props of luscious decay, degeneration, and violence to intimate social issues prevalent in the slavery and post-slavery American South, Charles Chesnutt's works reveal, however, that the important underlying factor for the Southern Gothic is a pervading notion of guilt. Subtly informing the Gothic works of William Faulkner, for instance, guilt over the practice of slavery and the continuing maltreatment of African Americans during and after Reconstruction is more overtly a topic in Chesnutt's works. While his 1899 collection of stories, *The Conjure Woman*, is a delicate and understated treatment of guilt with little impact on the predominantly white, reading audience, his later novel, *The Marrow of Tradition* (1901), is a much more direct, and consequently less popular, commentary on historical guilt. In order to either insinuate, as in *The Conjure Woman*, or expose this nation's underlying historical guilt, as in *The Marrow of Tradition*, Chesnutt utilizes Gothic tropes such as inversion, mirroring, doppelgängers, and haunting in these two works.

The combination of various Gothic tropes is not a novel idea, as the genre itself has been a malleable one from its inception by British writer Horace Walpole. The initial Gothic setting and props Walpole employed in his novella *The Castle of Otranto: A Gothic Story* (1764) had been quickly adapted in Britain and the United States, where the Gothic genre underwent many adaptations to the new geographical and social environment, resulting in, for example, the Southern Gothic and the frontier Gothic. Most importantly, Leslie Fiedler's declaration that "until the gothic had been discovered, the serious American novel could not begin; and as long as that novel lasts, the gothic cannot die" (143) suggests that there are attributes characteristic of the United States that can only be expressed and fictionally represented in Gothic literature.

Since the plot of Walpole's novella is the usurpation of an Italian estate by earlier generations whose current residents now have to atone for their fathers' sins, the theme of guilt is the main factor that inspired him to turn a nightmare into fiction. This nightmare derived from his anxiety over his family's victimization by political scandals that were based on disingenuous accusations that cost his cousin his post at the royal court. Accordingly, Walpole writes in his preface to the first edition that he wished the plot had been based on "a more useful moral than this, that *the sins of the fathers are visited on their children to the third and fourth generation*" (7; italics in orig.). Fiedler, therefore, seems to suggest that the nation's doubtful characteristics emerge in American Gothic literature, characteristics that are permeating history and perpetuating guilt.

Yet, Southern Gothic not only gets its name from its setting in the American South; rather, it is the historical setting of slavery and its repercussions that make this genre a particularly apt medium to discuss the nation's past. The relationship between the Gothic and guilt becomes clear when one understands the interconnectedness between culture and its literary production. Teresa A. Goddu explains that the intimate connection between Gothic stories and the "culture that produces them" (and thus historicizes them) must not be ignored (2). She further asserts that "slavery haunts the American gothic" (3), because, despite this nation's relatively young age, the United States has enough history to justify Gothic literature. Locating the site of historical haunting in slavery, Goddu explains that

> American gothic literature criticizes America's national myth of new-world innocence by voicing the cultural contradictions that undermine the nation's claim to purity and equality. . . . The gothic tells of historical horrors that make national identity possible yet must be repressed in order to sustain it. (10)

This suppression is closely linked with the feelings of guilt that have always been concurrent with the historical atrocities committed.

Regularly, writers such as J. Hector St. John de Crèvecoeur, whose *Letters from an American Farmer* (1782) already discussed the discrepancy between the slaveholders' alleged benevolence and their actual conduct, have voiced vague dissent and moral scruples indicative of feelings of guilt, and according to Charles L. Crow, additional early authors who exhibited such feelings are Cotton Mather and William Bradford. However, scholars have only glimpsed a tentative connection between historical and cultural guilt and American Gothic literature. Like Goddu, Crow also finds slavery and its aftermath a suitable topic for Gothic literature. And although Louis S. Gross recognizes the American Gothic as a genre that serves to provide an "alternative history of the American experience" (3), Eric Savoy clarifies that the object of the American Gothic is not to reiterate and reinforce history, but to reconstruct and rewrite it. This historiography, then, assists in dealing with the haunting influences and anxieties from the past.

These anxieties derive from the unacknowledged notion of historical guilt, which permeates generations long after the offenses if that guilt remains ignored and disregarded. In order to truly liberate oneself of anxieties and evoke healing, according to philosopher Margaret Urban Walker, both victims and perpetrators (even later generations of either) need to engage in a sincere and communicative act of restorative justice. A respectful acknowledgment of the victims' "moral vulnerability" establishes mutual accountability for a culturally shared past, present, and future, says Walker (31). American Gothic literature provides a medium with which to initiate acknowledgment because its anxiety-inducing tropes allow the readers to dispense with their defense mechanisms, engage in reader participation, and have their assumptions of historical accuracy challenged. In other words, the main feature of the American Gothic is its ability to challenge the readers' safe boundaries of aesthetic distance, which, in turn, allows them to emotionally and morally participate in the Africans' and African American's horrors endured during slavery and post–Reconstruction.

The Conjure Woman

Chesnutt's short story collection, set in North Carolina during Recon-struction, exemplifies the ways American national guilt was accrued during the times of slavery. Uncle Julius, a former slave, narrates con-jure stories from the past to the Northern couple, Annie and John. The tension that ensues between Annie's willingness to believe in the sto-ries, which John finds irrational and claims are unreal, mirrors con-temporary society's attitude toward the political situation at the turn of the last century. While some Americans dismissed the horrible treat-ment of African and African Americans slaves, others understood at least the emotional impact slavery had on the non-Anglo population. Altogether, the conjure stories serve three distinct purposes: First, An-nie empathizes with the characters and feels the emotional and moral impact in which readers can participate by reducing their aesthetic dis-tance to Chesnutt's text. Also, John continues to degrade the African American population by perpetuating the old racial distinctions that made the system of slavery possible and thus points out to the reader the false basis and perpetuation of those beliefs. Finally, Uncle Julius provides an elaborately emotional picture of slavery's aspects with-out belittling himself or his people, despite John's thinking otherwise. Thus, Uncle Julius's stories "prove" that African Americans are human beings with feelings and rational capacities, and they accordingly have a natural right to freedom and autonomy. By showing these aspects to the reader, he or she is made aware of a sense of guilt, which the Gothic features of the tales seek to emphasize.

The Conjure Woman tales resemble the popular genre of plantation stories, which were successful because of their pastoral representa-tion of slavery and the antebellum South and which served to rein-force the fallacy that slavery was a benign and benevolent system. Robert M. Farnsworth calls those stories "sentimental revery" and realizes that "the hunger for such fantasy indicates the retreat of the American white public from the demands of the Reconstruction effort made after the exhausting and enervating Civil War" (vi). Although

---

Chesnutt's tales were popular because of their entertaining qualities, their Gothic elements were meant to provoke reflection and to access buried emotions. Instead, Chesnutt's tales, partly written in local color dialect reminiscent of Joel Chandler Harris, gained him fame as a local color author. Chesnutt's political agenda was overlooked, despite critics' recognition of the especially gruesome or Gothic qualities of the stories. Still, few contemporary scholars besides Crow recognize Chesnutt's *The Conjure Woman* tales as Gothic; even Sandra Monlyneaux refrains from calling the tales Gothic, while simultaneously acknowledging their role of providing a mirror to conveniently forgotten history. She says that

> Chesnutt's "conjuring" voice negotiates the delicate discourse between clashing cultures—challenging faded memory, stubborn blindness, and divisive discourse. Chesnutt demonstrates that it is essential to remember the content of one's heritage. . . . *The Conjure Woman* remains a recorded legacy and model for a new generation willing to civilize itself—to extend beyond an alien dialect and into the "magic mirror" of story. (174)

This Gothic mirror, however, is what induces readers to engage in historical or genealogical accountability and moral vulnerability. The subtle empathy expressed by the character Annie, for instance, provides a model for the readers. In the story "Sis' Becky's Pickaninny," Annie's empathy with the character Sis' Becky overtly effects healing in the audience, as Annie recuperates from her depression after hearing and engaging in Uncle Julius's tale. Although Annie appears to have no children of her own, she empathizes with the slave woman Sis' Becky who is traded for a race horse. Already suffering from the loss of her sold husband, the separation from her little "pickaninny" results in both mother and son suffering from serious depression and a withering of health and spirit. Sis' Becky's master, described by the narrator as benevolent, offers to send Sis' Becky's son along with her, but the new master opposes, "fer niggers is made ter wuk, en dey ain' got no time fer no sich foolis'ness ez babies" (Chesnutt, *Conjure* 142).

Subtly exposing the proposed benevolence of slavery to be based on economic interests, the narrator continues that when the nanny Aun' Nancy reports little Moses's deteriorating health to her masters, they do send for a doctor because "Aun' Nancy's ole missis 'lowed he wuz a lackly little nigger en wu'th raisin'" (145). Understandably distrustful of Anglo American physicians, however, Aun' Nancy proceeds to take Moses to the conjure woman Aun' Peggy instead who then conjures Moses into a hummingbird and then a mockingbird so that he can fly and sing to his mother. Since this does not offer a permanent solution to improving her health, though, Aun' Nancy wishes to get Sis' Becky back to the plantation. Aun' Peggy therefore sends a hornet to sting the racehorse and make it seem faulty, while simultaneously conjuring nightmares for Sis' Becky that further diminish her health. Finally, the plantation owners' deal is reversed and Sis' Becky is returned to her son. After the "goopher" has been taken off, Moses grows up and buy his mother's and his own freedom.

The story and especially its ending emphasize African American autonomy and empowerment, thus subtly criticizing the institution of slavery. Furthermore, by realizing that mothers ought to have a right to raise their children and men should have the right to provide for their families, Annie, at least, recognizes that freedom is a ubiquitous human right. With Annie's face expressing "in turn sympathy, indignation, pity, and at the end lively satisfaction," her character mirrors the reader's response when engaged in reader participation (158). Her facial expressions reflect emotional stages leading up to the recognition that slavery was, indeed, not a benevolent system but an institution that was based on economic interests that denied basic human rights. As the readers become aware of these historical truths and their generational guilt, they also witness Annie's healing process. Uncle Julius's tale has provided Annie with an opportunity for catharsis; the experience of various emotions by vicariously living Sis' Becky's emotions described in the tale ignites Annie's own recovery from depression. The tale works similarly for the reader; even if Uncle Julius's tale within in the frame tale of Annie and John's listening to the narration were too remote for some readers, the surrounding story of the couple allows for easier reader participation. Furthermore, if one cannot identify with Annie, there is also the character of John, which has an effect on the reader.

John is an embodiment of rational, Western mentality that denied the validity of human rights to slaves as much as John still denies the validity of Uncle Julius's tales, however hidden by elements of folklore or conjure. Asserting and perpetuating typical Anglo American prejudices against former slaves, John comments on Uncle Julius's conjure tales saying,

> "Julius," I observed, half to him and half to my wife, "your people will never rise in the world until they throw off these childish superstitions and learn to live by the light of reason and common sense. How absurd to imagine that the fore-foot of a poor dead rabbit . . . can promote happiness or success, or ward off failure or misfortune!" (135)

However, it is John's rational curiosity that initiates the conversation in the first place because he asks Uncle Julius about the object in his hand, which "had not yet outgrown the charm of novelty" for John's inquisitive, analytical mind. Also, John never misses an opportunity to educate Uncle Julius on the dangers of irrational beliefs. Nevertheless, it is John's rational, and allegedly superior, mind that does not recognize Uncle Julius's reason for bringing the rabbit's foot along. Knowing that Annie has not been feeling well, Uncle Julius attempts to cheer her up with the story about Sis' Becky, but it is easier to make her listen if there is an unusual object, such as a tangible talisman, attached to it. Chesnutt uses Gothic inversion to emphasize the flaws in allegedly superior, but really detrimental, rational behavior. Uncle Julius's reply to John's tutelage thus satirizes John by playing toward John's prejudices of African Americans' ignorance:

> "It is ridiculous," assented my wife, with faint interest.
> "Dat's w'at I tells dese niggers roun' heah," said Julius. "De fo'-foot ain' got no power. Ihas ter be de hin'-foot, suh,—de lef' hin'-foot er a grabe-ya'd rabbit, killt by a cross-eyed nigger on a da'k night in de full er de moon." (135)

By purportedly feeding the stereotype that African Americans lack of rational capacities, Uncle Julius points out the shortcomings of this one-sided disposition of Western thought, which, of course, resulted in slavery as one of the atrocities committed by this nation whose founding ideologies proclaim liberty and justice for all. At the end of the narration, John calls Uncle Julius's story "a very ingenious fairy tale," because unlike his wife Annie, he still has not understood its point (159). Annie exclaims severely that the "story bears the stamp of truth, if ever a story did." She recognizes that the story's features that John ridicules are merely "ornamental details and not at all essential," because she realizes that "the story is true to nature, and might have happened half a hundred times, and no doubt did happen, in those horrid days before the war" (159). While Annie perceives the reality of the recounted horrors of slavery, John chooses to further ignore them and doubt the value of the tale altogether, arguing that the story has not proven the premise of a rabbit's foot bringing good luck. Uncle Julius knows that Annie understands more than even she lets on with her husband to whom she merely explains, "I rather suspect . . . that Sis' Becky had no rabbit's foot" (160).

It does not emerge until later when Annie has recuperated from her illness and has resumed her afternoon drives that she has kept the rabbit's foot Uncle Julius must have offered her during John's short absence from the porch. While it remains doubtful that Annie has kept the talisman for good luck, it has nevertheless helped her out of her depression by reminding her of Uncle Julius's tale and the effect it has had on her. Annie understands what the story is really about and wants her husband to see this too. Yet, rather than allow Uncle Julius's stories to challenge his devotion to potentially detrimental and guilt-accruing rational thought, John clings to the accustomed stereotypes.

Throughout all of the tales, John is suspicious of Uncle Julius's motives for telling the conjure stories and is eager to believe that Uncle Julius's tales serve an ulterior motive. The progression of the tales in the collection easily leads the reader to fall into the same trap, as the first tales indeed end in a way that induces the Northern couple to be more generous or benevolent to the African American community surrounding them. For instance, the first story, "The Goophered Grapevine," suggests that Uncle Julius tries to discourage the couple from buying the vineyard so that he may continue to profit from the product. The second story, "Po' Sandy," also seems to prove Uncle Julius's interest in the haunted timber to build a church for his dissented congregation. Any suspicion on the part of the reader is mitigated, though, by the number of stories that relate the exploitation and abuse of slaves and that emphasize that the Anglo American population does, in fact, owe the African Americans some sort of compensation.

The last tales in the collection, however, demonstrate Uncle Julius's genuine concern for the couple's well-being and are told in an effort to help Annie convalesce from her depression as well as mend a broken relationship between Annie's younger sister Mabel and Mabel's fiancé, Murchison. Stressing the juxtaposition of projected and real intentions of Uncle Julius, Chesnutt in "Hot-Foot Hannibal," for instance, summarizes the contemporary Anglo American attitude represented by John: After seeing Mabel and her fiancé reunited due to the mare's balking at the haunt of the slave woman Chloe, John surmises that Uncle Julius had chosen to drive the long route toward the allegedly haunted spot on purpose:

He was fond of Mabel, but I was old enough, and knew Julius well enough, to be skeptical of his motives. It is certain that a most excellent understanding existed between him and Murchison after the reconciliation, and that when the young people set up housekeeping over at the old Murchison place, Julius had an opportunity to enter their service. For some reason or other, however, he preferred to remain with us. (228–29)

John still cannot accept that a former slave's ulterior motives might be benevolent of other people outside his immediate (racial or cultural) community and adds that the mare "was never known to balk again" (229). John thereby diffuses the idea of ghosts as important symbols in African American folklore. More importantly, John simultaneously dismisses the validity of the story itself, which recounts the horrors slaves endured in their personal lives when they were separated from their loved ones and left to pine away, as Chloe in this story is recounted to have done. John thus represents the Anglo American population that refuses to acknowledge and take responsibility for the tragedies in slave families caused by their rational, calculating, and materialistic owners.

The Conjure Woman offers the reality of slavery but presents three different lenses through which to see it. While Annie is the empathetic, emotional character with whom one can easily connect and gain access to the narrations' horrible truths, John is the rational person representing most of the American population at the time of the book's publication. Additionally, Uncle Julius is depicted as the stereotypically old, slightly comical and cunning former slave whose tales portray African Americans as people with virtues and vices like anybody else. Although this approach made *The Conjure Woman* more palatable to its predominantly white audience and gained Chesnutt recognition as a writer, his political agenda of educating the white population had failed. In another literary attempt, his 1901 novel *The Marrow of Tradition* was therefore a much more direct approach.

The Marrow of Tradition

Forfeiting the subtlety of *The Conjure Woman* tales, Chesnutt's post–Reconstruction novel fictionalizes the 1898 Wilmington, North Carolina, race riots and delineates how slavery's accrued guilt remains unacknowledged. The title of the novel suggests that the noxious ideologies that made slavery possible were still feeding the nation in which a worsening infringement on African American rights during the post–Reconstruction period portrayed a deep-seated racist attitude. Different from his folkloristic approach for "the elevation of whites" (Render 9), Chesnutt's *The Marrow of Tradition* is classified by some as psychological realism. Willie J. Harrell Jr., for instance, finds the novel's display of verisimilitude an authentic exposition of Southern prejudice. Furthermore, Bernard W. Bell agrees with George Levine, who says that "nineteenth-century realism was a highly self-conscious attempt to explore or create a new reality" that questioned social relations (qtd. in Bell102). These social relations—characterized by the emergence of Jim Crow laws, the Ku Klux Klan, and lynchings—clearly discriminated against African Americans and elucidate the unresolved and remaining racist attitude with which they had to deal. Thus, presenting the reader with fictionalized, yet genuine, scenarios that reveal the emanations of historical, national guilt, Chesnutt prompts us to confront the truth and realize our "complicity in evil"—both past and present (Simmons 100).

The Marrow of Tradition is not generally recognized as a Gothic work though critics reluctantly acknowledge the Gothic elements of *The Conjure Woman*: Slavery and its aftermath are suitable topics for Gothic literature in, as Crow says, their exposure of hidden truths that shake the bourgeoisie out of its complacency ("Upas" 262). Gerald Ianovici classifies *The Marrow of Tradition* as Realist despite its Gothic tropes, which emphasize "the gothic quality of nineteenth-century racial discourse" (40). Justin D. Edwards, however, finds the Gothic elements in the novel representative of "the asymmetrical divisions of power across racial lines" that Chesnutt sought to depict (95). Edwards goes on to observe that the Gothic tropes of doppelgängers, which allude to the destabilization of racial boundaries represented by the mulatto and the horrors of lynching, aid Chesnutt in this representation of contemporary racial relations. Nevertheless, the combination of the novel's realistic setting and the Gothic tropes reveal social anxieties, which indicate notions of guilt underlying the concept of racism and therefore make the novel distinctly Gothic.

Since, as Render explains, "Chesnutt also felt that whites avoided thinking about their injustices to blacks and thereby invited the danger inherent in the denial of evil" (34), Chesnutt realistically represents the post–Reconstruction disenfranchisement of the African American population in *The Marrow of Tradition* with Gothic tropes that challenge the readers' aesthetic distance and therefore boundaries of safety. Using the mulatto as a doppelgänger motif, Chesnutt not only points out the Anglo American's inclination to stereotype African Americans, but also indicts the false scientific notion of racial inferiority upon which the institution of slavery had been based. Both of these realizations create Gothic anxiety in the Anglo American reader, who realizes that both actions reveal national, historical guilt.

One way in which Chesnutt critiques the stereotyping of African Americans is in his narration of a cakewalk, which the white character Tom Delamere utilizes to frame the black manservant Sandy for robbery and murder. Originally a Sunday night parody by slaves to ridicule their white masters, the show was quickly appropriated by Anglo Americans who performed the cakewalk in blackface to caricature African Americans, explains Eric J. Sundquist. It is easy for Tom to evade suspicion as the real culprit for murdering his aunt Polly Ochiltree for the money he needs to pay off gambling debts, because his blackface rendition of Sandy at a cakewalk is blindly accepted as a black man's "typical" criminal behavior and places Sandy near the crime scene. Even though the narrator points out that "Sandy's" performance at the cakewalk had "struck him as somewhat overdone, even for the *comical type* of negro" (*Marrow* 119; italics added), the citizens of Wellington are eager to arrest Sandy without further investigation. Sandy's confusion in this scene represents the Gothic reality of unfounded, yet customary, arrests of African Americans during and after Reconstruction:

> As it seemed to Sandy, he saw himself hurrying along in front of himself toward the house. . . . The figure ahead of him wore his best clothes and looked exactly like him . . . The situation was certainly an incomprehensible one, and savored of the supernatural.
>
> "Ef dat's me gwine 'long in front," mused Sandy, in vinous perplexity, "den who is dis behin' here? . . . Ef dat's me in front, den I mus' be my own ha'nt; an' whichever one of us is de ha'nt, de yuther must be dead an' don' know it." (167)

The comical effect aside, Sandy's vision of his Gothic doppelgänger foreshadows the Gothic nightmare of lynching. Not granted a trial with a jury of his peers, Sandy is stereotyped as the degenerate African American whose supposedly bestial inclinations have led him to murder. Afraid to recognize a flaw in the pseudoscientific mindset that had justified the enslavement of people of African descent for centuries, the Anglo Americans of Wellington are quick to dispose of Sandy to constitute an example. The former overseer, McBane, exclaims, "Burn the nigger. . . . We seem to have the right nigger, but whether we have or not, burn *a* nigger. . . . The example would be all the more powerful if we got the wrongone" (182; italics in orig.).

This stereotyping of African Americans as a mechanism to avoid dealing with the notions of guilt, which would emerge once Anglo Americans recognized their flawed concepts of racial inferiority that helped build the nation, developed into the nationwide custom of lynching. During Reconstruction, says Sandra Gunning, an estimated 3,300 to 10,000 African Americans were hanged, and often tortured and mutilated, without a trial (5). Gunning explains that the black man symbolized the social chaos against which all whites could unite to purge their fears over national unity, black emancipation, and European immigration (6). The description of the adamant behavior of Wellington's white population to justify this practice tells of Chesnutt's overt criticism of contemporary, racist politics. The narrator describes the "swift and terrible directness" of the proceedings as "impelled by the highest and holiest sentiments . . . [to] maintain the purity and ascendency" of the white race (182, 229). The Gothic, but real, horror of the scene lies in the white Judge Everton's condoning the circumvention of the nation's liberty and justice in the case of an African American, because he "maintained that there were exceptions to all rules" (193). Furthermore, all African Americans were implicated by the alleged crime of one, as even the well-liked and fairly accepted Dr. Miller is affected by the outbreak of open violence against African Americans.

While the acknowledgment of guilt over the pseudoscientific practice of stereotyping people of African descent as either benignly infantile (such as Mammy Jane) or criminally inclined (such as Josh Green or Sandy) is easily displaced by declaring them as distinctly Other from society, the recognition that the nation has prospered because of an inhumane system based on falsely fabricated scientific notions is harder to ignore with the presence of the mulatto. The mixed-race offspring as a result of white slave owners' sexual interactions with their slaves, often in the form of rape, can no longer be hidden in the slave quarters after the slaves' emancipation. Though generally considered African American, the features of many mixed-race people were Anglo American enough to pass as white. Since Charles W. Chesnutt himself was very light in complexion and could have passed as white, he knew well how to depict mulattos in his novel and utilize them as Gothic tropes that challenge the save boundaries of readers' self and Other.

As just one of many ironic twists in the novel, Chesnutt creates a conflict around Olivia Carteret, the wife of one of Wellington's main characters who attempts to keep African Americans away from the election polls and thus avoid the Fusion ticket, which would allegedly threaten the white supremacists' way of life.

Olivia's half-sister, Janet, is so light in complexion that she resembles her older sister to a frightening extent. The importance of racial distinction in Wellington emerges in the narrator's description of Janet's husband Dr. Miller, whom he describes as "a sensitive, educated man who happened to be *off color*" (75; italics added). The narrator further clarifies that "such a person was a sort of social misfit" without any hope of entering the white class above him (75). Olivia's fear upon seeing her doppelganger Janet indicates that racial distinctions determine equality in the post–Reconstruction United States. The uncanny likeness between the half-sisters frightens Olivia who begins to blame Janet for the mishaps that befall her baby, Dodie. Although Olivia feels haunted by Janet, she is actually troubled by the implications this relative has for her life; accordingly, she destroys all the papers proving her relationship to Janet after her aunt's Polly Ochiltree's death, yet she develops nightmares and often "lapsed into a troubled silence" (265) only interrupted by her questioning her husband about judicial intricacies in regard to her estate.

Olivia is finally horrified when she realizes that the destruction of her father's will would actually grant Janet half of her estate, more than the will had allotted her if their family relationship were ever to become public. Furthermore, Olivia realizes the arbitrariness of color determining human rights:

> If the woman had been white,—but the woman had *not* been white, and the same rule of moral conduct did not, *could* not, in the very nature of things, apply, as between white people! For, if this were not so, slavery had been, not merely an economic mistake, but a great crime against humanity. If it had been such a crime, as for a moment she dimly perceived it might have been, then through the long centuries there had been piled up a catalogue of wrong and outrage which, if the law of compensation be a law of nature, must some time, somewhere, in some way, be atoned for. (266; italics in orig.)

In her own attempts to protect both her privileged status as a white citizen and her conscience as guilt-free, Olivia becomes aware of the fact that racial distinctions, however arbitrary, are important in order to protect and justify her way of life. Dean McWilliams explains that an acknowledgment of human kinship would "require the recognition of black claims on the wealth blacks and whites had jointly created in the plantation South" (155), and that acknowledgment would seriously threaten the nation's claim to be founded on the ideals of liberty and justice for all. An admission of racial equality therefore threatens the very foundations of the nation, and the Anglo Americans' resistance to grant African Americans the privileges concomitant with full citizenship indicates an attempt to ignore the guilt that would have to be acknowledged and atoned for, as Olivia notices.

Conclusion

During a time when African American rights were increasingly infringed upon, and segregation and disenfranchisement worsened into terrorizing the black community with legally condoned lynchings, Chesnutt sought a literary genre with which to open the eyes of his predominantly white readership to the Gothic reality of the African American community. In an effort to eliminate "the unjust spirit of caste, which is so insidious as to pervade a whole nation, and so powerful as to subject a whole race and all connected with it to scorn and social ostracism" (qtd. in Render 9), Chesnutt was frustrated with the lack of recognition incited in the readers by *The Conjure Woman*. Since he considered this "spirit of caste . . . a barrier to the moral progress of the American people," he took to more realistic depictions of the contemporary American South in *The Marrow of Tradition*. But his novel was too didactic for public taste, and even his benefactor, the famous editor William Dean Howells, described the novel's realistic depiction of race relations as "bitter" (qtd. in H. Chesnutt 177).

Although his collection of conjure tales is a subtle indictment of the American nation that used pseudoscientific theories on race in order to build a nation with the help of slave labor, Chesnutt's novel is an open critique of contemporary political attitudes about race relations. Despite their different literary approaches of relying on folklore and realism, respectively, both works utilize Gothic tropes in order to portray the resulting horrors for African Americans. Since these works focus on the guilt incurred by wrongfully exploiting other humans in a nation that prides itself for providing justice and liberty for all, Chesnutt's tales and novel are works of the American Gothic in their attempt to address this guilt. By utilizing Gothic tropes that induce horror and fear by challenging the safe boundaries of long established race relations, Chesnutt sought to shake readers out of their complacency and induce rewcognition and reconciliation between the races. Doppelgängers, mulattos, and Gothic inversion show the readers that racial distinctions are arbitrary, while characters like Annie are models for readers to engage in what Walker calls emotional and moral participation. Chesnutt chose the Gothic as a suitable genre to portray the underlying guilt within this nation because its tropes cause anxiety as a result of our buried feelings of guilt. Reading his works, readers are confronted with and have to recognize the existence of alternative versions of the past that are at times markedly contrary to historical facts and challenge our traditional, yet harmful, notions of history and nationhood.

Works Cited

Bell, Bernard W. *The Contemporary African American Novel: Its Folk Roots and Modern Literary Branches*. Amherst: U of Massachusetts P, 2004. Print.

Chesnutt, Charles W. *The Conjure Woman*. 1899. Ann Arbor: U of Michigan P, 1969. Print.

___. *The Marrow of Tradition*. 1901. Ann Arbor: U of Michigan P, 1998. Print.

Chesnutt, Helen M. *Charles Waddell Chesnutt: Pioneer of the Color Line*. Chapel Hill: U of North Carolina P, 1952. Print.

Crow, Charles L. *History of the Gothic: American Gothic*. Cardiff: U of Wales P, 2009. Print.

___. "Under the Upas Tree: Charles Chesnutt's Gothic." *Critical Essays on Charles W. Chesnutt*. Ed. Joseph R. McElrath. New York: Hall, 1999. 261–70. Print.

Edwards, Justin D. *Gothic Passages: Racial Ambiguity and the American Gothic.* Iowa City: U of Iowa P, 2003. Print.

Farnsworth, Robert M. Introduction. *The Conjure Woman.* By Charles W. Chesnutt. Ann Arbor: U of Michigan P, 1969. v–xix. Print.

Fiedler, Leslie A. *Love and Death in the American Novel.* 1960. Normal: Dalkey, 2003. Print.

Goddu, Teresa A. *Gothic America: Narrative, History, and Nation.* New York: Columbia UP, 1997. Print.

Gross, Louis S. *Redefining the American Gothic: From Wieland to Day of the Dead.* Ann Arbor: UMI Research P, 1989. Print.

Gunning, Sandra. *Race, Rape, and Lynching. The Red Record of American Literature, 1890–1912.* New York: Oxford UP, 1996. Print.

Harrell, Willie J., Jr. "'The Fruit of My Own Imagination': Charles W. Chesnutt's *The Marrow of Tradition* in the Age of Realism." *Charles Chesnutt Reappraised: Essays on the First Major African American Fiction Writer.* Ed. David Garrett Izzo and Maria Orban. Jefferson: McFarland, 2009. 26–41. Print.

Ianovici, Gerald. "'A Living Death': Gothic Signification and the Nadir in *The Marrow of Tradition*." MELUS 27.4 (2002): 33–58. Print.

McWilliams, Dean. *Charles W. Chesnutt and the Fictions of Race.* Athens: U of Georgia P, 2002. Print.

Molyneaux, Sandra. "Expanding the Collective Memory: Charles W. Chesnutt's *The Conjure Woman* Tales." *Memory, Narrative, and Identity. New Essays in Ethnic American Literatures.* Ed. Amritjit Singh, et al. Boston: Northeastern UP, 1994, 164–78. Print.

Render, Sylvia Lyons. "Introduction." *The Short Fiction of Charles W. Chesnutt.* By Charles W. Chesnutt. Ed. Sylvia Lyons Render. Washington, D.C.: Howard UP, 1981. 3–54. Print.

Savoy, Eric. "The Rise of the American Gothic." *The Cambridge Companion to Gothic Fiction.* Ed. Jerrold E. Hogle. Cambridge: Cambridge UP, 2002. 167–88. Print.

Simmons, Ryan. *Chesnutt and Realism: A Study of the Novels.* Tuscaloosa: U of Alabama P, 2006. Print.

Sundquist, Eric J. *To Wake the Nations: Race in the Making of American Literature.* Cambridge: Harvard UP, 1993. Print.

Walker, Margaret Urban. *What is Reparative Justice?* Milwaukee: Marquette UP, 2010. Print.

Walpole, Horace. Preface to the First Edition. *The Castle of Otranto.* 1764. Ed. W. S. Lewis. New York: Oxford UP, 1996. 5–8. Print.

Revealing Faulkner: Religious Fall in *The Sound and the Fury*

Henry L. Carrigan, Jr.

Fellow southerner Flannery O'Connor once famously declared of William Faulkner, "Nobody wants his mule and wagon stalled on the same tracks the Dixie Limited is roaring down." Fifty years after his death on July 6, 1962, Faulkner's ferocious influence remains unchecked, and, wise enough to stay off the tracks, numerous Southern writers have instead hitched their wagons to Faulkner's speeding locomotive, hurtling through the pine barrens and lowland farms across the South, delivering a load of pathos, loss, apocalypse, love, and—in spite of a ragged company of grotesque, seemingly irredeemable, characters and dark settings—hope and redemption.

The haunting, spectral, and violence-laden novels of Harry Crews, Carson McCullers, Barry Hannah, Cormac McCarthy, and O'Connor herself are unthinkable without Faulkner's vivid creation of a mythical Mississippi county, Yoknapatawpha, whose denizens have inherited and must cope with a legacy of poverty, racism, and violence that often threatens to disentangle and separate them from the fabric of family and place into which they have been so intricately woven over time. Most, though not all, of Faulkner's novels and stories are set in a mythical place that provides at once both the safe haven from a distant, unfamiliar, harsh world ("The Bear"), as well a home from which its members are expelled into an exile in that distant world, permitted to return home again only in death (*As I Lay Dying*).

Most of Faulkner's characters are not attractive people—they commit incest, rape, murder—and many of them who might be sympathetic, like Caddy Compson in *The Sound and the Fury*, turn out to be hollow individuals whose sacrifice arises not out of heroic action but out of self-abnegation. Written in a time suspended between World War I and World War II, Faulkner's fiction also captures the anxieties of a South that never recovered from its defeat in the War Between the

States; many of Faulkner's characters are veterans of the Civil War and are trying to come to terms with what they perceive not only as a failure of their Southern country but also as an exile from the rest of America, which they feel has never and never will recognize their desires and concerns. In addition, Faulkner's writings capture the Southerners' deep sadness over the loss of land—not only the agricultural parcels that provided southern landowners with a livelihood but also the pristine and Edenic forests and groves where individuals felt close to nature—resulting from the increasing industrialization of the South after the war.

William Faulkner did not have to search very far for the settings, characters, events, or places that populated his fiction; with little exception, he modeled Yoknapatawpha on the Mississippi countryside and villages in which he grew up, and he based many of his characters on his own family of scoundrels, Confederate war veterans, planters, lawyers, and businessmen. Faulkner demonstrated a talent for writing when he was young and often imitated the poetry of Robert Burns and A. E. Housman, among others, in his own early poems. Dropping out of high school, he tried to join the army air force during World War I, but he was rejected because of his height. Soon after, he applied to join Canada's Royal Air Force (RAF), lying about his age, place of birth, and height. When the RAF accepted him as a cadet, he moved to Toronto to begin his training; the war ended before his training ended, but that did not stop Faulkner from returning to Mississippi wearing the RAF uniform and airman's wings and claiming to have participated actively in the war. His experience instilled in Falkner a love and fascination with flying, and it provided him with material for his first novel, *Soldiers' Pay* (1926) and his later and now little-known novel of barnstorming and aerobatics, *Pylon* (1935).

In 1919, even though he had never completed high school, Faulkner enrolled in the University of Mississippi in Oxford, thanks to a program for war veterans, where he spent three semesters before dropping out. During his short time at the university, however, Faulkner began to develop his writing talents, publishing a poem in the *New Republic* and writing fiction for the university newspaper. Encouraged by other novelists, Faulkner continued writing and by 1925, after a disastrous stint as Oxford's postmaster, he moved to New Orleans, where he wrote for a literary journal, *The Double Dealer*, and spent his time moving among various literary circles. In New Orleans, he wrote and published *Soldiers' Pay* and began work on his second novel, *Mosquitoes* (1927), a satire about his New Orleans literary circle.

Once he began publishing fiction, Faulkner never looked back, and during his most productive period between 1929 and 1942, he turned to stories of his region's history, especially its ambivalence surrounding the War Between the States and stories growing out of his family's history. He once remarked that "beginning with *Sartoris*, I discovered that my own little postage stamp of native soil was worth writing about and that I would never live long enough to exhaust it, and by sublimating the actual into apocryphal I would have complete liberty to use whatever talent I might have to its absolute top" (Meriwether 255). Over the next fourteen years, Faulkner wrote and published his most recognized novels, including *The Sound and the Fury* (1929), *As I Lay Dying* (1930), *Light in August* (1932), *Absalom, Absalom!* (1936), as well as his most enduring collection of stories, *Go Down, Moses and Other Stories* (1942). In some of these writings, Faulkner embraced the stream-of-consciousness narrative style of modernist writers such as Proust and Virginia Woolf that provided access to the rambling thoughts of the characters while at the same time invoking some spatial and psychological distance from the events being narrated. Faulkner quickly emerged as a Southern writer whose ability to capture and portray the deeply troubled mind of the South—and in the words of one of his characters, to "tell about the South"—launched him into the literary firmament with writers such as Hemingway, T. S. Eliot, Joseph Conrad, and fellow southerner Edgar Allan Poe. In November 1950, he accepted the 1949 Nobel Prize for Literature. In his acceptance speech, Faulkner remarked that his writings testified to the work of an artist who had created out of the materials of the human spirit something that had never before existed. Famously, he declared that humankind would not simply endure; it would prevail, and that the poet's task was to provide one of the voices to help humankind to this end ("Banquet").

In spite of Faulkner's own declaration of the writer's vocation, his own fiction is often difficult to read and is seldom uplifting. Generations of readers have struggled with his often confusing literary style with its labyrinthine sentences without punctuation and stream-of-consciousness narration. For example, at least one section of *The Sound and the Fury* is narrated by Benjy Compson, a young, mentally handicapped character whose mutterings vacillate between incoherence and insanity. Readers also often have difficulty keeping straight the enormous cast of characters, most of whom are related to one another and often share the same first name. Thus, in *The Sound and the Fury*, Caddy Compson's brother and her daughter are both named Quentin, and her brother Quentin shows up again in *Absalom, Absalom!* (even though the character committed suicide in *The Sound and the Fury*), which provides a complicated history of the Sutpen and Compson families and their interrelatedness. Moreover, Faulkner's fiction is full of grotesque characters who seem to have no regard for the well-being of others, often committing acts of rape, murder, and suicide in an effort to protect and preserve their land and their home.

Yet, at the center of Faulkner's fiction stands a hope that in the midst of a fallen and broken world, human dignity can survive and provide individuals the strength to go on. Without question, Faulkner's writings stand at the threshold of modern Southern Gothic with their depictions of primeval lands, families haunted by the ghosts of the past seeking to outrun them if possible, a society taunted and haunted by defeat and exile, and depraved men and women searching to survive any way they can in what seems to them to be a world without hope. Drawing upon the Gothic tradition of early nineteenth-century Europe, Southern Gothic offers powerful psychological studies of temptation and persecution involving a struggle between good and evil told against a backdrop of vast landscapes, and Faulkner's fiction contains many of these elements.

Missing from most discussions of Southern Gothic, however, is an emphasis on its religious dimensions. In the British Gothic tradition, religious figures, often monks, nuns, and priests, serve as either protectors or corrupters of the tale's protagonist, and the action of the story is often set in a monastery, church, or convent with mysterious passageways that lead characters further into isolation but also closer to enlightenment. Gothic literature grows out of a Catholic tradition, and thus characters in novels ranging from Ann Radcliff's *Mysteries of Udolpho* (1794), William Beckford's *Vathek* (1786), and Mary Shelley's *Frankenstein* (1818) portray a world where revelation of mystery comes through nature and where acts of absolution and confession—even if Victor Frankenstein is confessing his overvaulting pride (and its ruinous consequences) not to a priest but to Walton, a ship's captain—offer individuals the chance for redemption.

Although Flannery O'Connor writes from a Catholic perspective, Faulkner and many other Southern Gothic writers are baptized in the blood of the Protestant South where humans are fallen creatures who must see the light of true religion by encountering Jesus in the Bible and by declaring their faith in this incarnation of God. Indeed, Faulkner excels at portraying depraved, fallen creatures who appear either to mock religion, to have left it behind as a vestige of a failed past, or who are guided by it in some implicit or explicit fashion. Faulkner himself certainly never claimed to be writing from a religious perspective nor to be an adherent of any particular Christian sect; yet, in spite of himself, Faulkner's writings, regardless of their relentless focus on the despair, depravity, and damnation through which humankind must endure and over which it must prevail, nevertheless often offer a picture of hope and redemption, resurrection and renewal. Even more important, however, Faulkner's writings focus on ultimate concerns such as: What is nature of humanity? What is the nature of reality? What is the relationship between humankind and nature and reality? These are foundational religious questions and provide the structure for his novels and stories. While religious figures—preachers and priests—tend to be marginal characters in Faulkner and are unable to offer any hope of redemption, the central feature of his fiction is the never-ending struggle between good and evil where individuals possess the freedom to choose their destiny and in which some individuals function as God's instruments no matter how they in fact see themselves, leading others to ask these key questions about human nature and its relationship to ultimate reality.

Much as in the novels of Balzac, Dickens, and Dostoevsky, Faulkner's fiction features a parade of humanity—the lowly and the exalted, the rich and the poor, the grimy and the spotless, the conniving and the forthright—marching through a historical and natural landscape that palpably forces these individuals to come face-to-face with brokenness, hopelessness, guilt, and despair. Yet, given the religion-soaked soil out of which Faulkner grew, he could not help but get some grains of this dirt under his fingernails, and Faulkner's greatest novels derive their epic imaginative structure from the powerful biblical stories that so drenched his region and by which so many of his fellow southerners lived and arranged their lives.

Faulkner clearly witnessed the ways in which his community used the Bible as their manual for life, building their ideas of racial purity and social order on their interpretation of stories from both the Old Testament and New Testament. The very idea that God had chosen a certain community as God's own, zealously and jealously protecting it from its enemies—foundational to the narratives of the Old Testament—provided Southerners with a myth of their own specialness as they seceded from the Union and fought to preserve this hallowed identity throughout the Civil War. When the South suffered such bitter defeat, it felt much like the Jews who had been forced into exile in Babylon in the Old Testament; like the Jews, the Southerners had lost their beloved land, which provided them with their special identity.

After the war and throughout Faulkner's own life and beyond, southern preachers used the Bible to exhort believers to restore the racial purity of their country by recognizing that God continued (even after such great loss) to preserve the purity of the white race, which the preachers believed God had created as superior and favored, by maintaining a system that viewed blacks as lower creatures, just above animals, in God's created order. Thus, drenched as it is in the biblical headwaters of the South, Faulkner's fiction is saturated with biblical allusions, and it is often difficult to understand his fiction without reference to biblical literature and religious themes.

The Old Testament depicts a God electing a chosen people, requiring that people to follow certain teachings and to worship that God exclusively, exacting punishment on those individuals or communities who did not follow these teachings, and offering a new pastoral community out of the exile into which many of these individuals have been cast for disobedience. The Old Testament also provides the deep structure for many of Faulkner's writings. For example, *Absalom, Absalom!* takes its outline from the story of David and his family in 2 Samuel, chapters 13–18 in which King David's son, Absalom, vengefully kills his brother, Amnon, who has raped their sister, Tamar. Absalom's action creates a deep rift between father and son that eventually ends in Absalom's death at his father's command, an action that David mournfully regrets as he utters his son's name over and over. In 1939, Faulkner used Psalm 137, verse 5, "If I forget thee, Jerusalem," the psalmist's lament over his exile from his homeland, as the original title for his novel of estrangement and reconciliation that his publisher published as *The Wild Palms*. Finally, Faulkner's earliest title for his saga of the Snopes family—*The Town, The Hamlet, The Mansion*—was "Father Abraham."

Themes and references from the New Testament also abound in Faulkner's fiction. Faulkner's late novel, *A Fable* (1954), is built around Holy Week and Easter and some critics interpret the protagonist as a Christ figure; Holy Week provides the framework for *The*

Sound and the Fury; the central character of *Light in August* (1932) is named Joe Christmas, whose name and initials, J. C., recall Jesus Christ, and his death in the novel resembles a crucifixion. Faulkner's novella, *The Bear* (1942) also features a Christlike protagonist, Ike McCaslin, whose experiences in the wilderness end with his figural baptism into knowledge of purity and corruption, truth and beauty.

Although Faulkner did not set out to write explicitly theological or religious novels, all of his fiction is haunted by a religious sensibility, and fellow southern novelist Walker Percy once called Faulkner "a theologian in spite of himself" (Johnston 161). In his earliest novels, *Soldiers' Pay* (1926) and *Mosquitoes* (1927), Faulkner often cynically questions the ways of the world and wonders if it is possible to capture humankind's ongoing quest for truth and whether or not such a quest is indeed worth the trouble. Moreover, some of the characters in these novels question the nature of truth itself. In *Mosquitoes*, Mrs. Wiseman, whose name is an ironic reflection of her cynicism regarding the futility of the search for truth, asks, "What is there worth the effort and despair of writing about except love and death?" (247). In *Soldiers' Pay*, a skeptical Episcopal priest, in yet another ironic twist, declares that "truth is unbearable" (318). These two examples offer a mere glimpse of the intensity with which the mature Faulkner will plumb the depths of love, family, order, and truth in his laterfiction.

The title of Faulkner's *The Sound and the Fury* alludes to Shakespeare's *Macbeth*, the tragedy that "is a tale / Told by an idiot, full of sound and fury, / Signifying nothing" (Shakespeare 5.5). Like the play, Faulkner's novel narrates the decline and fall of a family of great importance, in this case a traditional upper-middle-class family of the Old South whose confrontation with the New South, illustrated most richly by Jason Compson's rejection of his parents' values, rips the family's fabric to shreds. Also like Shakespeare, Faulkner carefully weaves words and sentences into a rich, and very dense and multilayered story that delves into numerous perspectives on the same subjects. The novel is a meditation on the nature of time and the corruption of history, and it reflects Faulkner's deep debt to Modernist novelists such as James Joyce and Marcel Proust, but it's also a profound tale of beginnings and endings, loss and grief, and despair and hope.

The Sound and the Fury chronicles the sordid history of the Compson clan, an old aristocratic Mississippi family that has seen better days. Descended from the noble Civil War veteran, General Compson, the family has fallen into financial ruin and has lost some of its land through greed (a golf course has been built on a former pasture sold to an outsider by a family member) and selfishness. The action of the novel occurs mainly during a few days in 1928, though at least one section of the novel is set in 1910. In every part of the novel, one or another Compson (or an individual involved with the Compson family) tells his or her version of the events and his or her own responsibility for the events. Few individuals take direct responsibility for their own actions, often blaming outside forces for their choices, and the novel culminates in the family's telling of the sprawling tale of the family's dissolution.

The novel is divided into four sections, and Faulkner, perhaps in an effort to help readers keep all the characters straight and to help them sort of the main features of the story, in 1945 added an appendix in which he provided long descriptions and interpretations of each of the characters in the novel.

The first section of the novel, set on April 7, 1928, is narrated by Benjy (Benjamin Maury) Compson, a thirty-three-year-old autistic man-child whose burbling recollections provide not only a foretaste of what is ahead for the reader and for the family but also an outline of all the events that occur in the novel. Called an idiot child by his family, Benjy nevertheless recalls, through the tangled workings of his mind as well as his labyrinthine ramblings, many of the events that have shaped the Compsons but, more important, the personalities and the attitudes of each family member. As the novel opens, Benjy is staring through the fence at what used to be the pasture on the Compson Place but is now a golf course when he hears someone utter the word *caddie*.

This tantalizing linguistic morsel (much as the madeleine cookie in Proust's *Remembrance of Things Past* transports Marcel to an earlier time) carries Benjy back to memories of his sister, Caddy, and the love and care she always gave him. Faulkner uses italicized words to signal a shift from the external narrator's point of view to the interior, stream-of-consciousness perspective of the main character. Here Benjy sees Caddy "with flowers in her hair, and a long veil like shining wind," (*The Sound* 47) and he fondly, or out of his need to feel secure, repeats her name. This first section moves back and forth in time very frequently, covering a thirty-year time span from 1898 to 1928, and Benjy recalls numerous events from these years: his grandmother's death, Caddy's loss of virginity, the sale of the pasture (sold by the family to send their son, Quentin, to Harvard), Caddy's wedding, Quentin's suicide, his own castration, and his father's death.

The pivotal scene in this first section occurs thirty years earlier (1898) at his grandmother Damuddy's funeral. At the end of the nineteenth century and even well into the twentieth century, many southern families held funerals for their loved ones in their own homes, preparing the bodies themselves for burial and sitting up with the body as a part of the ritual of mourning and grief. Children were not allowed to be inside the house and were ushered outside during the funeral service itself. At Damuddy's service, the Compson servants pushed Benjy, Caddy, Quentin, and Jason outside where the older children took care of the younger ones. Curiosity about the goings-on inside the house prompt Caddy to climb a pear tree in the garden to look into the windows, and the boys all look up to see Caddy's muddy drawers—perhaps the most famous image in the novel—and thus experience on various levels temptation, lust, desire. In climbing the pear tree, Caddy seeks knowledge, which she'd been denied by being banned from the funeral in an attempt to protect her innocence from knowing the corruption of the physical body in death. Faulkner cannily has Caddy climb a pear tree rather than another kind of fruit tree, and in doing so he is alluding to one of the most famous scenes in literature in which a young Saint

Augustine and his companions climb a neighbor's pear tree in order to pluck fruit even though it was not yet ripe. In his *Confessions*, Augustine recalls this scene as the one in which he realized how deeply he wanted knowledge but also how profoundly he is motivated by a desire that he cannot control.

A few moments after Caddy climbs into the tree, the Compson's servant, Dilsey, who has her own section in the novel, spies Caddy looking into the house. As Dilsey sees the tree shaking, she calls out, "You, Satan; come down from there" (54). When Dilsey asks the children gathered at the base of the tree what they are doing back at the house, they all say that Caddy told them to come. When Dilsey asks after Quentin, Caddy tells her that Quentin has refused to join them because he is mad at having to do what Caddy tells him to do. Even more important, Caddy gains knowledge through her actions, but she is disappointed to discover that everyone in the house is just sitting and looking. This particular scene illustrates well Faulkner's deep debt to the religious stories that drenched the ground out of which he grew. The model for this scene is Genesis, chapters 2–4, which depict the fall of humankind much as Caddy's and the others' actions essentially depict the fall of a family. In the biblical myth, the innocent woman, curious about a world she cannot see but to which she gain access by following the advice of the serpent, grasps the fruit of the tree, eats it, and leads her male counterpart to eat it. When confronted with their actions, both the man and the woman deny responsibility, each blaming the other or another creature for their actions. Just as in the biblical story, Caddy seeks knowledge in the form of a fruit tree, which she ascends in order to become wise like an adult; her brothers follow her, watch her climb the tree, and upon seeing her muddy drawers lose their innocence and gain a new kind of knowledge about themselves and their sister. When Dilsey sees Caddy, she recognizes a crafty creature who is seeking a clue to a world to which Caddy is an outsider, but in that moment Dilsey calls Caddy "Satan" (a traditional interpretation of the serpent in Genesis) not only because she has seduced the boys back toward the house to gain knowledge of death, but also because Dilsey foresees and interprets this event at Damuddy's funeral as the shattering of the Eden in which Caddy and the Compsons live.

Quentin Compson narrates the second section of *The Sound and the Fury* (which is set much earlier in time than the three other sections, on June 2, 1910) in Cambridge, Massachusetts, on the day he commits suicide at Harvard University. Quentin awakes on this Thursday morning in his room at Harvard, acutely aware of his physical surroundings and deeply moved by his consciousness of time, both past and present. Looking at a watch his father gave to him, Quentin launches forth on a dialogue between himself and his father that dramatically reveals his father's traditional southern values and Quentin's own deep insecurities about his southern identity, his family, his lust for his sister Caddy, and his despair at ever being able to tell about the South to his northern roommate who sees the Old South as nothing but corrupt. Calling it the "mausoleum of all hope and despair," Quentin's father tells him that Quentin will be able to use the watch to "gain the reducto absurdum of all human experience which can fit your individual needs . . . I give it to you not that you may remember time, but that you might forget it now and then for a moment and not spend all your breath trying to conquer it" (93).

This second section reveals one of the most characteristic themes in conversation about the Christian religion: time and memory. Once again, in his *Confessions*, Augustine reflects on the nature of time, and he questions the ways in which humans find and understand themselves as creatures who define their existence in terms of past, present, and future. The burden of time and memory weighs heavily on humans, he observes, and individuals very often cannot bear this burden for they cannot live with the negative actions they have taken in the past.

Set on Maundy Thursday, the Christian observance as the day that begins Jesus' journey toward crucifixion, this section reflects once again the deep influence of the Christ-haunted South on Faulkner's fiction. The Gospels depict Jesus as an individual who lived in time but lived outside of it. Jesus teaches that the time in which he is living is a time that he himself will soon conquer, overcoming the forces of the world in which he lives; in other words, he is living in a time that is not his own. Yet, because Jesus lives in a time not his own and attempts to turn both his time and place upside down, those who cannot bear to live with Jesus's idea of a new time breaking into the present time crucify him. In Quentin's case, his own inability to bear the burden of time past and time present leads him to kill himself. As his father points out to him, "Man the sum of his climactic experiences Father said. Man the sum of what have you. A problem in impure properties carried tediously to an unvarying nil: stalemate of dust and desire" (153), and Quentin, unable to live with being the sum of all his "climactic experiences," commits suicide on the very day that led Jesus down the path to his own death for being unable to bear the burden of time.

The third section of *The Sound and the Fury* belongs to Jason, the Compson whose New South values do the most to bring ruin on the family. This section is set on April 6, 1928, on Good Friday, and the day before Benjy's section. After his father dies, Jason becomes the caretaker of the family, watching over, both financially and physically, his mother, Caroline, Benjy, and Quentin who is Caddy's daughter. Perhaps because of his narrow focus on material wealth and well-being, Jason's section is narrated in a straightforward fashion with none of the flashbacks associated with the other characters. Cynical, materialistic, selfish, Jason is the model of "Compson selfishness and false pride" (126). In order to capitalize on the sins of his sister, Caddy, he blackmails her into signing over guardianship of her daughter, Quentin, to him, and he then steals the checks that Caddy sends him to support Quentin. Eventually, Quentin steals his strongbox—though she does not suspect that it holds the money he has stolen from her—and runs away. Appropriately, Jason spends the day crucifying himself when Quentin runs away, but he cannot see past his own delusions of self-grandeur as the new patriarch of the Compson family and thus never gains any deep knowledge about the relationship between culture and family or between love and hope. Because he is mainly concerned for himself in spite of his paternalism, he represents the end of the values of the Old South—taking care of land and those who work it, keeping land in the family, protecting the family circle—and his materialism represents values of the New South that indeed crucify his family's and his culture's traditional way of life. With his section, the dissolution and fall of the Compson family is complete.

The final section of the novel belongs to the Compson's devoted black servant, Dilsey. Set on Easter Sunday—April 8, 1928—the day that Christians celebrate as a time of light and hope with the rising sun, Dilsey's day breaks "bleak and chill, a moving wall of grey light . . . that seemed to disintegrate into minute and venomous particles" (330). Bone-tired and worn down from her years of service to the Compsons—from whom she had often received physical abuse, no matter her devotion to them—Dilsey faces the day with an expression "at once fatalistic and of a child's astonished disappointment" (331). In contrast to the other sections of the novel, Dilsey does not narrate her own tale, and her own story of the decline and fall of the Compsons makes up only a part of the section. The remainder of part 4 of the novel completes the story of Jason's pursuit of the runaway Quentin and the final downfall of a once noble family. Yet, Dilsey's story is at the center of part 4 of *The Sound and the Fury*, and it provides an outsider's perspective on the Compson's tragedy but also a final strand of redemptive hope in the midst of utter destruction.

The tenacity of Old South values is almost nowhere better represented than in the South's attitude toward race and religion. A man of his times, especially in a pre–Civil Rights Mississippi, Faulkner held to the separation of blacks and whites, and his family still had domestic servants descended from slaves in the Faulkner household. In the South, white churches used the Bible to justify slavery, and they also used it to justify the South's secession from the Union, the rights of whites to hold land, and the subjection of women to men. White churches practiced segregation by providing galleries upstairs in the church for slaves, but white religion offered a spiritual message unsuited to the situation of most blacks. At least until the end of the Civil War, many blacks held prayer meetings in their own quarters, singing the spiritual songs that would describe their plight and would carry them away to another world. By the end of the Civil War, the black church became the centerpiece of the black community, often serving as a refuge for blacks still suffering persecution from whites and offering a community of solidarity and liberation in the midst of an unwelcoming and hostile community. In the postbellum, Reconstruction South, white churches in rural areas especially focused to large extent on dealing with the guilt over losing the war. Why would God, who had chosen the South as God's new Israel, have allowed the South to suffer in defeat to the hated Union? In contrast, black churches preached liberation from oppression in lively services that sometimes lasted all day and celebrated community and family on the one hand and the promise of a new heaven and a new earth through the preaching of apocalyptic texts such as Revelation on the other.

Dilsey's section represents this division very dramatically. As devoted as she has been to the Compsons, she realizes that the family has no interest in her opinions about them and their ways. Moreover, the individuals about whom she cares—with the exception of Benjy—are either dead (Quentin), estranged (Caddy), or distant (Quentin, Caddy's daughter). Neither Caroline, the Compson matriarch, nor Jason, her son, has any use for Dilsey, and they let her know as much when she arrives at their house on Easter Sunday morning. However, Dilsey loves Benjy, and she regards him as a child of God who still has a chance of being saved. Thus, on her way to church on Easter, she stops at the Compson house, endures their abuse, and leaves with Benjy in tow for her own church.

Once she arrives, her regular minister introduces the congregation to a visiting preacher, Reverend Shegog, who will deliver the sermon on that morning. Shegog's sermon constitutes the centerpiece of Dilsey's section, for it stands in vivid contrast to the language of the

Compson's. While the Compson's tale is one of sound and fury and signifies nothing, Shegog's tale is one of hope, solidarity, unity, and redemption. Shegog's very name is reminiscent of the biblical names Gog and Magog, which are two cities mentioned in both Ezekiel and Revelation—two books of the Bible that deal with destruction and renewal, exile and restoration. Shegog begins his sermon by shouting that he has "de ricklickshun en de blood of de Lamb!" (368), indicating to his hearers that he is baptized in the blood and the spirit of Jesus, which gives him the power to preach the message he is about to preach. In a typical striding rhythm, his voice wraps around the congregation, lifting them out of their everyday lives and transporting them to the time of Jesus, reimagining the days before Jesus's crucifixion and Mary's lamentations over her son's arrest by the Romans and then carrying his hearers to the bloody mount of Calvary where Jesus hangs on a tree among other thieves as his followers wail and mourn for him. With a thundering crescendo, Shegog powerfully rolls back the stone on Jesus' death, inviting the congregation to bathe in the Easter light of the resurrection:

> I sees the darkness en de death everlastin upon de generations. Den, lo! Breddren! Whut I see? Whut I see, O sinner? I sees de resurrection en de light; sees de meek Jesus sayin Dey kilt Me dat ye shall live again; I died dat dem whut sees en believes shall never die. Breddren, O breddren! I sees de doom crack en hears de golden horns shoutin down de glory, en de arisen dead whut got de blood en de ricklickshun of de Lamb! (370)

Shegog's sermon brings tears to Dilsey's eyes: "Two tears slid down her fallen cheeks, in and out of the myriad coruscations of immolation and abnegation and time" (368). No other character in the novel is capable of such deep emotional responses to the passage of time; no other character embraces time in the same way that Dilsey embraces time, for she is freer of time than any other individual in the book. Although she has been worn down physically by the ravages of time, literally burned up ("immolation") as it has passed through her body, and though she has never been recognized as a full human being ("abnegated"), she still recognizes—as God reveals to her through Shegog's sermon—that time is redeemed by Christ's death and resurrection. The black church provides her with a community that also recognizes the power of Jesus to liberate them from the woes of the world. At the end of the service, "she sits bolt upright, crying rigidly and quietly in the annealment and the blood of the remembered Lamb" (371). She is burnished and she is healed by the spirit of God.

On their walk home, her son asks Dilsey to quit crying, especially since they will soon be passing white folks. It no longer matters, however, who witnesses Dilsey's tears; white folks are not free enough to cry when they receive God's healing, and she is not about to stop crying, for she is now fully free to be herself in front of anybody. Her new freedom fills her with the knowledge and hope of restoration. Dilsey has seen the rise, the decline, and the fall of the Compson clan: "I've seed the first en de last . . . I seed de beginning, en now I sees de endin" (371).

While the Compsons have depended on themselves to get through life, Dilsey has depended on a power outside of herself to survive and to triumph over the mistreatment and abuse she has experienced in her life. Because the Compsons have turned inward, they have imploded and fallen apart. Like the great house of Atreus in Greek tragedy (Aeschylus's *Oresteia*) or King David's house in the Bible or Lear's family in Shakespeare's play, when families turn inward and rely on themselves for the power to survive, things fall apart because their languages clash and individual pride destroys the social fabric. Because Dilsey has turned outward, relying on a power outside of herself for liberation, she survives. As Faulkner writes of Dilsey and her family in his appendix to the novel, "They endured" (427).

The Sound and the Fury illustrates nicely the ways in which Faulkner's fiction deals with ultimate questions regarding the nature of humanity and the nature of reality. Even though he never called himself a religious writer or a writer consumed with a Christian world-view, he nevertheless lived in a world soaked in the blood of Jesus where the risen Christ haunted every white frame church and every stand of woods. Faulkner absorbed this religion of judgment and grace, especially as his ancestors and his friends' families struggled to make sense, even sixty years after the fact, of the South's loss in the War Between the States.

All of Faulkner's novels and stories contain images and portraits of individuals struggling with the meaning of life in a harsh world and struggling to make sense of loss, grief, and despair. Some characters might never find hope or redemption or renewal or restoration, and Faulkner often pokes fun at preachers, but in each of Faulkner's writings there is at least one character who endures by turning outside of a community already corrupt and weakened by pride to embrace the promise of a new South or a new community or a restored hope in the dignity of humankind. *The Sound and the Fury*, one of Faulkner's more difficult and challenging novels, provides one of the best examples of his work as a theologian in spite of himself.

Works Cited

Blotner, Joseph. *Faulkner: A Biography*. 2 vols. New York: Random, 1974. Print.

Brooks, Cleanth. *William Faulkner: The Yoknapatawpha Country*. New Haven: Yale UP, 1963. Print.

___. *William Faulkner: Toward Yoknapatawpha and Beyond*. New Haven: Yale UP, 1978. Print.

Faulkner, William. "Banquet Speech." *Nobel Prizes*. Nobel Media AB, 10 Dec. 1950. Web. 8 Nov. 2012.

___. *Mosquitoes: A Novel*. New York: Liveright, 1927. Print.

___. *Soldiers' Pay*. New York: Liveright, 1926. Print.

___. *The Sound and the Fury*. New York: Vintage, 1954. Print.

Fowler, Doreen, and Ann J. Abadie, eds. *Faulkner and Religion*. Jackson: UP of Mississippi, 1990. Print.

Howe, Irving. *William Faulkner: A Critical Study*. Rev. ed. New York: Random, 1962. Print.

Johnston, Araminta Stone. *And One was a Priest: The Life and Times of Duncan M. Gray, Jr*. Jackson: UP of Mississippi, 2011. Print.

Kazin, Alfred. *God and the American Writer*. New York: Knopf, 1997. Print.

Meriwether, James B. and Michael Millgate, eds. *Lion in the Garden: Interviews with William Faulkner, 1926–1962*. New York: Random, 1968. Print.

Parini, Jay. *One Matchless Time: A Life of William Faulkner*. New York: Harper, 2004. Print.

Shakespeare, William. *Macbeth*. New York: Simon, 1992. Print.

Watkins, Floyd C. *The Flesh and the Word: Eliot, Hemingway, Faulkner*. Nashville: Vanderbilt UP, 1971. Print.

Wells, Dean Faulkner. *Every Day in the Sun: A Memoir of the Faulkners of Mississippi*. New York: Random, 2012. Print.

Welty, Eudora. *On William Faulkner*. Jackson: UP of Mississippi, 2003. Print.

Williamson, Joel. *William Faulkner and Southern History*. New York: Oxford UP, 1993. Print.

Carson McCullers' Boardinghouse and the Architecture of Ruin

Julieann Veronica Ulin

On June 16, 1858, Abraham Lincoln delivered his famous and revolutionary House Divided speech at the close of the Republican State Convention when he accepted the Illinois Republican Party nomination for the US Senate seat. Referring to the growing threat that slavery and the transportation of slaves would become legal in all states, Lincoln warned: "A house divided against itself cannot stand. I believe this government cannot endure, permanently half *slave* and half *free*. I do not expect the Union to be *dissolved*—I do not expect the house to *fall*—but I *do* expect it will cease to be divided. It will become *all* one thing, or *all* the other" (Appelbaum 25). The central rhetorical image of Lincoln's speech depends upon the identification of the United States as a fractured house, one that threatens to collapse under the weight of its own conflicting and irresolvable divisions. The speech was widely disseminated in pamphlets and newspapers; the depiction of the country as a divided house became a way of designating political and racial conflict in the post–Civil War United States. Given the widespread recognition of this speech, the centrality of the boardinghouse in representations of the South comes as no surprise. With its ability to encapsulate Civil War history and its lasting divisions, the boardinghouse setting provides a space for considering both domestic and national schisms.

The most significant visual use of the boardinghouse to signal the "divided house" and the occupation of the South after the Civil War occurs in D. W. Griffith's controversial 1915 film *The Birth of a Nation*. In the film's opening, viewers are introduced to the Cameron estate in Piedmont, South Carolina, as a house in which "life runs in a quaintly way that is to be no more." From its first appearance in the film, the Piedmont estate is shadowed by its own impending ruin; it symbolizes a social, racial, domestic, and national order that is "no more."

Furthermore, the film's text indicates that this ruin is both irreversible and something to be mourned. *The Birth of a Nation* dramatizes the horrors of the Reconstruction period through the transformation of the Piedmont estate from a secure Southern home to a boardinghouse.

Immediately following the end of the Civil War, the film's screen text reads: "The South under Lincoln's fostering hand goes to work to rebuild itself." Viewers witness this process of "rebuilding" as the Cameron women exit the Piedmont home and hang a sign that reads "Boarding" on the pillars of the estate. The film signals the transition from romantic antebellum order to the chaos of the Reconstruction period in this moment, as the idealized plantation house gives way to a boardinghouse, which the film uses as a symbol for a shattered Southern social order. For Griffith, this shift in designation from a family estate to a boardinghouse is a critical one that signals not only the falling economic status of the family, but also a new model for considering the racial and social shifts in the South following the Civil War. For Griffith, the boardinghouse encapsulates this shattered unity and marks the transition to the Reconstruction period, which is described in the film as "a veritable overthrow of civilization in the South." To emphasize this degeneration, Griffith keeps the "Boarding" sign prominently within the frame in several key moments in the film, structurally linking the opening up of the Piedmont estate to the fracturing of the South in Reconstruction: both are depicted as previously coherent and closed spaces that are now subject to invasion by outsiders and in which any claims to control or ownership are tenuous.

In the film, Griffith repeatedly frames tense and violent interracial encounters between the Camerons and the newly freed former slaves with the "Boarding" sign visible, further underscoring the use of the boardinghouse to signal the shifting social order in the South. In one such scene, Gus, who is black and is described by Griffith as "the renegade, a product of the vicious doctrines spread by carpetbaggers," stalks two white women. Gus walks directly past the "Boarding" sign, watching the women enter the house. The Cameron son known as the

Little Colonel witnesses this and orders Gus to keep away from the house. The encounter between the two men occurs across the picket fence surrounding the Piedmont boardinghouse.

As Gus and the Little Colonel continue their argument, they are joined by the mixed-race Silas Lynch, newly elected lieutenant governor of the state. As Lynch towers imposingly over the Little Colonel, an armed black man joins Gus and Silas. Griffith tightly frames the scene directly underneath the "Boarding" sign hanging on the Piedmont column. The inclusion of the sign signals the Camerons' tentative hold on their house and social status. While the Little Colonel remains inside the picket fence, his position directly underneath the "Boarding" sign highlights his own identity as an occupant rather than a full owner. Furthermore, the shot shows him to be outnumbered by Gus, the increasingly politically powerful Silas Lynch, and the other armed black man. No longer the idealized estate to which we are introduced in the film's opening, the Piedmont house is now subject to invasion and occupation.

In *The Birth of a Nation*, the fate of the Piedmont estate may be viewed as a visual example of the shift from coherence to chaos, ownership to occupancy, antebellum social order to anarchy. In his essay "The World and the Home," Homi Bhabha identifies the presence of the "unhomely" in texts in which historical forces refuse to lie quietly outside the walls of the home. Rather than provide a space of protection from the outside world, the domestic spaces "become sites for history's most intricate invasions" (141). For Griffith, the transition from estate to boardinghouse underscores the invasion of the home by the outside forces and presences that it is designed to keep at bay. For Griffith, this displacement is not relegated to the domestic realm but is reflected by the invasion of national "houses" of political power. As one slide tells us, "The executive Mansion of the Nation has shifted from the White House to this Strange House on Capitol Hill." The designation of the houses of government as "strange" suggest that like the Piedmont estate, these national houses are subject to redefinition, upheaval, and chaos. Griffith's cinematic interest in the boardinghouse emerges from its ability to serve as a domestic and national allegory of disintegration, decay, and ruin.

In her epilogue to *The Boardinghouse in Nineteenth-Century America*, Wendy Gamber argues that by the dawn of the twentieth century, boardinghouses were viewed nostalgically as remnants of a bygone era:

> What's striking about twentieth-century representations of boardinghouses—as opposed to their nineteenth-century predecessors—is that they seem to have been uniformly benign. They drew on longstanding traditions of boardinghouse humor, poking fun at boarding places and their inhabitants, but rarely portrayed either as physical or moral threats. (168)

Within the Southern Gothic tradition, however, representations of boardinghouses persisted not as humorous or "benign" remnants of the past, but as evidence of the collapse of that past and as frightening architectural representations of a new social order. William Faulkner uses the boardinghouse to signal the irreversibility of the change in his 1946 appendix to *The Sound and the Fury* (1929). In the appendix, Faulkner twice records the fate of what is "already known as the Old Compson place even while the Compsons were still living in it":

> Jason IV . . . sold the house to a countryman who operated it as a boardinghouse for juries and horse- and muletraders, and [it was] still known as the Old Compson place even after the boardinghouse (and presently the golf course too) had vanished and the old square mile was even intact again in row after row of small crowded jerrybuilt individuallyowned demiurban bungalows. (*Novels 1926–1929* 1131)

In the entry on Jason, Faulkner again emphasizes the conversion of the Compson home to a boardinghouse. Jason "vacated the old house, first chopping up the vast oncesplendid rooms into what he called apartments and selling the whole thing to a countryman who opened a boardinghouse in it (1137). In Faulkner's final descriptions of the Old Compson place, the house is described as "forgotten," "weedchoked," and "ruined" (1130). A symbol of the "oncesplendid" South, the Compson house stands divided, vacant, and sold. Literally a fractured house, the boardinghouse recalls the "House Divided" of Lincoln's speech and the occupation of the South in the aftermath of the Civil War, and it signals the irreversible changes to the previous social order.

If Griffith's Southern boardinghouse, continually subject to invasion and destruction throughout the film, evokes a terrifying specter of irrevocable change, resistance to that change in Faulkner is equally terrifying. Much of Southern Gothic fiction depends upon the representation of enclosed and stifling spaces that seek to maintain a barricade against change. Such spaces facilitate what Sundquist calls the South's "most singular tradition—the tradition of stupefying nostalgia, the painful and tender looking backward toward the ever-living dead dream" (98). For one example, we may look at the opening of William Faulkner's *Absalom, Absalom!* (1936) in which Quentin Compson discovers Rosa Coldfield within

> a dim hot airless room with the blinds all closed and fastened for forty-three summers because when she was a girl someone had believed that light and moving air carried heat and that dark was always cooler, and which (as the sun shone fuller and fuller on that side of the house) became latticed with yellow slashes full of dust motes which Quentin thought of as flecks of the dead old dry paint itself blown inward from the scaling blinds as wind might have blown them. (*Novels 1936–1940* 5)

In closing the windows, Rosa Coldfield attempts to defeat both circulation and movement. The closed and "airless" room operates as a kind of mausoleum; the house appears to be closing in on itself. The "dead old dry paint" that is "blown inward" forecasts the fate of the Sutpen house in the novel's conclusion. Rosa Coldfield's house both preserves and imprisons the past. The air inside is hot "as if there were prisoned in it like in a tomb all the suspiration of slow heat-laden time which had recurred during the forty-three years" (8). The description of Rosa Coldfield's house reminds the reader of the similarly airless domestic scene in Faulkner's "A Rose for Emily" (1930), in which the narrator perceives the horrifying final image of a "long strand of iron-gray hair" through an atmosphere of "faint and invisible dust dry and acrid in the nostrils" (*Collected* 130). Faulkner continually aligns the choice to seal up the house and entomb oneself within it with a desire to hold change and its attendant chaos at bay. Indeed, Rosa's journey in *Absalom, Absalom!* may be viewed as moving among three such crypt-like spaces. First and foremost, there is her own house, which at one time entombed her father within its attic as it now likewise entombs her (*Novels 1936–1940* 8). Additionally, there is the Sutpen house, which she leaves her own house to infiltrate and destroy. When Quentin accompanies Rosa to Sutpen's Hundred, he discovers Henry Sutpen in

> the bare stale room whose shutters were closed too, where a second lamp burned dimly on a crude table; waking or sleeping it was the same: the bed, the yellow sheets and pillow, the wasted yellow face with closed, almost transparent eyelids on the pillow, the wasted hands crossed on the breast as if he were already a corpse. (306)

Both Rosa Coldfield's house and Sutpen's Hundred entomb a corpse-like figure in an enclosed space. Finally, there is Quentin's dorm room at Harvard, itself a cold and crypt-like space that Rosa, through her letter, again infiltrates. Read in this manner, Rosa's house is not merely a singular space that isolates her as a grotesque entombed by her own past, but rather a space that multiplies and proliferates throughout the novel, reflected in a host of isolated spaces that hold cadaverous inhabitants (variously Rosa, her father, Henry Sutpen, Quentin Compson). The degree to which such enclosed spaces and their entombed occupants dominate *Absalom, Absalom!* make it difficult to conceive of an alternative possibility.

It seems that there is little fate available to these spaces that entomb the past other than to collapse inward on themselves. In "Evangeline," an early version of what would become the ending of *Absalom, Absalom!*, Faulkner writes:

> We were standing beneath the wall, watching the clapboards peel and melt away, obliterating window after window, and we saw the old negress come to window upstairs. She came through fire and she leaned for a moment in the window, her hands on the burning ledge, looking no bigger than a doll, as impervious as an effigy of bronze, serene, dynamic, musing in the foreground of Holocaust. Then the whole house seemed to collapse, to fold in upon itself, melting. (*Uncollected* 607)

Here Faulkner emphasizes the house collapsing and folding in upon itself. Thus the destruction of the house emerges as a kind of wish fulfillment for those who would at all costs like to keep the home closed to outside influences. In the conclusion of *Absalom, Absalom!*, Faulkner describes the burning of the "doomed house" again as a move inward: "But the door was not locked; it swung inward; the blast of heat struck them" (308). The house and its entombed occupants appear one and the same: "It loomed, bulked, square and enormous, with jagged half-toppled chimneys, its roofline sagging . . . beneath it, the dead furnace-breath of air . . . seemed to reek in slow and protracted violence with a smell of desolation and decay as if the wood of which it was built were flesh" (*Novels 1936–1940* 301). Body and house fuse in "dead furnace-breath" and the wood made flesh. In *Absalom, Absalom!*, houses figure as mausoleums that pit the tremendous forces of closure and containment against the violent changes occurring in the New South. In other words, spaces are constructed as a means of containing or perhaps defeating time.

In the above examples from Griffith and Faulkner, the boarding-house stands in for that which has been ruined; its inhabitants may be set in opposition to those who would entomb themselves in "stupefying nostalgia" with other "back-looking ghosts" (Sundquist 98; *Novels 1936–1940* 8).

Southern Gothic literature has the proclivity for enclosed, stifling spaces and for dim, airless rooms where the occupant's chief objective is to defeat circulation and movement. Also in this genre, the transition of the estate or plantation to a boardinghouse signals the final defeat of closure, coherence, and order. Carson McCullers's *The Heart is a Lonely Hunter* (1940) announces a clear departure. In McCullers's novel, the boardinghouse does not appear either to deliver the epitaph of a defeated South or to function as a symbol for a national house irrevocably divided, but instead it serves as a possible platform upon which to construct a new Southern identity. Recent work by Sarah Chinn and Rupal Oza has posed the question, "What is (always) so bad about ruin?" (17). Such critical reconsiderations of ruin suggest its capacity for "intervening in history, for discovering the possibility of the new" (14). Ruin may offer spaces free of previous social and political constraints. McCullers employs the boardinghouse not to engender mourning, nostalgia, or a sense of the irrevocable fracturing of a once-coherent whole, but instead to ask what possible communities might emerge from that ruin.

In its concentration on the grotesque body, much of Southern Gothic criticism neglects the potential of architectural spaces such as boardinghouses to function as grotesque and to disrupt and defy categories. In "Revisiting the Southern Grotesque: Mikhail Bakhtin and the Case of Carson McCullers," Sarah Gleeson-White argues that all too often, the gothic is aligned with an "alienating modernity" and an "existential anguish" to the neglect of "the affirming qualities and practices of growth, promise and transformation" (109). For Gleeson-White, the bodies of McCullers's characters exhibit clear definitions and understandings and fulfill Bakhtin's conception of the grotesque as transgressive:

> In Bakhtin's account, the body is a body of excess, and so it queries borders and neat categories. Perhaps more importantly, it is a body in flux, in a constant process of reformation and reemergence: it is becoming. Strictly opposed to the aesthetics of the grotesque is the classic body and its accompanying poetics of closure, coherence, and stasis. The grotesque, then, by its very nature, unnerves the world of classic identity and knowledge, for it tests the very limits of the body and thus of being. Crucially, Bakhtin celebrates this strange body, for it is a site of production: "the grotesque . . . discloses the potentiality of an entirely different world, of another order, another way of life." (110)

Whereas Gleeson-White's argument extends from this reading of Bakhtin to focus on McCullers's characters, emphasizing their grotesque bodies as sites of resistance to a "poetics of closure, coherence, and stasis" (110), I wish to examine how McCullers's architecture functions as a similar site of resistance and potentiality. Rather than use the failing boardinghouse to signal ruin and to mourn the loss of a previous coherence, McCullers's boardinghouse allows her to move beyond a conception of the boardinghouse as signaling disintegration and decay toward a gesture of new possibilities for a more multifaceted Southern identity.

In "Some Aspects of the Grotesque in Southern Fiction," Flannery O'Connor writes that "the characters have an inner coherence, if not always a coherence to their social framework. Their fictional qualities lean away from typical social patterns, toward mystery and the unexpected" (40). O'Connor aligns the grotesque "strange skips and gaps" with incoherence and with a rupture of "typical social patterns." In choosing to set her novel in a boardinghouse, McCullers offers an acknowledgement of this lack of "coherence" and perhaps even a celebration of the "mystery and unexpected" encounters made possible by the dissolving of the previous social systems. What interests Mc-Cullers about transitional spaces such as the boardinghouse is their potential to continuously alter, change, and transform. As a domestic space that resists closure, the boardinghouse facilitates a number of dynamic interracial and intergenerational encounters within the text, resisting the mausoleum spaces typical of the Southern Gothic. The boardinghouse occasions a sense of openness both architecturally and in social terms.

The Kelly family's boardinghouse, which is at the center of McCullers's *The Heart is a Lonely Hunter*, "unnerves" the classic definition of a house as closed to the world to secure those inside from outsiders. As a boardinghouse, it instead "queries borders and neat categories" (Gleeson-White 110), disrupting the idealized boundary between the public and private realms. It is a domestic space and a place of business. The presence of tenants in the house makes any total claim to ownership over the space suspect. The house is eventually returned to the bank when the Kellys cannot make the payments on their mortgage, but they continue to rent the house from the bank, essentially becoming tenants themselves even while continuing to operate it as a boardinghouse.

Thus the boardinghouse at the center of McCullers's novel disrupts any clear boundaries and resists a closed or coherently stable identity. Throughout the novel, the boardinghouse is in a constant state of flux, reformation, and reemergence and is continually subject to transfers of ownership and the arrival and departure of tenants. For the purposes of my analysis, I want to examine McCullers interest in *The Heart is a Lonely Hunter* in the architecture that allows for a disruption and "testing" the limits of the domestic structure to reveal alternative conceptions of home and nation.

Too often, critics of *The Heart is a Lonely Hunter* misread the southern town of McCullers's novel as entirely closed to outside influences, mistaking the individual isolation experienced by the inhabitants for the isolation of the town itself. In fact, McCullers takes great pains to depict the openness of the town to external influences and inhabitants, an openness that she reflects in the structure of the boardinghouse.

The novel takes place in a factory town with a population of 30,000 in "the middle of the deep South" dominated by mills (*Complete* 6, 60). Of the first two characters we meet, one is a Greek and the other, Singer, is variously identified by the townspeople as Jewish, Turkish, and "pure Anglo-Saxon." Another main character, Jake Blount, declares himself to be "part nigger and wop and bohunk and chink. All of those. . . . And I'm Dutch and Turkish and Japanese and American. . . . I'm one who knows. I'm a stranger in a strange land" (23). Biff Brannon, owner of the New York Café, the main setting apart from the Kelly boardinghouse, identifies himself as "an eighth part Jew. . . . My mother's grandfather was a Jew from Amsterdam. But all the rest of my folks that I know were Scotch-Irish" (227). At a party the young Mick Kelly hosts at her family's boardinghouse, her classmates compare their various backgrounds (Scotch-Irish, French, and German), and Mick's next-door neighbor, Harry Minowitz, is a Jewish boy who fantasizes about killing Hitler (112). McCullers moves away from depictions of closed-off and isolated rural Southern towns. The openness of the town and the house at the center of *The Heart is a Lonely Hunter* function not as a sources of terror, but as revealing, in Bakhtin's terms, "the potentiality of an entirely different world" (Gleeson-White 110).

In bringing the national into the domestic, McCullers's boardinghouse allows for what O'Connor calls "seeing far things close up" (44). In her reconfiguration of the boardinghouse, McCullers achieves what she terms "the widening of an art":

> If only traditional conventions are used an art will die, and the widening of an art form is bound to seem strange at first, and awkward. Any growing thing must go through awkward stages. The creator who is misunderstood because of his breach of convention may say to himself, 'I seem strange to you, but anyway I am alive.' ("The Vision" 264)

Rather than use the failing boardinghouse to signal ruin and to mourn the loss of a previous (imagined) coherence, McCullers's boardinghouse allows her to widen the symbol beyond convention in order to incorporate multiple voices and perspectives and to achieve a textually democratic open space. Indeed, McCullers repeatedly flags intersections between the domestic and the national, inviting the reader to view the Kelly boardinghouse as reflecting issues beyond the domestic sphere. In a novel that continually threads the threat of Nazi Germany and its politics of a closed and purified nation throughout, McCullers's boardinghouse offers the possibility of an alternative to domestic and national politics of closure (223, 226, 299). The boardinghouse refutes what Benedict Anderson refers to as nationalism's belief in a homogenous identity constructed through coherent grand narratives (111, 208–10). Instead, McCullers offers us a complex and multiperspectival view of life within a "crowded house" (*Complete* 53).

From the beginning pages of *The Heart is a Lonely Hunter*, McCullers aligns the open and unfinished house with an atmosphere of possibility and becoming. In one of our first introductions to the adolescent Mick Kelly, she is heading toward "the big, new house that was being built" (34). Mick scales the ladder until she reaches the roof, "the place where everybody wanted to stand. The very top" (34). It is at the top of the incomplete house that Mick feels compelled to yell out a song she'd learned in high school. She explains that "there was something about getting to the very top that gave you a wild feeling and made you want to yell or sing or raise up your arms and fly" (34). Returning to the ground, Mick enters the "new, empty house" where she recognizes its temporary accessibility: "no matter how many Keep Out signs were put up, they couldn't run kids away until the house had been painted and finished and people had moved in" (37). Here McCullers designates the "finished," closed house as synonymous with a closing off of possibility and play. By contrast, the yet unfinished house is a place of both transgression and artistic production, a place where "some tough boys wee-weed all over one of the walls and wrote some pretty bad words" and where Mick encounters music: "She hummed one of the tunes, and after a while in the hot, empty house by herself she felt the tears come in her eyes. . . . Quickly she wrote the fellow's name at the very top of the list—MOTSART" (38). Along with Mozart, Mick scrawls the names of Edison, Dick Tracy, and Mussolini on the walls, marking the unfinished house with names that signify invention and discovery and that write the international into the domestic space. From this early moment in the novel, McCullers designates the open, unfinished, and incomplete house as the space of possibility.

In her "widening" of the closed, crypt-like spaces typical of the Southern Gothic, McCullers embraces the open and the unfinished. The house in which Mick Kelly sings, writes, and dreams is mirrored in the open structure of the Kelly house, which

> was one of the biggest houses on the whole north side of town—three stories high. But then there were fourteen people in the family. There weren't that many in the real, blood Kelly family—but they ate there and slept at five dollars a head and you might as well count them on in. . . . The house was narrow and had not been painted for many years. It did not seem to be built strong enough for its three stories of height. It sagged on one side. (40)

In its function as a boardinghouse, the Kelly home is subject to flux and reformation through its continuously changing residents. McCullers's boardinghouse is far from the tomb room of Rosa Coldfield; in the Kelly boardinghouse we have a space not of suffocation and dust, but of energy, circulation, and multiplicity. Though physically pushed to capacity and seemingly unable to hold up, the Kelly boardinghouse is used by McCullers as the locus of dynamic interracial and intergenerational encounters and as a potential space free of the past.

McCullers's novel departs from the enclosed Southern Gothic houses dominated by the "stupefying" collective memory of the Civil War (Sundquist 98). Early in the novel, Mick hosts a party in the boardinghouse. In decorating the house, Mick removes all traces of the family's connection to the Civil War:

> By the hatrack she stopped before the picture of Old Dirty-Face. This was a photo of her Mama's grandfather. He was a major back in the Civil War and had been killed in a battle. Some kid once drew eyeglasses and a beard on his picture, and when the pencil marks were erased it left his face all dirty. That was why she called him Old Dirty Face. . . . On both sides were pictures of his sons. . . . They had on uniforms and their faces were surprised. They had been killed in battle also. A long time ago. (105)

Mick removes the picture for the party, stating that it looks "common" and hiding it underneath the hatrack. The relegation of the Civil War and its toll to something that happened "a long time ago" and the desecration of "Old Dirty Face" clearly indicate that McCullers's characters occupy a very different attitude from Faulkner's characters toward the Civil War. In fact, this is the novel's only reference to the Civil War. Instead, the boardinghouse and the New York Café host debates about racism, fascism, communism, and socialism, with characters appearing far more concerned with Nazi Germany than with the history that entombs Faulkner's characters. This move from an obsessive remembering of the Civil War to an engagement with global debates underscores McCullers's "widening" of the Southern Gothic ("The Vision" 264).

The removal of "Old Dirty Face" to a space underneath the hatrack occasions a carnivalesque release of energy during the party Mick Kelly hosts at the boardinghouse. Despite Mick's attempt to keep her school friends separate from the neighborhood children, the party itself occasions mixing of all kinds: "The party was all messed up. Everybody was talking at once. The invited people from Vocational were mixed with the neighborhood gang" (114). The boardinghouse becomes "more like a crazy house" (113). That Jake Blount will later use the term *crazy house* to describe America highlights the intersections between the domestic and the national in the novel (152). In the description of the party given at the boardinghouse, McCullers connects such mixing with the potential for reinvention: "Excitement—that was the word. She could feel it all through the room and on the porch and the sidewalk. She felt excited, too. . . . Maybe it was the decoration and all these Vocational people and kids being jammed together" (115). McCullers's novel encodes a sense of excitement and vitality about the rejection of enclosed spaces, freedom from obsessive historical memory, and an embrace of circulation and movement.

McCullers's Mick Kelly fears the enclosure and the collapse inward that so characterizes the domestic spaces of the Southern Gothic:

> A queer afraidness came to her. It was like the ceiling was slowly pressing down toward her face. How would it be if the house fell apart? Once their Dad had said the whole place ought to be condemned. Did he mean that maybe some night when they were asleep the walls would crack and the house collapse? Bury them under all the plaster and broken glass and smashed furniture? So that they could not move or breathe? She lay awake and her muscles were stiff. (311)

By contrast to such enclosed spaces, McCullers characterizes the Kelly boardinghouse as "full of noise and unrest. In the room above the kitchen someone was moving furniture about. The dining room was crowded with boarders. . . . Doors banged and voices could be heard in all parts of the house" (258). What is remarkable about the Kelly house in the text is the way in which it provides not just the only communal space, but a space of movement and exchange in which a range of voices struggle to make themselves heard. McCullers consistently employs the boardinghouse to render a picture of interracial dialogue, political discussion, and aesthetic enjoyment. To this end, it is hard not to see the open structure as contributing to a vitality that rescues the boardinghouse from the epitome of ruin as seen in Griffith's film and Faulkner's novels, and then claims it as a space to reimagine a new social and racial order in the South.

The locus of the dynamic encounters within the space of the novel is Singer's room in the Kelly boardinghouse where the deaf-mute is regularly visited over seven months by four of the novel's main characters: Mick Kelly, Jake Blount, Biff Brannon, and Dr. Copeland. "From his room in the evening there was nearly always the sound of a voice," McCullers writes (90). Dr. Copeland believes Singer to be "the only white man I have ever encountered who realizes the terrible need of my people" (204). For Mick, Singer's room affords her one of the few private spaces to think about her music. Prior to coming to Singer's room, she thinks that "no place was left but the street" and that "Next to a real piano I sure would rather have some place to myself than anything I know" (51). As she wanders the town, Mick tries to imagine a space that will allow her to compose her music: "It was funny, too, how lonesome a person could be in a crowded house. Mick tried to think of some good private place where she could go and be by herself and study about this music. But though she thought about this a long time she knew in the beginning that there was no good place" (53). For her, Singer's room becomes such a space: "he understood every word she said. . . . She would tell him some of her plans that she would not tell anybody else" (91). In Singer's room, Jake Blount unleashes his rage at the system of labor exploitation and his frustration at being unable to organize those around him: "Often his voice would come out loud and angry from the room. But before he left his voice gradually quieted. When he descended the staircase . . . he walked away thoughtfully" (91). In an unsent letter to the asylum in which his friend Antonopoulos resides, Singer writes of the cacophony of voices and passions that the four visitors bring to his room:

Yah Freedom and pirates. Yah Capital and Democrats, says the ugly one with the mustache. Then he contradicts himself and says, Freedom is the greatest of all ideals. I just got to get a chance to write this music in me

---

and be a musician. I got to have a chance, says the girl. We are not allowed to serve, says the black doctor. That is the Godlike need for my people. Aha, says the owner of the New York Café. He is the thoughtful one. (216)

McCullers uses the multiplicity of voices within the text to offer something more democratic in the form of the novel than what had been achieved at the national level. Like Singer, the reader is forced into a deepening understanding of each of the characters: "At first he had not understood the four people at all. They talked and talked—and as the months went on they talked more and more. He became so used to their lips that he understood each word they said" (205). In both the form of the novel and in its setting, the text opens to reveal multiple perspectives and convey competing voices. More so than any other space in the novel, the boardinghouse accommodates the possibility for dialogue and exchange; its openness to visitors offers an alternative in the novel to race and class-based violence.

The precariousness of Singer's room with its potential to facilitate communication may be seen against the text's emphasis on class and racially motivated violence as a means of "vigorously asserting distinctions that have threatened to become obliterated (Sundquist 126). More often than not, the novel shows the failure of attempts to communicate, to organize against exploitation, or to replicate an open housing structure in an integrated town. Additionally, *The Heart is a Lonely Hunter* contains numerous violent episodes such as the shooting of a child, rape, self-castration, murder, and dismemberment. Dr. Copeland's son Willie, imprisoned for fighting in a brothel, has both of his feet cut off in jail. Lancy Davis, a boy whose eleven-year-old sister had been raped by her white employer, attempts to castrate himself (184). At the conclusion of the novel, Lancy is murdered. Collectively, these incidents serve to show the violence that comes from divisions between human beings. That McCullers includes these multiple violent incidents highlights the significance of the dialogue that occurs in the Kelly boardinghouse in the room of Mr. Singer (90–91).

In staging a series of encounters within Singer's room at the Kelly boardinghouse, McCullers raises the potential for communication that transcends divisions of age, race, and class. That this possibility is never actualized in the space of the novel does not discount the desire to construct an alternative "house" expressed by each of Singer's visitors. Far from offering a utopian space, the encounters within Singer's room reveal the degree to which human communication is marked by misunderstanding and difficulty.

After months of individual meetings with Singer, his four visitors arrive at the same time one day. McCullers's text emphasizes the failure of communication among the four visitors, each of whom has grown accustomed to having unrelenting access to the silent Singer:

> Always each of them had so much to say. Yet now that they were together they were silent. When they came in he had expected an outburst of some kind. In a vague way he had expected this to be the end of something. But in the room there was only the feeling of strain. (210)

In his letter to Antonopoulos, Singer writes, "They all came to my room at the same time today. They sat like they were from different cities" (216). Despite the seeming total failure of this group encounter, it in fact leads to a series of dynamic exchanges between Copeland and Blount, who struggle to align economic philosophies that approach one another but ultimately fail to cohere. Though the structure of the boardinghouse and Singer's room in particular allows for the opportunity for interracial and intergenerational communication, McCullers's novel does not discount the divisions that separate each of the visitors from one another, an early hint of the eventual failure of the open space of the boardinghouse to affect any lasting change.

Ultimately, neither the boardinghouse, Singer, nor the communication that his room engenders survives the novel. The Kelly family loses the boardinghouse to the bank. As Jake Blount asks Dr. Copeland, "Who owns the South? Corporations in the North own three-fourths of all the South. . . . Absentee ownership" (298). In its final role in Mc-Cullers's novel, the bank-owned boardinghouse stands not as a model for a New South, but as symbol of its failure.

Following Singer's suicide, his room is immediately rented to a typist and each of his visitors returns to a solitary existence (342). The novel's final section takes place on a single day, August 21, 1939, and is divided over the course of the day and in terms of the activities of Singer's former visitors. Dr. Copeland leaves his house, a move that appears to silence him: "He wanted to sit up and speak in a loud voice—yet when he tried to raise himself he could not find the strength. The words in his heart grew big and they would not be silent. But the old man had ceased to listen and there was no one to hear him" (336). When Jake Blount goes to visit Copeland, he finds an abandoned house reminiscent of the Southern Gothic spaces, "an abandoned kitchen" with "shutters . . . drawn" (341). The carnival at which Jake Blount works ends in a riot, described as "a fight with every man for himself" (337): "But [Jake] was caught. And without knowing when it happened he piled into the fight himself. . . . He did not see who he hit and did not know who hit him. But he knew that the line-up of the fight had changed and now each man was for himself" (339). Forced by her family's economic situation to give up school and music to get a job, Mick finds herself in a "trap—the store, then home to sleep, and then back at the store again" (350). Biff Brannon ends the novel by shutting off "a foreign voice . . . speaking over the radio" and descending into "silence . . . deep and unbroken" and "loneliness" (357). The future appears to him as one "of blackness, error, and ruin" (359).

With the main characters once again trapped in individual isolation, with Singer's suicide, and with the loss of the boardinghouse to the bank, it would be tempting to see only the failure of any form of lasting community. Yet McCullers closes with another (though unrealized) possibility. As Biff Brannon turns to head inside the café, he sees "at the far end of the next block two men, small from the distance and motionless, stood arm and arm together" (356). This image for the reader immediately recalls the novel's opening—the friendship between Singer and Antonopoulos—and later Antonopoulos's death, which leads to Singer's suicide. The image of these two men, arm in arm, is also a vision of the union and communication that stands together against the isolated fate of the book's characters. Though McCullers does not offer a novel in which such lasting community is realized or achieved, she creates an architecture in which it could be. In the boardinghouse, McCullers finds not a symbol of ruin, but an architecture of change and flux that is open to the stranger and that gestures toward "the potentiality of an entirely different world, of another order, another way of life" (Gleeson-White 110). As Blount argues in the novel, "The work has to start at the bottom. The old traditions smashed and new ones created. To forge a whole new pattern for the world. To make man a social creature for the first time" (304).

Musing on his dead wife and their life together, Biff Brannon thinks to himself that "only the past can be whole" (224). *The Heart is a Lonely Hunter* may be seen as an attempt to grapple with a fractured and incomplete present. As readers of the novel can attest, the competing voices in the novel are not resolved, neither is any lasting community formed. While McCullers shows the potential for alternatives to entombed spaces that preserve the past at the expense of the present, ultimately we do not see the survival of these alternative spaces. But to read *The Heart is a Lonely Hunter* as evidence of a failure is to miss the radical departure McCullers makes in moving away from enclosed spaces toward spaces that offer the potential for new possibilities beyond the "typical social patterns" (O'Connor 40). In her use of the boardinghouse setting and in her decision to "widen" it as a symbol, McCullers rescues it from the architecture of ruin and redefines it as the architecture of possibility.

In her critique of the Southern Gothic, a term which she coined, Ellen Glasgow feared that the emphasis on ruin and disintegration would lead to a literature with little power: "The literature that crawls in the mire will lose the power of standing erect. On the far side of deterioration lies the death of a culture" (4). As recent criticism on ruin has argued, it is too simple to view ruin as simply evocative of incoherence and decay and as leading to grief and nostalgia. The boardinghouse that encapsulates ruin in Griffith and Faulkner is transformed in McCullers into a site upon which to erect new possibilities. For McCullers, ruin is less a gravesite than a site of production, offering the potential for new configurations not only of the domestic but of the national sphere.

Works Cited

Anderson, Benedict. *Imagined Communities: Reflections on the Origin and Spread of Nationalism*. London: Verso, 2006. Print.

Appelbaum, Stanley. *Abraham Lincoln: Great Speeches*. Mineola: Dover, 1991. Print.

Bhabha, Homi. "The World and the Home." *Social Text* 10.31–32 (1992): 141–53. Print.

Chinn, Sarah, and Rupal Oza, eds. *WSQ: Ruin* 39.3–4 (2011). Print.

Faulkner, William. "A Rose for Emily." *Collected Stories*. New York: Vintage, 1995. 119–30. Print.

___. "Evangeline." *Uncollected Stories*. New York: Vintage, 1997. 583–609. Print.

___. *Novels 1926–1929*. New York: Lib. of Amer., 2006. Print.

___. *Novels. 1936-1940*. New York: Lib. of Amer., 1990. Print.

Gamber, Wendy. *The Boardinghouse in Nineteenth-Century America*. Baltimore: Johns Hopkins UP, 2007. Print.

Glasgow, Ellen. "Heroes and Monsters." *Saturday Review* 4 May 1935: 3–4. Print.

Gleeson-White, Sarah. "Revisiting the Southern Grotesque: Mikhail Bakhtin and the Case of Carson McCullers." *Southern Literary Journal* 33.2 (2001): 108–23. Print.

Griffith, D.W., dir. *The Birth of a Nation*. Perf. Lillian Gish and Mae Marsh. 1915. Image, 1998. DVD.

McCullers, Carson. *Complete Novels*. New York: Library of America, 2001. Print.

___. "The Vision Shared." *The Mortgaged Heart: Selected Writings*. Ed. Margarita G. Smith. New York: Houghton, 2005. 262–65. Print

O'Connor, Flannery. "Some Aspects of the Grotesque in Southern Fiction." *Mysteries and Manners: Occasional Prose*. New York: Farrar, 1969. 36–50. Print.

Sundquist, Eric J. *Faulkner: The House Divided*. Baltimore: John Hopkins UP, 1985. Print.

"Southern Fried Fairy Tales": Eudora Welty's *The Robber Bridegroom*

Tanya Carinae Pell Jones

Once upon a time, fairy tales were set in ambiguous (yet distinctly European) forests and castles in a period at which we could only vaguely guess. However, for Eudora Welty, "once upon a time" was eighteenth century Mississippi and Louisiana, about as far away from grand European castles as one could get. Instead, Welty's fairy tale world is one of bayous, plantations, alligators, and creeping kudzu. In true American Southern Gothic fashion, Welty exchanged the drafty castles for the remote Southern manse, a princess for a Southern Belle, and the elfin forest to one terrorized by "savage Indians." Her fairy tale is as Southern as she was herself.

A self-professed lover of fairy tales and folklore, Welty's 1942 debut novel *The Robber Bridegroom* is the perfect marriage of the two. She collected stories from the Grimm Brothers, Charles Perrault, and others, and she united them with her very own Southern style, creating a delightfully Southern fairy-tale montage. Crowded from beginning to end with classic fairy tales, it is merely a matter of pointing out features that are obviously taken from common childhood stories. Yet that is what makes it unique:

> You'll never come upon another mixture quite like it. If you'd like to try yourself, throw in some Mother Goose, Little Red Riding Hood, Alice in Wonderland, a dash of the Bible, Grimms' fairy tales, a smidgen of Mississippi History, and fill around with ginger ale, and lie back and close your eyes. (Kroll 10)

Regardless of how many folktales, ancient myths, and fairy stories Welty gleaned inspiration from, *The Robber Bridegroom* is not a perfect retelling of tried and true tales. Instead, her variations are amusing parodies or fractured fairy tales. Welty combined famous and decidedly Gothic fairy tales and myths like "The Robber Bridegroom," "Cinderella," "Rapunzel," "Cupid and Psyche," and "Snow White" to create her very own monomyth; a Southern Gothic fairy tale that follows a Southern merchant's daughter and her "robber bridegroom" while they struggle against villains both literary and historical and their own mistrust and dishonesty before they can begin to find their own happily ever after.

As the story opens, we are immediately catapulted into a fairy tale. Having found lodgings for the night, Clement Musgrove hides with Jamie Lockhart in a corner of their room while a third traveler, Mike Fink, attacks their beds, thinking that he will kill and rob his sleeping companions while they rest: "Then he proceeded to strike a number of blows with the plank, dividing them fairly and equally with no favorites between the two bundles of sugar cane lying between the feathers of the bed" (Welty, *Robber* 149). Mike Fink was "a brawny man six and a half feet high" and could easily be compared to the giant in the Grimms' story of "The Valiant Little Tailor" (47). In the German tale, a giant plots to kill a tailor as he sleeps, destroys the bed where he believes the hero is sleeping, and is frightened into flight when he wakes the next morning after his rampage to discover his "victim" without a scratch. Just like the little tailor, Jamie is not what he seems to be and has made himself indispensable to Clement with his quick thinking as they frighten off their own giant.

While her father is off meeting bandits and scaring giants, Rosamond—Welty's fairy-tale princess turned Southern Belle—is locked in her tower room by her stepmother. Ordered about when he is away on business by Clement's greedy second wife, Salome, Rosamond is anything but the meek and demure Cinderella Perrault envisioned: "Beautiful and loving, she is also an incurable liar" (Arnold 34). Though she is her father's joy and the heroine of Welty's story, she is no submissive and humble princess. Instead, she is strong-willed and "when she opened her mouth in answer to a question, the lies would simply fall out like diamonds and pearls" (an obvious reference to the

"Cinderella"–inspired "Toads and Diamonds" fairy tale by Perrault) (Welty, *Robber* 345).

It is likely this is one of the main fractures between Welty's fairy tale and traditional stories. The princesses, servant girls, and other heroines created by the likes of the Grimm Brothers, Hans Christian Andersen, and Perrault are usually obedient and mild young ladies, reluctant to sin for fear of tainting their souls. Yet, Rosamond is more interested in her own desires, curiosities, and simple self-preservation than modesty and tradition. When Jamie comes upon her in his robber disguise and robs her of her clothing, leaving her to go home as naked as on the day of her birth, he offers to kill her, a common fairy tale problem solver for virgins who may fear their name sullied:

> "But wait," he said, "which would you rather? Shall I kill you with my little dirk, to save your name, or will you go home naked?"
>
> "Why, sir, life is sweet," said Rosamond, looking up straight at him through the two curtains of her hair, "and before I would die on the point of your sword, I would go home naked any day." (454)

Sharp-tongued, prideful, and unapologetic, Rosamond is a curiosity in the fairy-tale world of Welty's creation. Not only has the princess chosen to live after having been humiliated and shamed, quite unlike her fairy-tale predecessors, she had even "imagined such things happening in the world" (Welty, *Eye* 442). Consciously aware of the dangers young ladies faced, Rosamond premeditated the likeliness of such an event and grew her hair as long as Rapunzel so that, when unpinned, it covered her naked body. It is in this state that she is sent home to face her stepmother and father.

Welty drew upon every fairy tale she knew to envision Salome, the quintessential wicked stepmother and evil witch of fairy-tale lore. Salome bears an uncanny resemblance to Cinderella's wicked stepmother, Snow White's evil queen/stepmother, and the witch that imprisoned Rapunzel in the tower. Stepmothers in fairy tales are prone to "actively persecute . . . their stepdaughters, who consequently take on the role of innocent martyrs and patient sufferers. They . . . can turn even the most aristocratic and beguiling girl into the humblest of scullery maids" (Tatar, *Hard Facts* 142). Salome, seeking to establish herself as the highest-ranking authority of her household, forces her stepdaughter to do the work of the slaves on the plantation while she plots and schemes against the girl, hoping to solidify her own place in Clement's household by orchestrating Rosamond's death. Blood is thicker than water, as Salome is quite aware.

After the death of Rosamond's mother, Salome seeks to rule over Clement with tyrannical fanaticism and uses his gentle nature against him: "As I grew weaker, she grew stronger, and flourished by the struggle" (Welty, *Robber* 230). Yet, as powerful as Salome grows, her power is wicked and—when considering the duality of the fairy-tale world—cannot overcome Rosamond's goodness. Like most fairy-tale stepmothers, Salome is extraordinarily vain and her narcissism is unwilling to tolerate competition. Thus, jealousy arises as her stepdaughter is young, beautiful, and beloved, whereas Salome is old, ugly, and feared.

It is possibly Clement's adoration and beguilement of his daughter's beauty that fosters this very deep resentment Salome has for Rosamond. Clement shows no affection for his spouse, but he lavishes it upon his daughter who so closely resembles his dead wife. Where Rosamond is showered with gifts and love, Salome must make demands in order to gain attention. Often, the fairy tale father is repeatedly called upon to pacify his impossible wife, though nothing he says or buys will every please her. However, it is frequently the father's very infatuation with another woman—in most cases his biological daughter—that causes the main source of family strife. Maria Warner suggests that the constant resentment the stepmother shows the daughter "could well be motivated in psychological terms by rivalry for the love and admiration of the absent husband and father" (Tatar, *Hard Facts* 154). Thus, Rosamond's budding sexuality is likely responsible for the majority of her stepmother's hatred as she becomes more and more like her father's fantasy (his dead wife).

A domineering, critical, patriarchal voice rings in the ears of Salome just as it did for Snow White's evil queen. The constant comparison Clement insists on pressing between Salome and Rosamond—both in public and in private—is as daunting for his wife as it was for the evil queen to hear she was not "the fairest of them all." Frequently judged by their spouses, the stepmothers resent their stepdaughters who have come to represent all areas in which they fail. In a society that puts so much stock in appearance, "women almost inevitably turn against women because the voice of the looking glass sets them against each other" (Tatar, *Classic* 293). Rosamond, as Clement's heiress and preferred family, is destined to replace Salome, just as Snow White and Cinderella were destined to replace their own stepmothers.

Salome—angry, jealous, and threatened by her stepdaughter's sound relationship with Clement—seeks to rid herself of the girl. She is constantly sending her on unnecessary errands into the woods in hopes that she will be eaten by an alligator or wildcat, killed by the Indians that inhabit the forests along the Natchez Trace, or murdered by Salome's very own lackey, Goat: a rather dull and dim-witted "huntsman" for Welty's little Snow White.

While Salome is obviously Welty's wicked stepmother pieced together from fragments of well-loved stories, Clement Musgrove is clearly the absent father of fairy-tale tradition. Though loving and kind, he is oblivious to the trials of his daughter and the animosity his wife holds for her. When away, Salome treats the girl brutally and Clement does nothing. This is the norm for fathers in fairy tales, especially in Cinderella stories. It is the father's remarriage that causes the family strife and forces him into a state of submission. But while the father's responsibility for creating turmoil by choosing a monstrous marriage partner recedes into the background or is entirely suppressed as a motif even as the father himself is virtually eliminated as a character, the foul deeds of his wife come to occupy center stage (Tatar, *Hard Facts* 150).

By removing himself from the action by refusing to take a stand for his child, Clement has handed the reins over to Salome and allowed her to dominate both Rosamond and himself.

Angela Carter remarked that the classic fairy tale father is "the unmoved mover, the unseen organizing principle, like God. . . . In every version of the story I have read, the father casts a remarkably blind eye over the circumstances of the household" (240). Without the absent father, there cannot be a story. Welty likely drew upon this motif for *The Robber Bridegroom*. Without Clement's blindness and misplaced trust, Jamie, Rosamond, and Salome's stories could never play out as they do. Because he is so honest, he believes everyone else is fair and thus he cannot see Jamie for what he is and turns a blind eye to Salome's "wicked" behavior. In fact, it is only after Salome suggests that Rosamond may not be a virgin that Clement finally asserts his authority over his wife. In both fairy tale and traditional Southern culture, a father with high social standing would have been horrified at the scandal that could erupt from having a daughter with a blight upon her name.

However, Rosamond does not remain physically unsullied for long. The day after their initial meeting, Jamie finds her again wandering in the forest, this time of her own volition. It could very well be suggested that Rosamond was in the forest with the vague hope of seeing her mysterious bandit again. And see him she does. Only, this time, Jamie carries her off and takes more than her clothing:

> Jamie Lockhart lifted Rosamond down. The wild plum trees were like rolling smoke between him and the river, but he broke the branches and the plums rained down as he carried her under. He stopped and laid her on the ground, where, straight below, the river flowed as slow as sand, and robbed her of that which he had left her the day before. (Welty, *Robber* 591)

Here again, Welty deliberately fractures the classic tales she knew so well. The idea of Prince Charming raping Cinderella might be viewed as obscene (though there are several accounts of rape or sex in fairy tales), but here is Welty's bandit prince molesting her Southern princess. Traditionally, having been "dishonored, a true fairy-tale heroine would probably beg for death" rather than face the humiliation associated with being a deflowered woman, but Rosamond only makes her way home in rapt surprise and confusion at the events that transpired (Arnold 35).

Welty's heroine is so thoroughly frazzled from her experience that she does not notice the beatings she is subjected to by Salome and replies to orders and cruelty as any good fairy-tale girl would: with complete obedience. Rosamond, overwhelmed with the day, does not even ready herself for her father's dinner guest and when he arrives she is a complete and utter "mess—unrecognizably dirty from house and yard chores, careless in serving dinner, mustard-stained on her mouth. No Southern Cinderella, she is not discovered by her prince" (35). Jamie, as unrecognizable as she is herself, is ignored by Rosamond as she struggles to deal with her turbulent emotions. Yet, instead of anger, shame, or regret for her circumstances after her abduction and subsequent "rape," Rosamond instead begins to feel a determination of spirit.

With her propensity for lying, her flippant disregard for authority, and her unrepentant attitude toward the loss of her virginity, Rosamond is, in effect, an antiheroine. She is not a fairy-tale princess imagined by the likes of the Grimms, Perrault, or Andersen. Rather than the epitome of decorum and restraint as a mild-mannered princess who answers meekly and is widely loved for her generosity and tenderness of spirit, Rosamond is bold, outspoken, self-serving, and even manipulative when the situation demands.

But Rosamond is not only the fractured princess of a fairy tale, but also a Gothic heroine. As such, she must face some dangers on her own, though she will not defeat her foes through strength. Gothic literature relies heavily upon very similar female stereotypes as do fairy tales. Gothic heroines are, traditionally, mild-mannered and meek, though compassionate and generous, quite like their fairy-tale counterparts (though Gothic heroines are certainly not often princesses). Yet, unlike fairy tales, Gothic heroines are usually the characters that drive the story and force the action by being curious and eager to please another (traditionally male) character. As the female hero of a Gothic fairy tale, Rosamond must prove her love and devotion to Jamie before their happily ever after.

Accordingly, Jamie Lockhart is also a fractured parody of the archetypal Prince Charming. If Rosamond is our antiheroine, Jamie is our antihero "as both Beast and Handsome Prince" (Weston 156). He is quite charming but also decidedly underhanded, mischievous, and a bandit by trade. Not only our prince but our Gothic hero, Jamie must remain reserved and emotionally unavailable as the story progresses. His fairy-tale counterpart is allowed to fall in love quickly, but a Gothic hero is not granted this ability. Jamie must remain a loner, bitter and distant until his trust is earned, broken, and then regained. This combination of charming prince and mysterious loner is what makes him the perfect Gothic robber bridegroom.

The Brothers Grimm collected and penned an early variation of "The Robber Bridegroom" and it was this piece that likely inspired Welty's novel in the first place, though it could be said that she also drew heavily on the "Mr. Fox" variant and the more widely known story of "Bluebeard." Of all the traditional fairy tales, "The Robber Bridegroom" and its variants are some of the darkest and most Gothic with their depictions of forbidden forests, secluded homes, murderous bridegrooms, and haunted heroines.

In the tale of "The Robber Bridegroom," a young woman is engaged to marry a charming and wealthy man, who she knows little about. Out of curiosity, she decides to visit his home unannounced, though her fiancé lives deep within the forest. When she arrives, a caged bird calls out to her and beseeches her to "turn back, turn back," as she has entered the house of a murderer. The girl hides behind a large barrel as the bandits enter the home with their leader, her betrothed. She witnesses them molest, kill, and then consume a young woman they have kidnapped.

In Welty's fractured retelling, while Jamie does not participate or condone the action, a young Indian girl is kidnapped by his thieves, whereupon she is drugged, raped, killed, mutilated, and consumed in an act of cannibalism. In the original tale of "The Robber Bridegroom," when the bride witnesses the attack, she is almost discovered when the girl's finger is severed and lands near her hiding place. Rosamond also witnesses this same scene and worries that the Indian girl's fate may be her own. Her saving grace comes in the form of Jamie, who arrives at the home and puts a stop to the horrors.

Welty's Jamie Lockhart is certainly no murderer with a proclivity toward cannibalism, but he is in every other aspect the original Robber Bridegroom or Bluebeard. Just as in the Grimm story and the other variations of the text, Welty's young girl is courted by a handsome, seemingly wealthy man. He is secretive, often foreign, but devilishly charming. Though there is little "courting" going on, Jamie still fills all other requirements in order to fit the Robber Bridegroom mold. He is quite charming—disarmingly so—and, in his stolen finery, he gives the illusion of vast wealth. He is also terribly mysterious and secretive.

However, before Jamie can begin his search for Rosamond's tormentor and take his place as the hero, she takes the initiative to search for him herself. Though she has no idea of his name or where to find him, she decides to begin her own quest to find her "prince." It is at this point that Rosamond moves from fairy-tale heroine to female hero. She is taking the initiative to change her life.

While Rosamond acts as the true hero of Welty's fractured fairy tale, she is also the most adaptable character. Welty's Southern princess is consistently reimagined as various fairy-tale heroines and female heroes to best fit the particular fairy tale Welty is reenvisioning. Not only does her fairy-tale character change from the likes of Cinderella to Snow White, her very nature is altered to fit the situation. This adaptability allows Rosamond the ability to choose to change her own fate; she is curious and brave as well as beautiful and rich.

Having fallen in love with her bandit lover, Rosamond seeks him out in the woods. She finds his hideout and chooses to venture beyond the threshold and into an adventure. She does this despite the warnings of a caged raven who pleads with Rosamond to "Turn back, my bonny, Turn away home," just as his fairy-tale counterpart tried to warn the young bride away from her own Robber Bridegroom's home lest she be killed and devoured. Here, Welty's fairy tale takes a decidedly Gothic turn. Instead of remaining in her world of light by moving from the familiar forest setting and into the darkness of the bandit's home, Rosamond is essentially moving from the known to the unknown and into her adventure. She is opting to control her own fate rather than wait for rescue at the hands of her prince and, fed up with her fate being controlled by her parents, she ignores the raven's insistence that she "turn back." She has crossed the portal into the unknown on a quest for her lover and there is no turning back for her.

Maria Tatar suggests that the bride in the Gothic fairy tales of "The Robber Bridegroom" and "Bluebeard" are figures "who suffer from an excess of desire for knowledge of what lies beyond the door" (Tatar, *Classic* 139). It seems obvious enough to the reader that Rosamond, like many sheltered Gothic heroines, was in search of sexual knowledge. After her encounters in the forest with Jamie and her subsequent "rape," Rosamond is desperate to see her lover again. Welty, who has often been described as a Southern feminist due to her strong and eccentric female characters, seems to have no qualms about creating a fairy tale princess with the same sexual desires as her prince. With this quality, Rosamond is put on much more equal footing with her hero because she is allowed to want and need Jamie sexually.

However, though Rosamond is allowed to have very heroic inclinations and unprincess-like desires, sadly, just like so many princesses in traditional tales, Rosamond does not go off and fight her own dragons. Regardless of her heroic courage, tenacity, and conscious sexuality, and even though she has decided to take control of her destiny by seeking out her lover, she is still not permitted to win him through acts of heroism. Instead, Welty's princess must submit to a life of domesticity and marriage in order to save herself and have the opportunity to live happily ever after. This is a common enough fate in both fairy tales and Gothic stories as, traditionally, a young girl is set up as a domestic servant or house guest while strange events unfold around her.

When Rosamond enters the hideout of Jamie and his gang and sees the absolute disorder of the home, she immediately sets out to clean it. When the bandits, led by Jamie, return and discover her and threaten to kill her, she offers them homemade cake rather than plead for her life. By proving her usefulness as a maid and cook, she has shown she has value. Without this ability, her life is in danger. Though Snow White was in little danger of having her head chopped off by the seven dwarves whose home she invaded, she did make a similar arrangement for shelter. Snow White makes an agreement with the dwarves who offer her refuge and safety when she promises to act as their domestic servant: "Will you look after our household, cook, make the beds, wash, sew and knit, and keep everything neat and clean? If so you shall stay with us and want for nothing" (Estes 5).

Even though she hangs up her questing armor to tie on an apron, thereby handing the control over to Jamie, the role of domestic servant seems to do Rosamond good. Her father remarks that her time with the bandits had cured her of her penchant for lying. Though she was never a "bad" girl, she was still not as "good" as her father felt she could be. Her talent for singing, her beauty, and her gentle nature was simply not enough to offset the pride of youth. Yet, by acting as housekeeper for the bandits, she earns her place in the kingdom, "for in serving them she learns essential lessons of service, selflessness, of domesticity" (Tatar, *Classic* 295).

Rosamond does not only play the role of servant; Jamie, the bandit-leader, takes her as his woodland bride. Though she is required to cook, clean, and sew for his entire gang, only he is allowed to sample her other favors. Again, Welty demonstrates a levity regarding fairy-tale tradition by permitting her prince and princess to "live in sin" in the forest. And, while they seem perfectly content with their arrangement, there are still issues of mistrust, a lack of commitment, and minor episodes of domestic violence.

Despite the fact that Jamie and Rosamond are "wed," he still refuses to tell her his name or show her his face. Though Rosamond claims she and her bandit lover "have a trust in one another," they are unwilling to share even the most basic information with each other. Rosamond "begged him every night to wash off the stains from his face so that she could see just once what he really looked like . . . but he would never do it" (Welty, *Robber* 746). He insists that she should be content with what is and love him regardless of his appearance. Like many a fairy-tale couple featuring a husband in disguise or animal groom, the bride is forbidden to see her spouse in his true form as a test of her love and faith. Here, we see another issue of inequality between the two. Though Rosamond has proven her capability to be the hero of her own story, she is unable to completely abandon her role as fairy-tale princess. She must curb her pride and demanding nature and in some sense be "rescued" so it is her prince who seems to be in control. Rosamond may not be pleased with the lack of trust her hero shows her, but the fairy-tale princess has little voice when pitted against her prince in a male-dominated household, so she must accept it regardless. (Oddly, she is more like her wicked stepmother than she realizes.)

Rosamond, though she does desire to see her lover without his berry-stain disguise, is relatively satisfied with their arrangement. She is blissfully happy in the hours he is with her, speaking to her and sharing words of love and adoration. However, she is plagued by the notion that he may abandon her. Jamie confesses that he is betrothed to an heiress, as he is still unable to reconcile the notion that his fiancée and his woodland bride are one in the same. Rosamond is understandably "afraid he might get up and fly away through the window while she was fast asleep" so she clings to him desperately until the sun is high in the sky and the bandits would already be on their way (757).

Yet, though Rosamond can hold Jamie sexually captive to a certain extent, she is the one who is truly ensnared: "Rosamond is captured by her bandit-lover, who tries to keep her, literally and figuratively, in the dark of his forest hideout" (Weston 136). By abandoning her lover, she would not only be giving up on her quest for happiness, she would also be condemning herself to a life as a ruined woman. She has lived in sin with her robber bridegroom and his gang of thieves in the forest without her father's consent, though she claims to have been married by a drunken minister. With her unconventional lifestyle and without her virginity, Rosamond is—essentially—damaged goods in the eyes of society.

Rosamond is not only held hostage by her own affections for her husband and her humble acquiescence to his demands regarding her role as servant and lover, but issues of domestic violence may also play a part in her captivity. As unapologetic a feminist as Rosamond is, she is still a woman bound by tradition to serve and obey her husband, so when Jamie lashes out, she is unwilling (or perhaps unable) to counter him. Jamie, though he speaks kindly to Rosamond at night, is still incredibly aggressive as a lover. Not only is Rosamond's first sexual experience with him a result of her kidnapping and his forcefully "robbing" her of her virginity, he is prone to kissing her "as hard as he could . . . since he was running things" and "when she tried to lead him to his bed with a candle, he would knock her down and out of her senses, and drag her there" (Welty, *Robber* 745).

Though their relationship is tense for a multitude of reasons, it is the secrecy that is the most difficult for Rosamond to submit to. The love affair of Rosamond and Jamie can be closely mirrored by the relationship of Cupid and Psyche. Psyche, who weds her husband but is forbidden to look upon him, fears she may be married to a beast. Unable to resist temptation, she gazes upon him while he is sleeping. Realizing her betrayal, Cupid abandons Psyche as "love cannot live where there is no trust," forcing her to undergo a quest to reunite herself with her lost husband, a common motif in animal/husband fairy tales (Hamilton 127). Rosamond also cannot deny her curiosity and, through trickery devised by her evil stepmother, she looks upon Jamie while he sleeps sans his disguise. Here again, the husband abandons his wife due to her curious nature with eerily similar words of parting: "Good-by . . . For you did not trust me, and did not love me, for you wanted only to know who I am" (Welty, *Robber* 1203).

Despite her lost love and her broken heart, Rosamond feels as betrayed as Jamie. Rosamond refuses to accept her role of fairy-tale princess by acting indignant as opposed to woebegone:

> "My husband was a robber and not a bridegroom," she said. "He brought me his love under a mask, and kept all the truth hidden from me, and never called anything by its true name, even his name or mine, and what I would have given him he liked better to steal. And if I had no faith, he had little honor, to deprive a woman of giving her love freely." (Welty 1302)

Rosamond is no ruined fairy-tale heroine to be cast off by her prince. Instead, she takes this as a personal challenge and sets off to prove to Jamie that she loves him despite his tantrums and lack of faith, as any good Gothic heroine would. Again, Rosamond must prove to be the hero of her own story; she is determined to rescue herself and her prince instead of waiting for him to get around to it. Hanging up her princess apron, she again dons her armor and sets off to find her husband, regardless of the perils and footfalls in her way.

This is, of course, necessary. In order for Rosamond and Jamie to truly be happy in their fairy tale, trials must be faced. In his unparalleled study on fairy tales and the psyche, Bruno Bettelheim concluded as much:

> If one wishes to gain selfhood, achieve integrity, and secure one's identity, difficult developments must be undergone: hardships suffered, dangers

met, victories won. Only in this way can one become master of one's fate and win one's kingdom. . . . Having truly become himself, the hero or heroine has become worthy of being loved. (278)

Rosamond, realizing her happiness is forfeited without Jamie, must search him out. Though she feels angry and betrayed at his lack of trust and flippant disregard for the love she has already shown him, she understands that she has not been entirely innocent. So, for the second time, she must play the female hero and venture into the world to earn her place by her husband's side, this time without any secrets between them.

However, the world is not a safe one by any means. Welty, a native of the American South, built her fairy-tale world from the very fabric of her surroundings. In genuine Southern Gothic style, Welty fractured the fairy stories of her childhood and reimagined them in her own kudzu-covered world in "that dank, primitive forest of Louisiana, some way above New Orleans, between the muddy Mississippi, and the old, murderous Natchez trace" (Bishop 86). It is this no-man's land of cypress swamps and dark, primeval forests that make Welty's novel a Gothic fairy tale.

Gothic scholar Judith Wilt once professed that there is nothing more authentically Gothic than a setting that boasts a great deal of mystery, darkness, and instability. The Natchez Trace has this in spades. With the naturally Gothic atmosphere of the ever darker woods along the Trace and the history of the area, it is no wonder Welty found such a source of inspiration for her singular Gothic fairy tale in her own backyard.

Welty's use of mysterious, deceitful men and haunted heroines bring to mind popular Gothic romances of her time, but it is the use of setting that truly provides the terror in her own Southern Gothic fairy tale. Gone are the enchanted woods where fairies seek to help the princess while sorceresses mean to do her harm. Welty's heroine must contend with a wilderness where Indians throw babies in boiling oil, bandits rape young women and then feast upon their flesh, and the law seems to be "anything goes." With her painstaking descriptions of the land and its ability choke the life out of careless travelers, the Natchez Trace Welty writes of is a character in itself; an accomplice to the villains to whom it provides sanctuary.

The use of the Natchez Trace as a land fraught with danger is certainly no stretch. The dense forests were home to many of the South's most horrific perils, harboring both marauding Indians and dastardly land-pirates in their dark recesses. The history of the area is more haunting than any fairy tale. In her essay "Fairy Tale of the Natchez Trace," Welty points out that real horror is to be found in history and not in fairy tales. Along the Natchez Trace alone, she recounts episodes of terror that haunt her beloved South when she writes of how many individuals "were scalped. Babies had their brains dashed out against tree trunks or were thrown in boiling oil when the Indians made their captures. . . . The Natchez Trace outlaws eviscerated their victims and rolled their bodies . . . into the Mississippi River" (Welty, *Eye* 309). It is in this world that Rosamond must maneuver if she is ever to be with her beloved again. However, not only does Welty draw from the Gothic setting and the evils perpetrated there, but she draws also from area folktales that sprang up around specific, historical individuals like the Mike Fink and the notorious Harpe Brothers.

Known as the "king of the keelboaters," Mike Fink was once described by Davy Crockett as being "half horse, half alligator." Very much human despite his reputation, Mike Fink managed to make a significant name for himself in Southern folklore. As an Indian scout, river boatman, trapper, and mountain man, Mike Fink was larger than life:

> He was the marksman who could not miss, the bully-boy who could not be felled, unmatchable in drink, invincible to wenches. He was a Salt River roarer. . . . He fought a thousand combats. . . . He was superior to the ethics of timid souls and no court could restrain him. . . . Casanova, together with

Paul Bunyan, merges into Thor, and Mike is a demigod of the rivers even before he dies—the boatman immortally violent, heroic, unconquerable. (DeVoto 60)

It is this image of Mike Fink—brutal, lawless, formidable—that Welty drew upon when imagining her giant for *The Robber Bridegroom*. Though Fink does not play a major role in the fairy tale as a whole, his presence is very much felt as the tall-tale figure he is. It is with Mike Fink that Welty opens her novel, as he is the giant Clement and Jamie must face together.

And the affection Welty had for her Southern folk hero is obvious as Fink recounts his exploits on the river, his ability to carry whole loads of oxen and pigs on his back, and his habit of trouncing any man or Indian in his wake. Welty even uses his familiar catchphrase, allowing him to tell his companions that he "can outrun, out hop, out jump, throw down, drag out, and lick any man in the country" because he is Mike Fink: "a he-bull and a he-rattlesnake and a he-alligator all in one" (Welty, *Robber* 93).

Mike Fink is, for all intents and purposes, as Gothic of a folk hero as there could be. The legends of his adventures are both true and untrue, for no one can be sure where the real tale ends and the tall tale begins. He was by all accounts a man of rough manners and a ferocious nature but one of admirable talents. Portrayed as both hero and villain in Southern lore, he is also both comic relief and Gothic villain for Welty. He may play the fool by drinking to excess and dancing naked with Clement, but with his raven companion acting as a dark oracle and his monstrous presence, Fink is a Southern Gothic giant for Welty's fairy tale.

And if Fink is the giant, then the Harpe brothers must be the ogres. Though it is up for debate as to whether they were brothers or cousins (the literature is quite vague on this point), historians often agree on their crimes, and credit the Harpes with the title of America's first serial killers. The Harpes were land-pirates and murderers who, it has been suggested, derived more pleasure from the killing than the actual robbery. Between the two of them—Micajah "Big" Harpe and Wiley "Little" Harpe—they slaughtered upward of forty men, women, and children during their reign of terror on the Southern wilderness.

It is not so much their reputation as killers that inspired Welty to add them to *The Robber Bridegroom*, but the means by which they dispatched their victims. Like the flesh-eating, nefarious ogres of fairy tales, the Harpe brothers were inclined to treat murder as a macabre art. They would often rip and tear at the bodies of their victims with their bare hands, as if the kill was a pleasure to not be wasted upon implements. Some accounts are more horrific than any fantasy. The son of one of their pursuers was "shot, kicked, tomahawked, pummeled. His body was macerated by their blows, almost dismembered by their knives" (Coates 39). Another of their more ruthless murders ended with a settler "tomahawked, disemboweled, his belly filled with gravel, and his body flung in the river" (11). Mutilation, it seemed, became the calling card of the Harpes as more and more of their victims were found gutted and filled with stones or gravel.

It is likely Welty saw a distinct parallel between the villainous bridegroom in the original, darkly Gothic tale of "The Robber Bridegroom" and the historical abominations by the bloodthirsty Harpes. In her fairy tale, it is Little Harpe who sets in motion the rape, mutilation, and murder of the Indian maiden by Jamie's gang. As the bridegroom in the story, Little Harpe slices off the finger of the young girl before hurling her upon the dinner table among the knives and forks where she will be consumed.

Yet, while Little Harpe is acting out atrocities, he is also haunted by his past. Keeping in mind the appearances of the supernatural so prevalent in both fairy tales and Gothic fiction, Welty was not remiss in using one of the darkest elements of the Harpes history in her story. When Big Harpe was captured by a posse, the husband and father of two of his victims severed his head and nailed it to a tree; the spot is still known as "Harpe's Head." In *The Robber Bridegroom*, it is Big Harpe's head that haunts his little brother, screaming from a trunk that Little Harpe is cursed with. His brother, though dead, continues to haunt his existence, extolling his weaknesses and ruling over his decisions. A significant villain of Welty's Gothic fairy tale, Little Harpe is plagued by his past by the supernatural, patriarchal voice of his brother, a voice that he cannot escape.

Perhaps it was a similar voice that haunted Eudora Welty. It may not have been the disembodied voice of the past, but one can certainly imagine the darkness of the woods around her home and the well-thumbed pages of fairy stories whispering to her, urging her to write. A true Southern Gothic fairy tale, *The Robber Bridegroom* is a testament to the American ability to adapt. In a land founded upon the echoes of other countries, Welty's novel is an echo in itself as both a fracture of European fairy tales and Victorian Gothic romances.

Works Cited

Arnold, Marilyn. "Eudora Welty's Parody." *Critical Essays on Eudora Welty*. Ed. W. Craig Turner and Lee Emling Harding. Boston: Hall, 1989. Print.

Bettelheim, Bruno. *The Uses of Enchantment: The Meaning and Importance of Fairy Tales*. New York: Vintage, 1975. Print.

Bishop, John Peale. "The Violent Country." *The Critical Response to Eudora Welty's Fiction*. Ed. Laurie Champion. Westport: Greenwood, 1994. Print.

Carter, Angela. *Burning Your Boats: The Collected Short Stories*. London: Penguin, 1997. Print.

Coates, Robert. *The Outlaw Years: The History of the Land Pirates of the Natchez Trace*. New York: Macaulay, 1930. Print.

DeVoto, Bernard A. *Mark Twain's America*. Lincoln: U of Nebraska P, 1997. Print.

Grimm, Jacob, and Wilhelm Grimm. *Tales of the Brothers Grimm*. Ed. Clarissa Pinkola Estes. New York: Quality Paperback Book Club: 1999. Print.

Hamilton, Edith. *Mythology: Timeless Tales of Gods and Heroes*. New York: Hatchette , 2011. Print.

Kroll, Harry Harrison. "Unusual Story by Eudora Welty Among Latest Fiction Publications." *Memphis Commercial Appeal* 25 Oct. 1942: 10. Print.

Tatar, Maria, ed. *The Classic Fairy Tales: Texts, Criticism*. New York: Norton, 1999. Print.

___. *The Hard Facts of the Grimms' Fairy Tales*. New Jersey: Princeton UP, 1987. Print.

Welty, Eudora. *The Eye of the Story: Selected Essays and Reviews.* New York: Random, 1978. Print.

___. *The Robber Bridegroom.* New York: Houghton, 1978. Kindle ebook file.

Wetson, Ruth D. *Gothic Traditions and Narrative Techniques in the Fiction of Eudora Welty.* Baton Rouge: Louisiana State UP, 1994. Print.

Sexuality, Insanity, and the Old South in Tennessee Williams's *Suddenly Last Summer*

Tanfer Emin Tunç

Tennessee Williams's one-act play *Suddenly Last Summer* (1958) is considered by critics to be a prominent example of mid-twentieth-century Southern Gothic drama because it not only captures the darkness and decay of the New South, but it also questions the metaphoric meaning of the plantation both as a physical space and as a state-of-mind. Southern Gothic traces its roots to the first American Gothic writers, Edgar Allan Poe, Nathaniel Hawthorne, and Washington Irving. The genre uses elements of traditional European Gothic literature, such as the supernatural, Gothic architecture, extreme weather conditions, misfits, "freaks," madness, secrets, love triangles, guilt, "deviant" sexuality, and death. These elements deconstruct the "magnolia myth" of the chivalrous planters, demure southern belles, and content slaves of the Old South, as well as the archetypal Southern setting—the plantation itself. Southern Gothic also involves highlighting the tensions between the conventional values of the Old South and the grotesque realities—the flawed characters, haunted places, racism, sexism, violence, alienation, oppression, corruption, and materialism—of the New South. Thus, inherent in the Southern Gothic genre is a reexamination of the plantation as a matrix of darkness, death, and decay that shapes the South; a reconsideration of the impact of the ghosts of the past on the present; and a reevaluation of the place of women, homosexuals, and peoples of color, whose domination contributes to this haunted geography.

The play's dramatic arc centers on the Venable family's Victorian Gothic mansion in New Orleans, whose internal flora and fauna substitute for the modern plantation. Its sinister secrets—including the mental decline of Catharine Holly, who is diagnosed as insane following her cousin Sebastian Venable's mysterious death during a vacation to the fictitious Cabeza de Lobo—represent the grotesque realities of this decaying world. Sebastian had used Catharine as a means to procure, sexually exploit, and thus, like a plantation master, recolonize the bodies of dark-skinned (slave) boys who caught his fancy. In an attempt to obscure Sebastian's homosexuality, sadism, and abuse of Catharine, his mother, Violet Venable, threatens to lobotomize the hysterical Catharine. She hopes this will curtail Catharine's incoherent and potentially damaging mumblings about Sebastian's death, thus maintaining his reputation as a poet and bon vivant. However, under the guidance of psychiatrist Dr. Cukrowicz, Catharine is saved from a lobotomy and, after a dose of truth serum, reveals the events surrounding Sebastian's death by dismemberment and cannibalism at the hands of the local boys whose sexual favors he sought.

By substituting herself in the role of the plantation mistress, Violet obscures the sins of her son Sebastian, who substitutes as the modern, morally corrupt, and ethically bankrupt plantation master. This role assumption is complicated by Sebastian's deviant sexual excesses, which not only bring to mind the sexual coercion enacted by plantation masters, but when Violet's and Catharine's positions are considered, also suggest the extent to which white women functioned as both victims and victimizers. Although Catharine eventually remembers the horror of her cousin's death, thus suggesting the New South's desire to grapple with the troubling realities of its past, Violet dedicates her life to upholding the "honor" of her son—and therefore the Old South—which becomes her lost cause. As this essay will elucidate, *Suddenly Last Summer* not only exemplifies the elements commonly associated with mid-twentieth-century Southern Gothic literature, but also positions death, haunting, and the oedipal relationship between Violet and Sebastian as part of the geography of secrets of the Old and New South.

Williams's framework of the decaying, grotesque, and secret-laden plantation is established through the setting of the play:

> [A] mansion of Victorian Gothic style in the Garden District of New Orleans. . . . The interior is blended with a fantastic garden which is more like

a tropical jungle, or forest, in the prehistoric age of giant fern-forests. . . . The colors of this jungle-garden are violent, especially since it is steaming with heat after rain. There are massive tree-flowers that suggest organs of a body, torn out, still glistening with undried blood; there are harsh cries and sibilant hissings and thrashing sounds in the garden as if it were inhabited by beasts, serpents and birds, all of savage nature. (Williams 9)

Clearly, Williams's description of the Venable mansion, with its adjacent garden or "well-groomed jungle" (11), suggests "an atmosphere of lush, sickly decay" mixed with sophistication, violence, and disarray (Sofer, "Self-Consuming Artifacts"). A grotesque and terrifying Garden of Eden, Sebastian's garden functions as a demented microcosm of the plantation fields, where both the land and its cultivators (bondspeople) have been exploited, with the blood of slavery seeped in its soil. The garden is also home to all sorts of wild beasts and birds, whose shrill, echoing sounds throughout the play underscore the Gothic landscape. Even the plants themselves are much like their owner— barbarous, monstrous, and carnivorous. While Sebastian, the Gothic "Adam" or perhaps serpent, which is emphasized by the multiple "s" sounds in his name, subsisted on the bodies of young men, his Venus flytrap ate expensive fruit flies originally used in genetics experiments, suggesting that Sebastian also behaved like a "crazed scientist," a staple character in other Gothic works such as Hawthorne's short story "Dr. Heidegger's Experiment." Like Sebastian himself, "the flytrap is kept under glass from early fall to late spring and emerges only in summer" (Sofer, "Self-Consuming Artifacts").

In this gruesome context, "the *ante-bellum* mansion—a decrepit dwelling, a common metonymy for the crumbling Southern culture— becomes the theater for a series of burlesque scenes . . . [in which old southern] civilization is turned into ridicule" (Tuhkunen 27–29). A romantic trope of the plantation past, the pastoral garden is now the locale of death and disorder, "an entranceway to what lies behind the respectable façade of the old house: a mysterious hinterland created by

Sebastian Venable, a dead poet whose haughty, castrating mother, Mrs. Violet Venable . . . is committed to transforming his deceased son into a monument" (20–23). The plantation-esque setting also highlights the debased reality of their present by suggesting that the Garden District, traditionally considered to be an aristocratic quarter of New Orleans, is now, like its decadent and degenerate inhabitants, doomed, decaying, and grotesque.

Violet Venable, whose name evokes a traditionally Gothic color, the word "violence," as well as, ironically, the word "venerable," is an equally grotesque figure, and thus an appropriate mistress for this ghastly garden. As Williams informs the reader in his stage directions, the wealthy Southern dowager "has light orange or pink hair and wears a Victorian lavender lace dress." Additionally, "over her withered bosom is pinned a starfish of diamonds" (Williams 9), and she sports a "silver-knobbed cane [which] acts successively as crutch, magic wand, and weapon" (Sofer, "Self-Consuming Artifacts"), simultaneously suggesting a witch-like domination over nature. Moreover, "ice-cold daiquiris run in her veins instead of blood" (Sofer, "Self-Consuming Artifacts")—she drinks one every day at exactly five o'clock in the evening, so promptly that "you could set a watch by it" (Williams 37). Much like Brick from Williams's *Cat on a Hot Tin Roof*, Violet depends on alcohol to give her the strength and courage to forget her son's death and her loneliness, alienation, and abjection. Recovering from what she calls "a slight aneurysm" and what Catharine calls "a stroke" (57), "Violet is [also] supported by a bevy of 'brave utensils,' from the [elevator paneled in black and gold Chinese lacquer with birds] she has had installed to get her up and down stairs, to the chair whose back her hapless maid cranks up and down" (Sofer, "Self-Consuming Artifacts").

Violet is in retreat from life, choosing, instead, to preserve the archaic order of the aristocratic, antebellum Old South in the New South. This not only adds a note of tragedy to her reclusive and introverted life but also transforms her into a grotesque figure who is chronologically displaced, shocked by, and in denial about Sebastian's world, because it does not fit her ladylike sensibilities and standards of propriety. Violet is traditional, prudish, and proper, and suffers from a fear of sex—especially homosexual and extramarital—that borders on psychosis. She feels uncomfortable and alienated in this new society with its changing values, increasing sexual freedom, foreign influences—e.g., Dr. Cukrowicz, whose name she cannot pronounce—and the blurring of the borders between the Garden District and the French Quarter, where Sebastian maintained an atelier and sexual mores were looser. The disability, disfigurement, detachment from reality, and the loss of vitality among the Southern elite—from Violet's stroke that leaves her handicapped, to Sebastian's deviant lifestyle that results in his death, to Catharine's supposed insanity that causes her to oscillate between sedation and sexual aggression—thus serve as a continuous thread throughout the play, and one that Williams returns to on numerous occasions.

Dr. Cukrowicz, the other main character in the play, also represents a Gothic archetype: the scientist. While not insane himself, the neurosurgeon works with the mentally deranged, wild, animalistic patients at Lion's View, the state institution where he performs experimental lobotomies. The physician is lured into Violet's black widow spider web by promises of research funding, which he will receive only if he performs the procedure on Catharine. Violet believes that the insulin and electroshock therapies that Catharine is receiving at St. Mary's are not effective enough and that only surgery will cut out Catharine's "babbling" about Sebastian's lifestyle and shocking death. Dr. Cukrowicz is also significant because he represents the New South:

His foreign name—like Stanley Kowalski [in *A Streetcar Named Desire*], he is of Polish descent—is here, as in other plays by Williams, a sure sign of vigor. He resists both bribes and persuasion; he refuses to be swallowed alive by [Violet], a superannuated gargoyle. The measure of his success is the coolness he maintains in the face of Mrs. Venable's mounting fury. (Popkin 49)

The fact that Violet cannot pronounce Cukrowicz, which is not particularly difficult to pronounce—"Cu-kro-wicz," as the physician conveys—may be an indication of Violet's resistance to this new world: calling a physician by an ethnic name would taint the "pure" white Anglo-Saxon Protestant plantation world she has attempted to create. Instead, she calls him Dr. Sugar, sugar being a common Southern term of endearment as well as the English translation of the physician's Polish name.

The play starts in medias res and is partially told through flashbacks. Moreover, the main focus of the dramatic arc, Sebastian Venable, is already dead and never actually participates in the dialogue. Sebastian is the ultimate Gothic ghost: not only did he die young and under mysterious circumstances, but he also continues to haunt his family from beyond the grave. Throughout the play, Sebastian is associated with the binaries of black/white and dark/light, with the motif of whiteness—of Sebastian's white race and white clothing—reinforcing his position as "master" phantom. Sebastian is described by Catharine as being "white as the weather. He had on a spotless white silk Shantung suit and a white silk tie and a white panama and white shoes, white—white lizard skin—pumps! He . . . kept touching his face and his throat with a white silk handkerchief and popping little white pills in his mouth" (Williams 82). While his whiteness, and thus potency as a plantation master, is clearly queered and questioned throughout the play—he wore white pumps and touched his throat effeminately with a white handkerchief, and was ultimately devoured by dark boys, which suggests metaphorical miscegenation—Sebastian's spectral presence is nonetheless a powerful motif. He appears and reappears through the "very, very good-looking" (10) Dr. Cukrowicz, who, like Sebastian, is seemingly "angelic"—blond, dressed all in white, and is white like sugar. Sebastian also appears through Catharine's brother George, also blond, who inherits his cousin's clothing and wears it throughout the drama, serving as a ghost of the deceased man. As Andrew Sofer contends:

Suddenly Last Summer is unique in the Williams canon in that its protagonist is literally and figuratively absent. The poet Sebastian Venable
dies before the action takes place . . . [yet] images of Sebastian repeat and
refract until the play becomes a dizzying hall of mirrors. . . . No Williams
play is more haunted by the body, its directives and disguises; yet in no
other play is the body in question so elusive. ("Self-Consuming Artifacts")

Sebastian's white clothing is supposed to suggest youth and purity,
though he was neither: he harbored a desire to whitewash his past, with
white as a symbol of innocence, rebirth, and cleanliness/godliness. His
whiteness also creates a stark contrast with the darkness of the boys he
exploited, both in terms of race, if the boys are taken as stand-ins for
plantation slaves, and socioeconomic position: impoverished, the boys
were forced to occupy the shadows of the homosexual underworld, or
the world of darkness, whereas money allowed Sebastian to frequent
the world of light. In fact, before he died, Sebastian expressed a desire
for whiteness and white meat, specifically for Scandinavian boys:

CATHARINE. Cousin Sebastian said he was famished for blonds, he was
fed up with the dark ones and was famished for blonds. All the travel
brochures he picked up were advertisements of the blond northern
countries. I think he'd already booked us to—Copenhagen or—Stock-
holm.—Fed up with dark ones, famished for light ones: that's how
he talked about people, as if they were—items on a menu.—"That
one's delicious-looking, that one is appetizing," or "that one is *not*
appetizing"—I think because he was really nearly half-starved from
living on pills and salads. . . . (Williams 39)

Although Violet portrays her son as a sensitive poet who spent
his time in the pursuit of beauty—art, and not young men—as Dr.
Cukrowicz soon discovers, Sebastian was a dark and egocentric sa-
dist who had a voracious appetite for pain and destruction. While
he suffered from a weak heart after a bout of rheumatic fever as a

teenager, Sebastian nevertheless traveled to the ends of the earth to pursue that which he considered to be holy. As Violet states, "Sebastian had no public name as a poet . . . he refused to have one. He *dreaded, abhorred*!—the false vales that come from being publicly known, from fame, from personal—exploitation" (13). Yet, while the sophisticated and understated Sebastian certainly rejected the vulgar materialism of modernity, he was an amoral hedonist who was not above using or "devouring" others if it suited his purposes. Supernaturally trying to defy aging and the passage of time, Sebastian attempted to achieve perpetual youth in order to reach his ends. Like the aristocratic vampire Dracula, he avoided water and the sun—which makes his trip to Cabeza de Lobo in search for "dark ones" all the more desperate—drawing life-blood from the young he devoured sexually. He always had "a little entourage of the beautiful and the talented and the young!" (22), most likely to make him feel beautiful, talented, and young. Sebastian was obsessed with his body, and might even have been anorexic, fixated on maintaining his lean and youthful physique so he could attract younger and younger prey.

To prove that Sebastian was successful—at least in the type of lifestyle he led—Violet shows Dr. Cukrowicz two pictures of her son, taken twenty years apart in the same Renaissance pageboy's costume. Violet, who believes that her son was like a Renaissance prince, notes that they are indistinguishable. She proudly states that he "refused to grow old," a process which required "discipline" and "abstention," especially with respect to pleasures such as food and sex:

MRS. VENABLE. One cocktail before dinner, not two, four, six—a single lean chop and lime juice on a salad in restaurants famed for rich dishes. . . . Sebastian, was chaste. Not c-h-a-s-e-d! Oh, he was chased in that way of spelling it, too, we had to be very fleet-footed I can tell you, with his looks and his charm, to keep ahead of pursuers, every kind of pursuer!—I mean he was c-h-a-s-t-e!—Chaste. (23–24)

However, as Robert F. Gross elucidates:

These denials . . . repeatedly betray the strength of what they seek to negate. For example, her assertion "my son was chaste" immediately summons up its opposite, as denial always indirectly implies the state of affairs it explicitly denies. Violet herself is shown to be susceptible to that which she denies, as she moves from "chaste" to its homonym, "chased," and then backs off the point. . . . Quickly, the assertion of chastity degenerates from a simple celibacy to a frenzied race in an atmosphere of lust. (236)

Sebastian was insatiable like his Venus fly trap. However, he did not eat food; he, "ate" people, yet was above procuring men himself. Thus, part of this "chaste chase" involved using women—first his mother and then, after her stroke, his cousin Catharine—for this purpose, even though the prudish, repressed, Victorian Violet elides her son's sexuality, probably intentionally. Sebastian's world fell apart when he turned forty and entered middle age: he lost his original procuress, his good looks, and his ability to write poetry, and he spiraled into the desperation and despair that culminated in his summer of death.

The perfect antihero—a mix of Southern planter, Renaissance prince, devil, and "saint"—Sebastian's life was art, and art his life. Violet painted a world of grotesque illusion in which her son was the ultimate creator, not destroyer; in reality, Sebastian embodied both good and evil, beauty and beast. Guarding Sebastian's honor and poetic legacy thus became Violet's lifework and lost cause, for protecting Sebastian's reputation—or conveying "the truth" and recreating the past as she sees it—is crucial to maintaining Violet's own social standing. Sebastian knew that he was destined to die young, and he probably hoped for it since he had a irrational fear of aging. Consequently, he granted his mother permission to dedicate herself to his legacy after his death: "You're going to live longer than me, and then, when I'm gone, it will be yours, in your hands, to do whatever you please with" (Williams 13). Violet defends her son's work—his annual "Poem of Summer" series—religiously, displaying them to the doctor as if "elevating the Host before the altar" (13). Sebastian wrote one poem per year, for a total of twenty-five, which "he printed himself on an eighteenth-century hand-press at his—atelier in the—French—Quarter so no one but he could see it" (14), the admission of which makes Violet dizzy, most likely due to what the quarter represents—sexual debauchery—and the possibility that printing was not all that was occurring at the atelier.

Sebastian did not produce a poem the previous summer, the summer of his death, because according to Violet, she was his "mother, muse, and midwife" (Hall, "The Stork and the Reaper"). Each poem took nine months of preparation, "the length of a pregnancy," and was "hard to deliver," even with Violet, and without her, "impossible. . . . Without me he died last summer" (Williams 14). It is clear from this exchange that Violet and Sebastian had a grotesque relationship that breached the boundaries of normal mother and son behavior. As his benefactress, procuress, companion, and "mother of his poems" or children, Violet was the keeper of her son's artistic, sexual, and personal secrets. Mother and son were bound to each other: they had a "special understanding" or "an agreement, a sort of contract or covenant" (Williams 76). Their relationship bordered on oedipal, with Violet even claiming that her son was asexual and celibate, even at age forty, because she "was actually the only one in his life that satisfied the demands he made of people" (25). She ultimately chose her son over her husband, allowing him to die alone while accompanying Sebastian on a trip to the Himalayas. In fact, for all intents and purposes, they were a couple. As Violet expresses, "We were a famous couple. People didn't speak of Sebastian and his mother or Mrs. Venable and her son, they said, 'Sebastian and Violet, Violet and Sebastian'" (25).

At best a dilettante, Sebastian was not a poet or an artist, yet Violet maintained the facade because it was the best cover for his real passions. Sebastian derived a perverse sense of pleasure from pain and suffering, which, he believed, provided personal meaning and order to the hostile, indifferent, meaningless universe. His purposeless wanderings were in essence his attempts to find God, and in his opinion, he came close on his trip to the Encantadas—the Galapagos Islands—where he witnessed a horrific carnivorous spectacle which foreshadows his own fate of cannibalism: flesh-eating birds "were diving down on the hatched sea-turtles, turning them over to expose their soft undersides, tearing the undersides open and rending and eating their flesh" (16). When Dr. Cukrowicz asks "What was it about this that fascinated your son?" Violet hesitates before admitting "my son was looking for God and I stopped myself [from saying it] because I thought you'd think 'Oh, what a pretentious young crackpot'—which Sebastian was not" (17). In reality, what Sebastian was searching for was for proof that "God shows a savage face to people and shouts some fierce things at them" (20), most likely as an explanation for his own tormented state. Sebastian also searched for God in the Himalayas with Buddhists while has father was dying, living on a grass mat and devoting his life to prayer, as well as in other locations, such as Paris and Cairo, worlds of light and shadow where he engaged in his decadent and morbid quest for love and his evil and perverse brand of idealism.

Catharine enters the play in scene 2, where she is attempting to smoke in Sebastian's garden in the Venable mansion to the dismay of Sister Felicity, her caretaker from St. Mary's mental institution. Forbidden to smoke at the asylum because she dropped a lit cigarette on her lap and almost set her dress on fire—as Catharine claims, she burned a hole in her dress not because she is crazy but because she was heavily sedated—she attempts to snatch this one sliver of freedom in the outside world, but she is threatened with being placed back in the violent ward if she does not comply with the sister's wishes. In an outburst of cruelty, "she thrusts the lighted end of the cigarette into the palm of the Sister's hand. The Sister cries out and sucks her burned hand" (36). While Catharine claims that the action was provoked by the fact that she is "sick—of being *bossed* and *bullied*" (36) and not because she is mentally ill, her sanity is clearly called into question.

The possibility that Catharine is not insane and that she is being portrayed as such by members of her family for their personal gain is revealed in the next scene with the appearance of her brother George and her mother Mrs. Holly, who is Mr. Venable's (Sebastian's father's) sister. Described by Williams as a "fatuous Southern lady," Mrs. Holly may seem foolish but is actually a wolf in sheep's clothing. (The motif of the "vicious wolf" is also emphasized in other parts of the play, especially through Cabeza de Lobo, which means "Wolf's Head" in Spanish.) Named as the recipients of $50,000 each in Sebastian's will, the Hollys are afraid their inheritance might be in danger if Catharine continues to recount her "fantastic story" about the events of last summer. The money is still in probate, and Violet repeatedly threatens to contest the will if Catharine does not keep quiet. George and Mrs. Holly beg Catharine "to forget that story" because they do not have the funds to fight for their inheritance and soon will not even have "a pot to—cook *greens* in!" (46).[1] The Hollys are greedily willing to trade the truth, and if necessary Catharine's brain, for their inheritance, and plead with her not to "let them down"—in other words, to forget the events of that horrendous summer afternoon and stop insisting on talking about the gruesome details of Sebastian's death. As George states:

> We won't get a single damn penny, honest t' God we won't! So you've just GOT to stop tellin' that story about what you say happened to Cousin Sebastian in Cabeza de Lobo, even if it's what it *couldn't* be, TRUE! . . . Mama she IS going to tell it! . . . You are a BITCH! . . . She's just, just— PERVERSE! Was ALWAYS! (47)

Robert F. Gross explains that "from the moment Catharine witnesses Sebastian's death, she becomes the archetypal persecuted maiden of gothic fiction. Violet has worked to keep her confined from the outside world. . . . The effect of this persecution is to ally the audience's sympathies clearly with Catharine Holly, and against Violet Venable"

(233). In this context, "Catherine easily stands for the Madwoman-in-the-attic" while answering important questions:

> What does an oppressive patriarchal society do with women outcasts, women full of rage, who find refuge in madness? What does it do with women who dare have a mind of their own or who will not 'shut up' and do men's bidding? . . . It locks them up in a psychiatric institution (possibly considering lobotomy). . . . Things may get worse when the disturbing—more than disturbed—women are the depositories of secrets . . . when they hold the keys to the closet. (Guilbert 89)

Catharine holds the keys not only to Sebastian's legacy but also to his homosexual closet, and unlike the typical patriarchal woman (Violet) she refuses to do the bidding of men—Sebastian, George, and even to a certain extent Dr. Cukrowicz, who undoubtedly would like to receive patronage from the Sebastian Venable Memorial Foundation. Thus, like Blanche DuBois in Williams's *A Streetcar Named Desire* (1947), Catharine "suffers a similar fate at the hands of family members who cannot accept the validity of personal experience" (Fisher, "The Angels of Fructification"): she is threatened with imprisonment in an insane asylum until the end of her life, and, in Catharine's case, lobotomy.

While Catharine, like Violet, may have unwillingly played the role of procuress/victimizer for Sebastian, Williams aligns Catharine with the marginalized and powerless—the "dark boys" of society—as repeated victim. Not only has she witnessed the mauling of her cousin, but her word is now in doubt. She has also been labeled "insane" and "hysterical," and is subjected to countless therapeutic tortures, with the most serious yet to come. George calls his sister perverse because of her sexual dalliances—even Catharine admits that she knew what she was doing when she was procuring for her cousin, because she "came out in the French Quarter years before she came out in the Garden District" (Williams 81). However, rather than being empowering,

Catharine's sexual experiences are a source of guilt and shame, and reinforce her victimization by elite, patriarchal, New Orleans society.

According to Violet, during her debutante season, Catharine "lost her head over a young man, [and] made a scandalous scene at a Mardi Gras ball, in the middle of the ballroom" (57), after which all of polite society dropped her from their invitation lists. Sebastian pitied his cousin and invited her to Cabeza de Lobo as his companion. Catharine, however, conveys a far different interpretation of these events. While she admits that "He liked me and so I loved him . . . [in the] only way he'd accept:—a sort of motherly way" (63), thus suggesting a grotesque love triangle between herself, Violet, and Sebastian that hints of incest, her love for him was actually a mixture of gratitude and dependence. He saved her from the bitter tongues of New Orleans society and thus she wanted to save him—"to keep the web from—breaking" (76), by preventing his inevitable self-sacrifice; however, Sebastian was beyond redemption. Moreover, the incident at the Mardi Gras ball was not the result of a frivolous infatuation, but the outcome of a sexual encounter, possibly a rape, at "the Duelling Oaks at the end of Esplanade Street" (65). Although dueling evokes a chivalric tradition of the Old South, in this case it is a grotesque allusion that traumatized Catharine to such an extent that she began writing in her journal in the third person. The scene that she created on the ballroom floor was not the whim of a capricious girl; rather, it was the anger of a woman who had been used and manipulated by a man she barely knew who casually wanted to forget the incident, citing that his wife was pregnant and that nothing would come of the encounter.

Nevertheless, Catharine is "considered a *bona fide* liar and troublemaker. . . . Violet finds it easy to convince everyone that her niece is a psychopath, determined to destroy men whose only crime is rejecting *her* sexual advances" (Siegle 543). Exploited by New Orleans society and psychologically damaged, Catharine eventually fell into Sebastian's lap, who exploited her sexuality to actuate his own, using her for personal gain. Determined to reveal the truth, Dr. Cukrowicz injects her with truth serum and begins to extract how Sebastian saved her from the Duelling Oaks by taking her away on a six-day cruise, during which he was so attentive that passengers thought they were a honeymooning couple until they discovered they were staying in separate staterooms. The cruise was followed by a whirlwind shopping trip in Paris where Sebastian turned Catharine into a peacock, decked out in fine clothing no doubt to attract the attention of other dandies like himself. Catharine, however, "made the mistake of responding too much to his kindness, of taking hold of his hand before he'd take hold of mine, of holding onto his arm and leaning on his shoulder, of appreciating his kindness more than he wanted me to, and, suddenly, last summer, he began to be restless" (Williams 74). First cousins Catharine and Sebastian become the ultimate Gothic pair: they are coupled much like the incestuous brother/sister–husband/wife duo Roderick and Madeline in Edgar Allan Poe's short story "The Fall of the House of Usher." Likewise, Catharine and Sebastian are also doomed, and their house crumbles beneath their feet: Sebastian breaks "that string of pearls that old mothers hold their sons by like a . . . sort of umbilical cord" (77), and they take the fatal trip to Cabeza de Lobo.

Sebastian was able to conceal his homosexuality, personal depravity, and exploitive, manipulative, and cruel nature through wealth, youth, sophistication, and his mother's assistance. However, once Violet was no longer able to maintain the facade of civility, decorum, and seductive mystery due to poor health and was substituted with the young and attractive Catharine, Sebastian's veneer was shattered. As Catharine conveys, "all I know is that suddenly, last summer, he wasn't young anymore" (77). The formerly fastidious man who "had to go out a mile in a boat to find water to swim in" (79) desperately began to pursue street urchins in broad daylight at public beaches, rather than elegant men in private salons and fancy restaurants in the evenings, automatically rendering his powers as a vampire ineffective. At the mercy of "the dark ones," he tactlessly dressed Catharine in a white bathing suit that was transparent when wet which, he believed, would increase her value as a procuress. As Catharine describes:

> He bought me a swim-suit I didn't want to wear. I laughed. I said, "I can't wear that, it's a scandal to the jay birds!". . . . It was a one-piece suit made of white lisle, the water made it transparent! . . . I didn't want to swim in it, but he'd grab my hand and drag me into the water, all the way in, and I'd come out looking naked! . . . To attract!—Attention. . . I was PROCURING for him! . . . *She* used to do it, *too*. [*Mrs. Venable cries out.*] *Not consciously!* She didn't *know* that she was procuring for him in the smart, fashionable places they used to go to before last summer! Sebastian was shy with people. She wasn't. Neither was I. We both did the same thing for him, made contacts for him, but she did it in nice places and in decent ways and I had to do it the way that I just told you! (80–81)

As D. A. Miller states, Catharine served as "queer bait" for the "dead queer" (36). The fact that he was an aging, desperate forty-year-old homosexual pederast becomes blatantly clear—a secret that was concealed behind Violet's well-sculpted exterior of elegance—especially in the presence of the youthful, heterosexual Catharine. While he once cruised for young prey in the shadows of the night, with Catharine he searched in broad daylight, in the afternoon. The situation intensified, however, when the weather became warmer and the "homeless young people . . . [the] scavenger dogs, [the] hungry children" (Williams 81) came out and began to climb over the fence that separated the free beach from the public beach where Catharine and Sebastian spent their days. At that point, Catharine was permitted to wear dark bathing suits and write in her journal in a remote part of the beach while Sebastian frequented the bathhouses—well-known locations for homosexual activity—from which he would always emerge followed, presumably by the young men with whom he engaged in homosexual acts. The notion of homosexual acts is important here because as Guilbert suggests:

Indeed, in Cabeza de Lobo, the boys were certainly heterosexual. Starving as they were, they were prepared to comply for a few coins. . . . After he had had a few Cabeza de Lobo boys, Sebastian, feeling poorly and possibly satiated, stopped going to the public beach with Catherine. The boys were still starving, though [which is why they continued to hound him for money]. . . . To make it clear for the spectator/reader that Sebastian's activities were more pederastic than pedophilic, Williams makes her [Catharine] specify: "I think he recognized some . . . of the boys, between childhood and—older. . ." So presumably Sebastian has not had sex with *all* the boys who eat him, only some of them, the older ones. "That gang of kids shouted vile things about me to the waiters [of the café]," says Sebastian. No doubt they called him queer. (89)

Ultimately, the boys engaged in homosexual acts out of poverty—they were so hungry that they, like the vultures at the Encantadas, "looked like a flock of plucked birds . . . crying out *'Pan, pan, pan!'* [bread, bread, bread in Spanish] . . . they made gobbling noises with their little black mouths" (Williams 84). They despised their keeper (and were also possibly homophobic), and this—coupled with Sebastian's martyr-like attraction to self-sacrifice (like St. Sebastian), his possible self-loathing (the need to inflict punishment upon himself due to his "deviance"), and his pursuit of perfection and personal fulfillment (or "God")—killed him.

Sebastian, who had lost the magic which obscured his lifestyle, was now a grotesque monster, which was reinforced by the chilling serenade the boys played for him with tin cans and pieces of metal they had strung together to create rudimentary instruments. No longer able to hold them off with coins, Sebastian was surrounded and under the white-hot sun was chased up a steep street by the dark-skinned boys. There, he met his inevitable death by corporeal mutilation (he was also stripped nude), dismemberment, and cannibalism by the sexually exploited, ravenous boys—too poor to resist his offer of money for sex, too desperate to allow their source of income to escape—who greedily devoured him and left him looking like "a big white-paper-wrapped bunch of red roses [that] had been *torn, thrown, crushed!*—against that blazing white wall," much like the plants in his Gothic garden (92). The tables turned, and this time brutal violence was directed at the older, wealthy man by his younger, lower-class sexual partners. Thus, as Michael Portillo conveys, Sebastian, like his Venus fly trap, also "thrived in warm climates, but fed not on little black flies but little black boys down in Cabeza de Lobo, one of those wretched resorts where rich and poor come together and the gringo's dollar can buy services from the local youths" (44). Sebastian, who epitomizes the "Ugly American" stereotype, was unable to escape the scenario he created, and the victimizer became the victim and the hunter (or predator) became the hunted (or prey).

Catharine's confession frees her from the burden of the truth, the onerous shadow of the past on the present, and the secrets and lies of self-preservation—or what Big Daddy characterizes as "mendacity" in *Cat on a Hot Tin Roof*—that stifles this Southern family. However, her confession results in the demise of Violet, the catalyst of Sebastian's exploitive and destructive behavior, who collapses under the weight of her hideous story. Clearly, "*Suddenly Last Summer* . . . sketches a vision of a predatory universe. . . . In a sense, Sebastian, who is apparently incapable of real love, is devoured by his own promiscuous appetites in a frightening cosmos where only the most efficient predators survive" (Fisher, "The Angels of Fructification"). According to Williams, in this grotesque world, we all "eat" each other. In fact, Catharine universalizes what happened to Sebastian by conveying the point that "we all use each other and that's what we think of as love, and not being able to use each other is . . . hate" (Williams 63). While this is certainly a pessimistic and gruesome way of looking at human nature, it is one that compliments the Gothic motifs of the drama. As Williams explains:

Sometimes the truth is more accessible when you ignore realism, because when you see things in a somewhat exaggerated form you capture more of the true essence of life. The exaggeration gets closer to the essence. This essence of life is really very grotesque and gothic. To get to it you've got to do what may strike some people as distortion. (qtd. in Brown 264).

Sebastian, like many, was ultimately devoured by what he desired. This reinforces the ending of the play not as a literal devouring through cannibalism, but rather as "a dramatic *metaphor*. . . . [The play] was about how people devour each other in an *allegorical* sense" (Williams qtd. in Siegel 568). As the grotesque plantation master, Sebastian was as debauched as those of the Old South, sexually exploiting anyone who took his fancy, especially the young boys of color over whom he could exert power. Like his antebellum counterparts, he met his ruin because of his excessive decadence, cruelty, and inability to adapt, specifically to the fact that he was aging and that he was no longer attached to Violet's umbilical cord. Floating helplessly without his seducing, suffocating, overbearing, and protective mother, the weak Sebastian was devoured by those who were now stronger than him. Ultimately, those who can adapt to this new world, the New South, with all of its flaws, like Catharine and Dr. Cukrowicz, will survive. Those who cannot, like the manipulative and dark-hearted Sebastian and the physically and socially paralyzed Violet—both of whom insist on living in a Gothic fantasy world—will meet their demise.

Notes

1. The Hollys' lower-class status is also conveyed through their accents and their overt social climbing: George wears Sebastian's clothes, attends Tulane, and pledges a fraternity, and he uses anti-Semitism as a way to elevate his class position.

Works Cited

Brown, Cecil. "Interview with Tennessee Williams" (1978). *Conversations with Tennessee Williams*. Ed. Albert J. Devlin. Jackson: UP of Mississippi, 1986. 251–83. Print.

Fisher, James. "'The Angels of Fructification': Tennessee Williams, Tony Kushner, and Images of Homosexuality on the American Stage." *Mississippi Quarterly* 49.1 (1995): 13–32. Print.

Gross, Robert F. "Consuming Hart: Sublimity and Gay Poetics in *Suddenly Last Summer*." *Theatre Journal* 47.2 (1995): 229–51. Print.

Guilbert, Georges-Claude. "Queering and Dequeering the Text: Tennessee Williams's *A Streetcar Named Desire*." *Cercles* 10 (2004): 85–116. Print.

Hall, Joan Wylie. "The Stork and the Reaper, the Madonna and the Stud: Procreation and Mothering in Tennessee Williams's Plays." *Mississippi Quarterly* 48.4 (1995): 677–700. Print.

Miller, D. A. "Visual Pleasure in 1959." *October* 81 (1997): 35–58. Print.

Popkin, Henry. "The Plays of Tennessee Williams." *Tulane Drama Review* 4.3 (1960): 45–64. Print.

Portillo, Michael. "Hothouse Flowers." *New Statesman* 31 May 2004: 44. Print.

Siegel, Janice. "Tennessee Williams' *Suddenly Last Summer* and Euripides' *Bacchae*." *International Journal of the Classical Tradition* 11.4 (2005): 538–70. Print.

Sofer, Andrew. "Self-Consuming Artifacts: Power, Performance and the Body in Tennessee Williams' *Suddenly Last Summer*." *Modern Drama* 38.3 (1995): 336–47. Print.

Tuhkunen, Taïna. "Tennessee Williams's Post-Pastoral Southern Gardens in Text and on the Movie Screen." *Transatlantica: Revue d'Études Américaines* 1 (2011): 3 Jan. 2012. Web. 22 Oct. 2012.

Williams, Tennessee. *Four Plays*. 1976. New York: Signet Classics, 2003. Print.

"Fantastic terrors never felt before": Southern Gothic Poetry

David J. Rothman

> And the silken sad uncertain rustling of each purple curtain
> Thrilled me—filled me with fantastic terrors never felt before;
> So that now, to still the beating of my heart, I stood repeating
> "'Tis some visitor entreating entrance at my chamber door —
> Some late visitor entreating entrance at my chamber door; —
> This it is and nothing more."
>
> —Edgar Allen Poe, "The Raven" 13–18

A Place for Poetry

Most critics and scholars assume that Southern Gothic is primarily prose. This is understandable, because so many of the major figures associated with the Gothic in all its variants have been novelists and writers of short stories. Even the anonymous writers of guidelines for Oprah Winfrey's book club assume without comment that Southern Gothic is a prose genre:

> Southern gothic writers leverage the details of the American South—the lonely plantations, aging Southern belles, dusty downtowns, dilapidated slave quarters, Spanish moss and Southern charm—to bring life to their slice of history. Steeped in folklore, oral history, suspense and local color, southern gothic is first popularized by 19th-Century short story masters Edgar Allan Poe, Nathaniel Hawthorne and Ambrose Bierce. ("Genre: Southern Gothic")

Here is another such definition, from a reader's guide to Carson McCullers's *The Heart Is a Lonely Hunter* (1940), from the Big Read program of the National Endowment for the Arts (NEA). The aesthetic concepts are unexceptionable, but once again the assumption is that the Gothic is inherently a prose fiction genre:

> The predecessors to modern horror, gothic novels use ghost stories, madness, vampires, and perversity to develop a pleasant sense of fear in the reader. From the 1790s through the nineteenth century, gothic literature comprised everything from Nathaniel Hawthorne and Edgar Allan Poe's macabre stories to Mary Shelley's *Frankenstein* and Bram Stoker's *Dracula*. Only in the early to mid-twentieth century did such writers as Carson McCullers, Flannery O'Connor, Tennessee Williams, and William Faulkner use it to explore less supernatural, more earthly monsters, thus pioneering what came to be called the "Southern Gothic" literary tradition. ("The Southern Gothic")

Scholars begin with the same notion. In *American Gothic Fiction: An Introduction*, Allan Lloyd-Smith takes a far more nuanced and thorough approach to how the genre works than to what appears in the brief excerpts quoted above, but still implicitly argues—beginning with his title—that the Gothic is almost everywhere and is always prose: "In exploring extremes, whether of cruelty, rapacity and fear, or passion and sexual degradation, the Gothic tends to reinforce, *if only in a novel's final pages*, culturally prescribed doctrines of morality and propriety" (5; italics added).

Lloyd-Smith's second chapter, a Gothic timeline, lists hundreds of American novels, short stories, and films in over fifteen pages, and includes almost no poetry other than Philip Freneau's "The House of Night," Poe's "The Raven," and some mentions of Emily Dickinson. Like many others, Lloyd-Smith therefore obscures the foundational contributions that poets have made and continue to make. This contribution is so significant that the entire notion of the Gothic and its history as a literary movement become quite murky without it, indeed almost impossible to read coherently.

The neglect of poetic sources of the Gothic as a whole, including in Southern Gothic, is surprising, given the history of the kinds of stories that poets tell—that poets originated—in ancient literature and retell again and again in modern times. Lloyd-Smith's definitions of the thematic direction of Gothic fiction, and of American Gothic, are compelling and convincing, but he ignores this background almost entirely. He argues that many see the Gothic beginning as an offshoot from "largely realist and morally respectable fiction" to concern itself with "extreme circumstances of terror, oppression and persecution, darkness and obscurity of setting, and innocence betrayed" (5). This kind of fiction, whether supernatural or more realistic, gives the reader "a vicarious experience of forbidden excess, with punishment and retribution offered in the eventual return to psychic normality" (5). He points out that Gothic writers explore taboos such as "religious profanities, demonism, occultism, necromancy, and incest" (6) and then observes that explorations of these topics might represent "a dark side of Enlightenment freethinking or the persistence of an increasingly excluded occultist tradition in Western culture" (6) in the late eighteenth and early nineteenth centuries. Hence the Gothic became and remains today a secular outlet for irrational forces that used to be accounted for in daily life, but had been figuratively driven underground to reemerge as fictional monsters.

And yet, were not the poets writing about monsters, hauntings, and extreme emotional states from the very beginning? The prose writers in both England and America most strongly associated with the Gothic were the inheritors of literary conventions that stretch back to the beginning of imaginative literature in the West, which they only modified to suit their contemporary aims. The poetry of classical Greece and Rome, along with that of medieval Europe, includes themes that Southern Gothic poets have developed to their own ends. This is most evident in representations of the uncanny, such as visits to the underworld in classical and Renaissance epics, and even in the entire elegiac tradition of lamentation for the dead. If the Gothic is a vision that may include decaying castles, ghosts, treachery, madness, and a dark, extreme vision of human nature, it seems reasonable, for example, to consider a play like *Macbeth* in that category as a precursor to the blossoming of the genre, and that is a work of mostly verse, not prose.

Even *Macbeth*, however, is a latecomer to Gothic themes. Homer, Virgil, and Dante all include visits to the underworld, where corpses speak and act as if alive. Dante's *Inferno* is a Gothic carnival, a catalog of human beings destroyed by horrifying passion who suffer eternal, terrifying torment. In the famous Ugolino passage, that character, who was in historical actuality betrayed by one Archbishop Ruggieri and left to starve to death with his sons in a locked tower, endlessly gnaws on his betrayer's head, foreshadowing contemporary zombie narratives:

> I saw two shades frozen in a single hole
> packed so close, one head hooded the other one;
> the way the starving devour their bread, the soul
> above had clenched the other with his teeth
> where the brain meets the nape. (Canto XXXII, 124–129;
>   Pinsky)

The classical Greek and Latin tragedies are filled with a smorgasbord of Gothic thematic and iconic prototypes, from incest, bestiality, and suicide to mania, madness, and flesh-eating monsters. At the opening of Sophocles's *Oedipus Rex*, Thebes is under a mysterious curse that suggests a poisoned past, in which King Oedipus has unknowingly killed his father and slept with his mother; this inescapable curse drives the entire plot. The Roman playwright Seneca's tragedies still stand as examples of some of the most lurid narratives on the page. In his *Thyestes*, based on classical myth and previous sources, the title character's brother, Atreus, slaughters his nephews at the altar; dismembers, roasts, and boils them; and serves them up to their own father in a soup. Ovid's *Metamorphoses*, the source of the vast majority of

Shakespeare's classical narratives and allusions, includes hundreds of tales of monstrous transformations and irruptions of the magical and supernatural into everyday life. Even the Old English epic *Beowulf*, perhaps less known to early writers of the modern Gothic period as it only began to be translated into modern English in the early nineteenth century, revolves around a monarchy in decline—in a castle that is indefensible and presumably in rather bad repair—that is beset by monsters. If the Gothic is characterized, as the NEA introduction to McCullers puts it, by "ghost stories, madness, vampires, and perversity to develop a pleasant sense of fear in the reader," or, as Lloyd-Smith argues, by "extreme circumstances of terror, oppression and persecution, darkness and obscurity of setting, and innocence betrayed," its ultimate sources do not lie in prose, but in ancient and venerable modes of poetry in which artists have always sought to evoke, portray, describe, and convey uncanny and sublime extremity.[1]

Differences abound between the Gothic and its thematic sources in the sublime violence of earlier work, notably the fact that in earlier times much of that work was taken as either literal, historical, or legendary, whereas in the modern Gothic it becomes a symbolic and aesthetic rebellion against Enlightenment rationality. Still, the larger point stands: poetry always comes first. The themes underlying many Gothic fictions first emerged in poems and continue in them today. Southern Gothic is no exception.

To his credit, Lloyd-Smith acknowledges just a bit of this in passing, pointing out that the Gothic drew on earlier work such as Jacobean tragedy (3, 61), which is stuffed to the brim with extreme and monstrous behavior—and even monsters, such as Shakespeare's Caliban in *The Tempest*, and ghosts, such as Hamlet's father. Lloyd-Smith also very briefly but rightly cites a late eighteenth-century poem, "The House of Night," by the American poet Philip Freneau as an early example of American Gothic.

Freneau's poem, which was published in 1779 and then revised in 1786, deserves longer treatment than Lloyd-Smith gives it. The poem is historically significant because it was widely read and admired at the time; it is a foundational work in the genre by an American and, significantly for my argument, is poetry. In its longest published version, Freneau's poem is in 136 heroic quatrains (iambic pentameter, rhyming *abab*). In a number of ways it echoes earlier English Gothic poems such as Thomas Parnell's "A Night-Piece on Death" (1721), Edward Young's *The Complaint: Or, Night Thoughts* (1742), and Robert Blair's "The Grave" (1743), and it also looks forward to the Gothic poetry of the Romantics in volumes such as William Wordsworth and Samuel Taylor Coleridge's *Lyrical Ballads* (1798), which appeared even as Freneau was publishing his own work.

"The House of Night" is set in America (near "the Chesapeke," 37) but is completely imitative of English models in diction and imagery. Freneau sets his scene in typical Gothic fashion:

> Let others draw from smiling skies their theme,
> And tell of climes that boast unfading light,
> I draw a darker scene, replete with gloom,
> I sing the horrors of the *House of Night*. (9–12)

Exactly as Lloyd-Smith suggests, the poet self-consciously turns from light to gloom and darkness, to horrify intentionally. As the narrative begins, a traveler comes upon a desolate but "noble dome" (42). There he meets an anthropomorphized death who is himself dying and who is attended by a young man who ministers to him out of a perverse Christian charity. This young man, Cleon, instructs the traveler how to care for Death, who then revives and delivers a sententious speech. That revival almost seems to come straight out of a modern Gothic zombie novel:

> Then slowly rising from his loathsome bed,
> On wasted legs the meagre monster stood,

Gap'd wide, and foam'd, and hungry seem'd to ask,
Tho' sick, an endless quantity of food.
(233–36, stanza 59)

In its second, longest, and most famous version (published in 1786),[2] the poem is lurid and evocative, but somewhat disjointed. In the end of the poem, Death appears to be vanquished, allowing a righteous moral order of salvation to be reestablished, and the poet abandons his sublime terror for a more rationalistic philosophy:

What is this *Death*, ye deep read sophists, say? —
Death is no more than one unceasing change;
New forms arise, while other forms decay,
Yet all is Life throughout creation's range.
(524–27, stanza 132)

Yet, at this moment, day breaks, the vision vanishes, and the poet awakens to close with a brief, yet nonetheless dull homily of salvation:

When Nature bids thee from the world retire,
With joy thy lodging leave a fated guest;
In Paradise, the land of thy desire,
Existing always, always to be blest.
(541–44, stanza 136)

Again, as Lloyd-Smith and others argue, the Gothic aesthetic functions by whipping up a frenzy of terror and horror, then dissipating it with a return to order.

Freneau's poem begins to convey the influence of Gothic poetry as it came to America and eventually to the South. That poetic tradition eventually came to embody the conflicting prerogatives of terror and reconciliation as powerfully as any prose work. If anything, it is the poets who have most compellingly imagined the contradictions of the

---

modern Gothic theme, allowing terror free rein at the same time as they represent it as merely psychological and therefore ironic.

Southern Gothic Poetry and the Diction of Reality

Many American poets since Freneau have written poetry with Gothic themes, and many have been from the South. In its earliest manifestations, such work includes the violent, horrifying, and occult elements still frequently associated with the Gothic in all of its variants, but in the twentieth century, much of the major poetry takes a different tack, becoming either less overtly dramatic, or even ironic when it does venture into dramatically taboo territory. Even James Dickey's "The Sheep Child" (1967) is essentially a comic poem, and the most violent event in Donald Justice's "Southern Gothic" (1960) is the peeling of wallpaper in an abandoned house. Yet this poetry, in which violence and extremity are sublimated or assimilated into the diction of reality, resonates with the aesthetics of the greatest of Southern Gothic prose writers (led by Faulkner) and may well show us how the Gothic sensibility can make its greatest contribution to literature.

As he is for Southern Gothic fiction, Edgar Allan Poe is one of the sources of Southern Gothic poetry in works such as "The Raven" (1845) and many others. In Poe's Gothic poetry, as in his Gothic fiction, we find all the regalia of the genre on full display: inexplicable dread, dreary landscapes, madness, graveyards, corpses, decaying mansions, rot, sadism, horror, terror, and sorrow. Poe's aim is clear enough and he hardly hides it. As he states in the stanza from "The Raven" that serves as the epigraph to this essay and provides its title, he feels and is eager to tell the reader of "fantastic terrors never felt before," terrors that have "thrilled" him as only the sublime can: "And the silken, sad, uncertain rustling of each purple curtain / Thrilled me—filled me with fantastic terrors never felt before" (13–14). Poe's raven certainly derives from earlier versions of that bird as a bird of ill omen, a scavenger and companion of death. Poe may have even known earlier American poems that treat it that way, such as "Advice to a Raven in Russia"

(1812) by Joel Barlow. In that explicitly political poem, Barlow addresses the raven and advises it that if it can no longer find corpses to pick at on the Russian steppe because Napoleon's armies have withdrawn, it can still find the general at work in other countries, slaughtering people by the thousands and thereby providing the raven with food. Barlow gives a good sense of the raven's historical iconography, connotations that Poe also draws on:

> You fear perhaps your food may fail you there [Russia],
> Your human carnage, that delicious fare
> That lured you hither, following still your friend
> The great Napoleon to the world's bleak end. (5–8; Ellman 28)

The primary difference between Barlow's poem and Poe's is exactly the introduction of the Gothic element, an extreme sense of dread and doom that has no direct or obvious political correlation, but exists in and of itself as a sublime aesthetic experience. Whereas Barlow's raven may be able to understand the poet's address, in Poe's poem the raven itself has learned to speak—it has become uncanny and supernatural. Barlow uses the raven to signify the terror wrought by Napoleon's armies; Poe uses the same animal to evoke a deeply personal terror without any such objective correlative. Many of Poe's other poems operate in a similar way, exploring extreme states of mind for their own sake, much as his best stories do. Frequently, Poe is so focused on that generic state of mind that he even withholds his characters' names, suppressing any personal history or individuation in favor of pure sensation.

While Poe can be considered a Southern writer, his scenes rarely if ever draw directly on the landscapes and history of the South, a theme that seems to distinguish Southern Gothic in particular, as even the notes for Oprah's Book Club rightly make clear. One defining characteristic of Southern Gothic seems to be its regionalism. If a writer is from the South and writes Gothic prose or poetry, that is not enough to classify the work as such. The genre is regionalist first and thematic second; the thematic focus, such as the emphasis on the psychological brutalities of slavery, depends on the setting.

We begin to see more regionalist forms of Southern Gothic at about the same time as Poe wrote, in poems such as "The Marshes of Glynn" (1878) by the Georgia-born Sidney Lanier, a fine poet who was once far better known than he is now. The marshes Lanier describes are in Glynn County on the Georgia coast, and while his poem is a testament of faith in the wake of the Civil War, that faith is sorely tested by terrors that evoke a Gothic sensibility:

> Ay, now, when my soul all day hath drunken the soul of the oak,
> And my heart is at ease from men, and the wearisome sound of the
> stroke
> Of the scythe of time and the trowel of trade is low,
> And belief overmasters doubt, and I know that I know,
> And my spirit is grown to a lordly great compass within,
> That the length and the breadth and the sweep of the marshes of
> Glynn
> Will work me no fear like the fear they have wrought me of yore,
> When length was fatigue, and when breadth was but bitterness sore,
> And when terror and shrinking and dreary unnamable pain
> Drew over me out of the merciless miles of the plain –
> Oh, now, unafraid, I am fain to face
> The vast sweet visage of space. (25–36; Ellman 368)

Lanier may claim to be unafraid, but the way he evokes his fear is rooted in a sense of dread where one feels a Gothic muse lurking nearby.

Four Modern Southern Gothic Poets: Allen Tate, John Crowe Ransom, Donald Justice, James Dickey

While there are other suggestively Southern Gothic poems from the nineteenth century, the genre enjoyed an extraordinary flowering beginning in the 1920s. In other parts of the country, this rejuvenation of Gothic poetry may be considered to have happened somewhat earlier. We might consider especially the poems of Edwin Arlington Robinson beginning in the 1890s, when he wrote many dramatic poems about the twisted internal lives of New England villagers in his fictional Tilbury Town, which appears in volumes such as *The Torrent; and The Night Before* (1896), *The Children of the Night* (1897), *Captain Craig and Other Poems* (1902), and *The Town Down the River* (1910). We might also consider Edgar Lee Masters's *Spoon River Anthology* (1915), in which each poem is the dramatic monologue of a ghost.

Those works were of course well known to Southern poets, but the contributions these poets then made to Gothic poetry were quite original and distinct. Among them, Allen Tate, John Crowe Ransom, Donald Justice, and James Dickey stand out because of the drift of their work and because of particularly strong poems they wrote in the tradition. Robert Penn Warren, John Gould Fletcher, Donald Davidson, and other members of the Agrarian or Fugitive Poets of this period also participated in the Southern Gothic movement, along with many more over the last several decades and into the present.

Tate's "Ode to the Confederate Dead" appeared in his first book of poems, *Mr. Pope and Other Poems* (1928). It is a lengthy, painful meditation by an unnamed speaker at the gate of an unnamed graveyard filled with Confederate soldiers. While Tate lived and worked in a number of places in America and abroad, he is closely associated with the South of his upbringing—he was born in Kentucky and lived for long periods of his life in Tennessee—and this poem expresses a tortured relationship with the region and its history. Tate was a prominent member of the Southern Agrarians, a group of about a dozen poets and critics affiliated with Vanderbilt University in the 1920s who published a journal titled *The Fugitive*. All in the group shared the view that the modern industrial and urban world was destroying an agrarian tradition that had been crucial to the success of democracy in the early United States, a success that depended on a political and social individualism that industrial society everywhere undermines.[3] Without explicitly discussing politics, Tate's poem explores these problems in a dark and somber yet ironic mood, setting the tone and approach for all subsequent Southern Gothic poetry.

Tate's title is telling. He calls his poem an ode, not an elegy. The latter genre would seem to be a more appropriate title for such a poem to the dead. The irony is intense, as this ode hardly participates in the joyous or ecstatic feelings usually associated with the ode tradition. The irony comes to seem all the more pointed when we consider that one of Tate's models was probably "Ode Sung on the Occasion of Decorating the Graves of the Confederate Dead, at Magnolia Cemetery, Charleston, S. C., 1867," by Henry Timrod. Timrod's well-known and much shorter poem is a song of eulogistic and extravagant praise:

> Sleep sweetly in your humble graves,
> Sleep, martyrs of a fallen cause;
> Though yet no marble column craves
> The pilgrim here to pause. (1–4)

Where Timrod foresees marble monuments to the still newly fallen, valorous yet defeated Confederate soldiers, sixty years later Tate finds only a graveyard where "the headstones yield their names to the element" (2). The defeat, failure, humiliation and decadence could hardly be more complete.

While Tate's poem contradicts the assumptions about tone in an ode, in other ways he observes its typical modern English structure far more completely than Timrod. As the poet and critic Edmund Gosse (who wrote the entry on "Ode" for the eleventh edition of the *Encyclopedia Britannica* in 1911, a definition Tate may well have known) and others have pointed out, odes in the classical world were highly structured affairs, imitated by a number of English Renaissance writers with sections of strophe, antistrophe, and epode, but these parts mostly fell away by the time of the Romantics. What did survive was a sense, apparently based on misreadings of Pindar's metrics, that the ode could be a poem of ecstatic emotion that motivates abandonment of predictable stanzaic and metrical forms. In English, the ode therefore came to be a poem of indeterminate length with highly varied line lengths in each stanza, and with the stanzas highly irregular as well, varying both in rhyme scheme and in feet per line. Tate's poem, unlike Timrod's more regular verse, is exactly like this, with long stanzas of unpredictable rhyme schemes and line lengths, occasionally punctuated by short-lined couplets of indeterminate syntax that sound almost like pained cries or exclamations of sorrow and suffering. Tate takes this tradition of ecstasy and turns it to lamentation. It is a vision of sublime dread, not joy or celebration.

Irony also motivates how Tate uses Gothic tropes and themes. The setting of the poem seems immediately Gothic. The speaker stands in a scene reminiscent of Poe and many other Gothic writers: he is at the gate of a deserted, decaying graveyard in autumn, hardly the triumphal scene of Timrod's new graveyard where "There is no holier spot of ground / Than where defeated valor lies" (18–19). The season and the setting in Tate's ode are ominous enough, and then, in the opening of the second stanza, the decaying corpses of the Confederate dead, do not "sleep sweetly," but seem about to return to life in a terrifying resurrection that suggests a Gothic nightmare:

> Autumn is desolation in the plot
> Of a thousand acres where these memories grow
> From the inexhaustible bodies that are not
> Dead (10–13)

Then, exactly at this moment, comes the turn that separates the best modern Southern Gothic poetry from the more literal Gothic sensationalism of what came before. Line thirteen of the poem continues "but feed the grass row after rich row." The dead are not literally undead; they are not going to rise from the dirt like zombies, ghosts, or vampires. Rather, they do what corpses literally do: become the dirt that feeds the grass, just as in Walt Whitman.[4] They are just fertilizer. That simple word "but"—the very word that signifies so much in the history of poetry, the word that figures so frequently as the turn or volta of the English sonnet—here crucially and self-consciously turns the poem away from explicit Gothic fantasies into something ultimately far more interesting, where the Gothic impulse fully survives in the acknowledgment of emotional, spiritual, and historical darkness, but never surrenders to mere aesthetic sensation. Tate will not surrender to a ghost story—he must live with his painful confusions as confusions.

Throughout the poem, Tate returns to this tactic of the suggestion of, and then careful and ironic avoidance of fantastic mayhem, crystalliz- ing it for all future strong Southern Gothic poets. Again and again he invokes the situations, settings, and themes of Gothic sensationalism— what we might call "Splatter Gothic," the world of explicit sadism and horror, the world of chainsaws, disembowelments, bloodsuckers, and flesh eaters—but turns away from the predictable denouement to em- phasize the psychological reality of dark Gothic feeling without trotting out all the props. Again and again the Gothic vision of a painful history haunting the present threatens to erupt out of the graveyard—and again and again it does not: "Turn your eyes to the immoderate past, / Turn to the inscrutable infantry rising / Demons out of the earth—they will not last" (44–46). Even though history assaults him, accuses him, and terrifies him with its horrific defeats, Tate's dead stay dead.

It would be difficult to overestimate the influence of "Ode to the Confederate Dead" in modern American poetry. The poem is a difficult and obscure testament of a spirit at war with itself and with a past that is both horrifying and strangely seductive. Tate himself wrote an essay on the poem, "Narcissus as Narcissus," in which he argues that his ode "is 'about' solipsism, a philosophical doctrine which says that we create the world in the act of perceiving it; or about Narcissism, or any other *ism* that denotes the failure of the human personality to function objectively in nature and society" (136).

Odd, perhaps, that a poet who claims to be doing battle with solipsism and narcissism would write an essay about his own poem that supposedly fights this battle. In any case, Tate's essay is something of a deception, obscuring the poem's larger aesthetic debts in a bramble of rhetoric. The strength of the poem comes not from some ideational contemplation of narcissism, an explanation that satisfies about as much as T. S. Eliot's notes to "The Waste Land" (1922) explain that somewhat similar work. Instead, the strength of Tate's ode lies in his willingness to confront and articulate his own passionate paralysis in the face of history. He invokes the ghosts of the dead soldiers again and again, he can hear "the furious murmur of their chivalry" (73), and we may feel the terrors, but we never get to see them as if they were present:

> We shall say only the leaves whispering
> In the improbable mist of nightfall
> That flies on multiple wing;
> Night is the beginning and the end
> And in between the ends of distraction
> Waits mute speculation (76–81)

We are in a typically Gothic scene, a decaying autumnal graveyard at dusk, a place of dark, sublime emotional distress where Tate conjures with the living dead—but in the end he does not indulge any fantasy of their resurrection. Such "speculation" remains "mute." Tate is a strong poet because rather than fleeing with his feelings into lurid fantasy, he insists on articulating his feelings *as feelings*.

Tate's Gothic irony in "Ode to the Confederate Dead"—invoking it and drawing upon it for his poetic power, only to frustrate and dismiss it as insufficient to his ends—sets the model for all subsequent powerful renderings of the genre in Southern poetry. In "Prelude to an Evening," John Crowe Ransom takes a similar tack with a different subject. Ransom was also a member of the Fugitives (or Agrarians) and the strongest literary critic in the group; he was one of the leading figures of the New Criticism, a school that transformed American literary criticism by emphasizing close technical reading of poetry and precise attention to matters of versification and form. He first published "Prelude to an Evening" in the *American Review* in 1934, but then revised and expanded the poem for republication in the *Kenyon Review* in 1963, adding five quatrains and, as Tate did for his "Ode," a lengthy commentary on his own poem.

Ransom strongly identified at times in his career as a Southern writer, but "Prelude" has only one indication that it is a Southern poem. That single word, however, seems carefully chosen to insure the poem must be placed in its region. The poem is quite dense, yet ultimately dramatically clear. In his *Kenyon Review* explication, Ransom provides a summary of his own work that is far more accurate than Tate's discussion of his own work, including a concise description of the setting and situation:

Here is a man returning in the evening from his worldly occupations to his own household. He has had plenty of encounters with the world's evils, and his imagination is immoderate and wayward; it has blown the evils up, till now he manages to be attended habitually by a vague but overwhelming impression of metaphysical Powers arrayed against him; he can say even to others (if they are capable of sympathy) that he is a man pursued by Furies. And he cannot but think it an anticlimax, a defeat unworthy of his confrontation of his fate, to spend the evening with children at their lessons. The poem is the man's soliloquy as he approaches his house. He is addressing the mother of his children who awaits him, as if rehearsing the speech he will make in her presence in order to persuade her to share his fearful preoccupations and give him her entire allegiance. He seems to think he will win her over; there is no intimation that it may turn out quite differently. But suppose he succeeds: will not that be a dreary fate for the woman? And what of the children? Those are not his questions. But they came to be mine. By the end of the eighth stanza he pictures her prophetically as rapt in her new terrors, almost to the point of forgetting the children; if they are hungry, she will absent-mindedly smooth their heads. (72–73)

In his essay, Ransom then discusses why he revised and extended the poem, referring to several events and books that made him wish to rescue the homecoming man from being a "brutal character" and a "villain" (74). He primarily cites a 1962 article by his colleague Charles Coffin, "Creation and the Self in *Paradise Lost*," which emphasizes the endlessly generous willingness of John Milton's God to "extend his grace" to Adam, despite Adam's repeated "misdemeanors" (Coffin 74). Contemplation of this theology led Ransom to revise the poem in such a way that the man reconsiders his submission to the Furies, and agrees once again to be a good, bourgeois father—even to babysit:

> In the last stanza Adam stands on the threshold of his house, but he stops a moment to fortify his wiser self against his own self-defeating eloquence. The final utterance of his soliloquy, and of the poem, is a two-line homage, half mystical, perhaps half maudlin, to the formidable yet beneficent dignity of her status and that of the children. We imagine that he is going to enjoy her favor, but his immediate motive is under the familial sign. He will sit with the children dutifully and, we will think, proudly. It is not the happiest ending that he could possibly conceive, but it is the best he had the right to expect. (*Kenyon Review* 80)

Both versions of the poem matter, and Ransom revised it throughout for its later publication, but the latter version is more complete, because it fulfills the Gothic irony that he intuited was crucial to making the poem stronger.

While Ransom never mentions the term or refers to the tradition of the Gothic in his commentary, hewing to theological categories, the diction of the literary genre nevertheless permeates the poem's imagery. The man is "the tired wolf / Dragging his infected wound homeward" (1–2). He imagines the erasing of boundaries between the real and the world of dark dreams, "a miracle of confusion:— // That dreamed and undreamt become each other / And mix the night and day of your soul" (8–10). No sweet crying of the wife, no return of daylight has ever permanently broken "the improbable black spell / Annihilated the poor phantom" (15–16). The ghosts always return "in the shadowed places // Invisible evil, deprived and bold." (20–21). The "swamp of horrors" (34) to which the speaker invites his wife seems to have far more to do with the terms and icons of Gothic horror than with Milton's theology. To be more precise, the terms of Ransom's horror, the "conniving Furies" (30) of his narrator's dark, diseased imagination may have developed out of a Christian and pagan past (as with all such imagery), but in terms of their immediate aesthetic correlatives, they are far more Gothic than they are Puritan.

If Ransom had left the poem with only its first eight stanzas, he would have abandoned his hero on the doorstep of his home about to burst into it like hell unleashed, trying to resist terror yet with both he and his wife undone by it:

> Finally evening. Hear me denouncing
> Our equal and conniving Furies;
> You making Noes but they lack conviction;
> Smoothing the heads of the hungry children. (29–32)[5]

In the revised version, however, the Splatter Gothic impulse is ultimately restrained, contained, and ironized. The later version closes with these eight lines:

> I went to the nations of disorder
> To be freed of the memory of good and evil;
> There even your image was disfigured;
> Then the boulevards rocked; they said, Go back.
> I am here; and to balk my ruffian I bite

The tongue devising all that treason;
Then creep in my wounds to the sovereign flare
Of the room where you shine on the good children. (41–48)

The imagination, the Gothic imagination, is real, but will not be allowed to stand as merely real. It is fully acknowledged but also fully psychologized. As in Tate's "Ode," it becomes a state of feeling, a "mute speculation," not the unleashing of a fantasy. It is this deep acknowledgment of the impulses that underlie the Gothic genre at the same time as they are not allowed, even in a work of art, to dominate the sensibility, which creates the aesthetic power at the poem's core, a power few novelists have ever touched. The ironic embedding of the Gothic impulse in the diction of reality is exactly what makes it that much more compelling, elevating the dramatic situation of the poem from pulp to poetry.

The Southern element in Ransom's "Prelude" is muted, unless a reader recognizes one crucial fact, alluded to above, that explicitly sets the poem in the region. In both versions, the husband imagines his wife awaiting his return with foreboding, arranging "buck berries" in "blue bowls":

Freshening the water in the blue bowls
For the buck berries with not all your love
You shall be listening for a low wind,
And the warning sibilance of pines. (25–29)

Not only is the desolate wind in the pines evocative of Gothic dread, but the buckberry is a plant found only in the South. According to Charles Wilson Cook, an associate in research at the Nicholas School of the Environment at Duke University, it is also known as black huckleberry, *Gaylussacia ursine*: "Common within its limited range in the southern Appalachians, it is found only in the southeastern corner of North Carolina and nearby counties in southeastern

Tennessee, northeastern Georgia, and northwestern South Carolina" ("Black Huckleberry").[6] Ransom was born and raised in precisely this area, in Pulaski, Tennessee, about twenty miles north of the Alabama border. He is not writing of just any home, but of one he knows, and it is purposefully Southern.

Ransom was familiar with the Gothic tradition, even though he does not discuss it in the commentary on his poem. Almost forty years earlier, in 1925, in a letter to the English poet and critic Robert Graves, he had proposed applying for a Guggenheim Fellowship with a project title "The Gothic Principle in the English Literary Tradition." As Kieran Quinlan points out in *John Crowe Ransom's Secular Faith*, Ransom had been wrestling with the question of how to find a path for his own poetry between the skeptical claims of science and the credulous claims of orthodoxy. He was moving "from a concern with the truth or falsehood of religious claims to speculation on their importance for the well-being of the imagination" (40), issues that eventually found their way into his critical work *God without Thunder: An Unorthodox Defense of Orthodoxy* (1930). Kieran then quotes the letter to Graves, which makes it clear that Ransom saw this core of the religious imagination as inherently Gothic, by which he seems to mean medieval and primitive more than aesthetic, although the connections are there. Ransom wrote that in his book he will have:

A very fine chapter, I think, on Religion and Gothic, in which I show that all religions that are vital are a folk product first, and contain sensational and obscene features in plenty: but get themselves taken up by the higher critics, theologians, and Liberals, who try to emasculate them of their Gothic quality—whereas they cannot survive this process if they are to stay the religions of the whole society. (*Selected Letters* 148; qtd. in Quinlan, 41)

Ransom goes on to compare this quality to the skepticism of science as Platonic and therefore "anti-Gothic," and argues that only religion and art can save the sense of existence of "human personality" and even "the thinghood of things" (41).

When Ransom's narrator says "I am here" (45) in the revision to "Prelude to an Evening," his grand compromise, a tremendous argument with himself, works itself out in exactly the way his criticism describes. His narrator would not be a complete personality, a true sensibility, without acknowledgment of the primitive, Gothic elements of his spirit. At the same time, despite the tremendous power of the Gothic Furies in the poem, they are domesticated and ironized. In the land of the Gothic "the boulevards rocked; they said, Go back" (44). The feelings stand by themselves and require no further insistence on actual horror.

The serious yet ironic representation of the Gothic as articulated in Tate and Ransom's poems is the model of all strong Southern Gothic poetry. Donald Justice, who was born and raised in Miami, Florida, embraces this mode directly in his poem "Southern Gothic," which appeared in his first book, *The Summer Anniversaries* in 1960. Gothic fictions are filled with lurid action, yet in Justice's short poem (an unrhymed sonnet) nothing whatsoever happens, except a bee appearing to be puzzled that there are no flowers on the trellises of a decaying house, trees growing and casting shade, and wallpaper peeling under the moon. The poem opens:

> Something of how the homing bee at dusk
> Seems to inquire, perplexed, how there can be
> No flowers here, not even withered stalks of flowers,
> Conjures a garden where no garden is
> And trellises too frail almost to bear
> The memory of a rose, much less a rose. (1–6)

As David Yezzi states, "Concrete objects, deftly observed and presented, convey the real subject of the poem" (24), and yet the title suggests more. This is a self-identified Gothic poem that refuses to go beyond its typically Gothic setting. There are no horrors whatsoever in the Gothic sense, only that which "conjures" memory. Whatever dark events may have transpired, or might transpire in this abandoned home, Justice is not going to reveal them. The poet trusts us to supply our own demons. The ironic juxtaposition of the title and the poem require us to imagine what he does not say, an effect that would be impossible if Justice had simply titled the poem "An Abandoned House" or "Some Peeling Wallpaper." Irony permeates the entire work, holding us as surely in its grip as any self-inflicted terror or sorrow it both encourages us to imagine and simultaneously undercuts.

James Dickey deploys a far more extravagant and comic irony in "The Sheep Child." Dickey was born in Atlanta, served in the air force in World War II, and then attended Vanderbilt before pursuing a career in advertising and writing. He is best known for his Southern Gothic novel *Deliverance* (1970), which was made into the highly successful film of the same name (1972). Both the novel and the film are filled with explicit horror, including a graphic depiction of a male rape by satanic, gleeful crackers.

Despite the novel and film's success, Dickey spent far more of his writing life as a poet. "The Sheep Child," which first appeared in *Poems 1957–1967*, is a graphic work, but it deploys the Gothic in a far more ironized way than does *Deliverance*. The poem begins as a narrative about "Farm boys wild to couple / With anything" (1–2), then gives a long, comic list of those things and how the boys "keep themselves off / Animals by legends of their own" (4–5). Those legends are Gothic tales delivered in an imagined dramatic monologue by such boys of how the monsters born of boy-sheep unions are kept pickled "in a museum in Atlanta" (9).

In the second part of the poem, Dickey observes with comic sadness of such wild imaginative acts, that

> this is now almost all
> Gone. The boys have taken

Their own true wives in the city,
The sheep are safe in the west hill
Pasture (17–21)

The turn back toward the intensely comic Gothic irony of the second half of the poem comes in the ending of the same line and what follows, in which the speaker identifies himself as one of those imaginative boys: "but we who were born there / Still are not sure" (21–22). What follows is surely the most horrifically funny passage in Southern Gothic, where the boys go from imagining the Sheep Child, to imagining it speaking its own thirty-five-line dramatic monologue, which closes the poem.

Dickey's Sheep Child is represented as speaking in italics. The monster offers an explicitly artificial dramatic monologue, conjured by a plural male first person speaker who is apparently less interested in the sheep child itself than in the imagination of the young boys who could have dreamed it up it as a way to keep themselves from committing bestiality. All of these layers create an ironic distance around the central act and imbue it with absurd, horrific charm. The poem is a comic masterpiece, a Southern Gothic parody of Ovid, Dante, *Frankenstein*, and many other works so complete that it rises to their level. The poem closes:

> *Dead, I am most surely living*
> *In the minds of farm boys: I am he who drives*
> *Them like wolves from the hound bitch and calf*
> *And from the chaste ewe in the wind.*
> *They go into woods   into bean fields   they go*
> *Deep into their known right hands. Dreaming of me,*
> *They groan   they wait   they suffer*
> *Themselves, they marry, they raise their kind.* (55–62)

Like Tate, Ransom, Justice, and others in the tradition of modern Southern Gothic poetry before him, Dickey ironizes the tropes of the

Gothic at the same time as he honors them. Dickey's boys may "suffer," but in a cunning enjambment—a tool available only to a poet—he points out that they first and foremost actually "suffer / themselves," not some external reality. Like the other poets considered here, Dickey fulfills Marianne Moore's dictum about what poetry can be, providing "imaginary gardens with real toads in them" ("Poetry" 24; *Others for 1919*). Tate, Ransom, Justice, and Dickey treat the Gothic as imaginary, and yet they insist on the reality of the primal feelings that motivate it.

Conclusion

Southern Gothic poetry came into its own as a genre in the 1920s, when the strongest poets working in the tradition discovered ways to treat the genre seriously and ironically at the same time. The range of ironic response has varied from Tate's feelings of Eliotic historical paralysis, to Ransom's dark Walter-Mittyesque domestic fantasies,[7] to Justice's minimalism, to Dickey's slapstick, but that variety only serves to confirm the vitality of the tactic. Keeping careful distance from a Gothic tradition that presents its traditional props and tropes perhaps too literally—what I have affectionately called Splatter Gothic—these poets created a high or literary Southern Gothic tradition equaled by only a few prose writers, such as Faulkner and Flannery O'Connor. Further, while these strong novelists and others such as Cormac McCarthy have tended to take Gothic tropes and redomesticate them to realism, the stronger poets in the genre have managed to do what generally only poets can: *sustain the real and the fantastic simultaneously*, where both are concurrently true in what John Keats called "negative capability." Are Tate's Confederate soldiers alive or dead? Is Ransom's narrator a monster or a husband? Is Justice's setting an abandoned home or a haunted house? Is Dickey's Sheep Child a fantasy or a reality? The only answer to these questions is "Yes." These are questions that very few novelists even know how to ask.

The tradition of Southern Gothic poetry is very much alive, and while few poets ever write works as powerful as those considered closely here, many contemporaries are aware of what can be done and are pursuing ambitious work. Among others, Andrew Hudgins, Jake Adam York, Natasha Trethewey, and Jennifer Reeser have all been characterized at times as Southern Gothic poets. Of particular note are Hudgins's *After the Lost War* (1988), a poem recounting the life of poet Sidney Lanier in a series of dramatic monologues, and Tretheway's 2007 Pulitzer Prize–winning volume, *Native Guard*, which deals with her own background as a mixed-race child growing up in Mississippi, and with the story of the first Union Army regiment of African American soldiers, who were stationed in New Orleans. Many of these writers deal explicitly with painful historical subjects—York's recent books *A Murmuration of Starlings* (2008) and *Persons Unknown* (2010), address murders of the Civil Rights movement—but the violence and emotional pain of the subjects conjures with the Gothic, if not always as explicitly as in the poems more closely examined above. There has even been a recent Southern Gothic poetry competition, sponsored in 2011 by the South Carolina art journal *Undefined* and won by a poet named Kendal Turner for a poem titled "Ghosts."

Genre formation and development are odd and almost always surprising. As Lloyd-Smith and others have argued, the Gothic tradition in itself seems to have grown out of a response to Enlightenment realism. Like other fantasy genres such as science fiction, Gothic writers have been interested in keeping speculative and primal aspects of storytelling alive in ways that modern realist fiction, with its prohibitions on the supernatural or nonfactual, has proscribed. If the history of art is any guide, human beings seem to need, or at any rate to desire, such stories for complex reasons, but not least because while we no longer see them as literal, we do understand that they speak to psychological truths that we ignore at our peril.

In the case of the Gothic, beginning with Horace Walpole's *The Castle of Otranto* (1764) and in America with Washington Irving,

Poe, Hawthorne, and Charles Brockden Brown, the presentation of terror and horror came to take on specific generic characteristics that long ago became clichés: decaying mansions, ghosts and monsters, mad scientists, and so on. In America, these themes developed with a heightened sense, especially in the South, of racial violence, a stronger sense of the wilderness as malicious, and with rather more modest—though no less ruined—estates replacing crumbling castles. In this rich generic history, the great achievement of the major poets is the way they have deployed irony to achieve their effects. For whereas in most Gothic fiction, terror and horror are highly stylized and therefore more easily kept at a distance, or fully reincorporated into the real, an ironic juxtaposition of such terrors with daily life may, in the hands of a particularly strong poet, have the effect of bringing its psychological power and its ancient moral sublime that much closer to the bone. This achievement, which can occur in such compressed form only in what we call poetry, has always undergirded the sublime. Southern Gothic is no exception.

Notes

1. The primary influence on English notions of the sublime at this time, and a work that had a decisive impact on the development of the Gothic genre with its emphasis on the aesthetic pleasure of horror and terror, is Edmund Burke's 1757 work *A Philosophical Enquiry into the Origin of Our Ideas of the Sublime and Beautiful*. The argument of that book is too lengthy to summarize fully here, but its primary result was to articulate a vision of aesthetic pleasure that includes and explains extreme feelings of fear and awe, such as terror.

2. The poem was first published in 1779, was republished as a much longer piece in the best-known version of 1786, then heavily cut for its final appearance in Freneau's self-published volume of his own poetry in 1795. See *The Poems of Philip Freneau: Written Chiefly During the Late War* for the full text of the 1786 edition, with Freneau's prose introduction.

3. The defining manifesto of the Southern Agrarian movement is *I'll Take My Stand: The South and the Agrarian Tradition* (1930). The views expressed in the book's twelve essays combine an unregenerate reactionary tone on matters of race (including support for segregation) with more progressive notions of resistance to "overproduction, unemployment, and a growing inequality in the distribution of

wealth" (xli) caused by industrialism. The book is unapologetically nostalgic for agrarian values that the authors saw as both social and political counterweights to the modern urban and industrial society emanating from the North.

4. "I bequeath myself to the dirt to grow from the grass I love." (Walt Whitman, "Song of Myself" Section 52, 1340)

5. In the 1934 version, the full stanza reads:

   You like a waning moon, and I accusing

   Our too banded Eumenides,

   While you pronounce Noes wonderingly

   And smooth the heads of the hungry children. (29–32)

6. Cook's webpage "Trees, Shrubs, and Woody Vines of North Carolina" provides a detailed list of over four hundred of the state's various native and naturalized species.

7. Walter Mitty is the eponymous protagonist of James Thurber's 1939 short story "The Secret Life of Walter Mitty."

Works Cited

Alighieri, Dante. *The Inferno of Dante: A New Verse Translation*. Trans. and ed. Robert Pinsky. New York: Farrar, 1996. Print.

Burke, Edmund. *A Philosophical Enquiry into the Origin of Our Ideas of the Sublime and Beautiful*. 1757. *The Works of the Right Honourable Edmund Burke*. Vol 1. London: Nimmo, 1887. 67–262. Print.

Coffin, Charles Monroe. "Creation and the Self in *Paradise Lost*." *ELH, A Journal of English Literary History* 29.1 (1962): 1–18. Print.

Cook, Charles Wilson. "Trees, Shrubs, and Woody Vines of North Carolina." Duke University. *Duke University*, 2012. Web. 25 Oct. 2012.

Ellman, Richard, ed. *The New Oxford Book of American Verse*. New York: Oxford UP, 1976. Print.

Freneau, Philip. "The House of Night: A Vision." *The Poems of Philip Freneau: Written Chiefly During the Late War*. Philadelphia: Bailey, 1786. 101–23. Print.

"Genre: Southern Gothic." *Oprah's Book Club*. Harpo Productions, 2012. Web. 25 Oct. 2012.

Gosse, Edmund. "Ode." *Encyclopedia Britannica*. 11th ed. Vol. 20. Cambridge: Cambridge UP, 1911. 1–2. Print.

"Handout Two: The Southern Gothic Literary Tradition." The Heart Is a Lonely Hunter *Teacher's Guide*. National Endowment for the Arts: The Big Read, 2012. Web. 25 Oct. 2012.

Hudgins, Andrew. *After the Lost War: A Narrative*. Boston: Houghton, 1988. Print.

Justice, Donald. *Collected Poems*. New York: Knopf, 2004. Print.

Lloyd-Smith, Allan. *American Gothic Fiction: An Introduction*. New York: Continuum, 2004. Print.

Quinlan, Kieran. *John Crowe Ransom's Secular Faith*. Baton Rouge: LSU P, 1989. Print.

Ransom, John Crowe. "Prelude to an Evening." *American Review* (May 1934): 262–63. Print.

___. "Prelude to an Evening: A Poem Revised and Explicated." *Kenyon Review* 25.1 (1963): 70–80. Print.

___. *God without Thunder: An Unorthodox Defense of Orthodoxy*. New York: Harcourt, 1930. Print.

Rubin, Louis Decimus Jr., ed. *I'll Take My Stand: The South and the Agrarian Tradition*. 1930. 2nd ed. Baton Rouge: LSU P, 1977. Print.

Tate, Allen. "Narcissus as Narcissus." *Reason in Madness: Critical Essays*. New York: Putnam, 1941. 132–51. Print.

Tretheway, Natasha D. *Native Guard*. Boston: Houghton, 2007. Print.

Turner, Kendal. "Ghosts." *Undefined* 12 (2011): 34–35. Print.

Yezzi, David. "The Memory of Donald Justice." *New Criterion* 23.3 (2004): 21–25. Print.

York, Jake Adam. *A Murmuration of Starlings*. Carbondale: Southern Illinois UP, 2008. Print.

___. *Persons Unknown*. Carbondale: Southern Illinois UP, 2010. Print.

Cthulhu Visits the South, or Fred Chappell's Three Levels of *Dagon*

Michal Svěrák

"There's something in that house. . . . Something living in it. Hidden in it. It has been out there for four years, living hidden in that house."

—William Faulkner, *Absalom, Absalom!*

The air of death and desertion was ghoulish, and the smell of fish almost insufferable . . . .

—H. P. Lovecraft, "The Shadow over Innsmouth"

In the socially restless year of 1968, the writer-in-residence at the University of North Carolina at Greensboro, Fred Chappell, published his third novel, *Dagon*. From one point of view, the short but disturbing book is a thematic and aesthetic follow up to his two previous Southern novels, *It Is Time, Lord* (1963) and *The Inkling* (1965). From another, it contains an array of quite different contextual components intentionally absorbed from the American macabre fiction of the magazine *Weird Tales*.

The primary context of *Dagon* and its prominent source of ideas is Southern literature, especially the imaginative strain of Southern Gothic that includes ancestral curses, feverish visions, and psychological abnormalities. This thematic string connects *Dagon*, in particular, with Chappell's second novel. The context drawn from *Weird Tales* came specifically from the highly original literary imagination of the prominent New England dreamer Howard Phillips Lovecraft and his so called Cthulhu Mythos, which represents a series of thematically interconnected stories that concentrate on the negligible significance of human life in a vast and indifferent cosmos.

The writing of *Dagon* was not easy. According to Casey H. Clabough, it took three years (50) of exhausting struggle with its numerous and frequently inconsistent themes, particularly those connected with a secret American religion, moral consequences of the Puritan spiritual legacy, an American inclination to mindless consumerism and wastefulness, a modern reinterpretation of the Biblical story of Samson and Delilah, and a colorfully seductive Lovecraftian cosmic mythology. By the end, Chappell was almost overcome by his own manuscript (Clabough 50–51). After subsequent months of rewriting and numerous changes, the novel finally came to light. Fortunately, the literary result of the agonizing creative process was not a failure; *Dagon* presents Chappell as one of the most original and experimental voices of contemporary Southern literature.

The novel is divided into two interrelated parts that are composed of six chapters each. In the first part, the reader is introduced to thirty-two-year-old Methodist minister and scholar Peter Leland and his patient and intelligent wife, Sheila. Peter is rather naive, anxiety-driven, and obsessed with the obstacles of living, whereas Sheila is a more practical, caring, and generally happy person. At the very beginning of the novel, the couple has moved to a remote farm in western North Carolina, which Peter has recently inherited from his grandparents. The reason for the move is Peter's book, *Remnant Pagan Forces in American Puritanism*, on which he desires to work in the tranquility of Appalachian nature. Already, this initial situation connects the novel with the tradition of Gothic literature and its fascination with secrets from a hidden but still lurking past. Such a place as Leland's familial farm presents a mental trap, in which the protagonist usually confronts his or her unconscious desires and fears. The past itself is buried in the deserted location, and the coming of the young, unaware couple brings it back to life. This past is never empty, but always filled with malevolent forces calling for renewal.

In chapter one of the first part, a weary Peter Leland conducts a search around his inheritance. Even now the interior of the rustic mansion is full of wickedness and strangled malevolency. The two windows of the downstairs salon are "eyed and wavy" and the curtain in the door's window resembles "fingers of the dead" (Chappell 3). Everything in this uncovered mausoleum is coated with dust, and the low sofa is described as the "obese horror" (5). Peter speculates on whether all the wooden floors are rotting. Perceptive observers should be warned by these early signs, because there is no doubt that Peter's family house is haunted. It is haunted and animated by the ghosts of the past, like many houses in the rich American Gothic tradition: Edgar Allan Poe's House of Usher, Nathaniel Hawthorne's House of the Seven Gables, William Faulkner's plantation mansions, Shirley Jackson's Hill House, and of course H. P. Lovecraft's New England attic witch dwellings and dilapidating backwoods farmhouses. In *Dagon*, the motif of the haunted house is crucial, as its aesthetic and symbolic function is closely connected to the function of the room. But just like Lovecraft's houses, the house of *Dagon* is a fateful harbor of the irrational.

Subsequently, Peter contemplates two embroidered companion pillows on the sofa and equates them with "twin tombstones" (5). These pillows strangely depict a dualistic conception of the Puritanical worldview and unpleasantly refer to Peter's spiritual inheritance. On one of the cushions, there is a motto that refers to a dreamy state of innocence, and on the other, a reference to a woken state of a fallen and strictly dutiful life. Through this sofa and pillows, which cause Peter to reflect on his Puritan ancestors, the house slowly lures Peter into its mighty grasp. Puritanism in *Dagon* is only a kind of mental catwalk to the more hideous caverns of Peter's personal history, but it functions as a vehicle of human bodily deprivation, constant fear, and mental corruption, too. This approach is at least partially inspired by H. P. Lovecraft, who was deeply disgusted and simultaneously fascinated by the persistent legacy of seventeenth-century Puritanism in Massachusetts. In a discussion with Frank Belknap Long, he wrote: "Verily, the Puritans were the only really effective diabolists and decadents the world has known; because they hated life and scorned the platitude that it is worth living" (Joshi, *I am Providence* 375). Even more complex portraits of Puritan oppressive theocracy can be found in Lovecraft's short story "The Picture in the House":

> In such houses have dwelt generations of strange people, whose like the world has never seen. Seized with a gloomy and fanatical belief which exiled them from their kind, their ancestors sought the wilderness for freedom. There the scions of a conquering race indeed flourished free from the restrictions of their fellows, but cowered in an appalling slavery to the dismal phantasms of their own minds. Divorced from the enlightenment of civilization, the strength of these Puritans turned into singular channels; and in their isolation, morbid self-repression, and struggle for life with relentless Nature, there came to them dark furtive traits from the prehistoric depths of their cold Northern heritage. By necessity practical and by philosophy stern, these folk were not beautiful in their sins. Erring as all mortals must, they were forced by their rigid code to seek concealment above all else; so that they came to use less and less taste in what they concealed. (34–35)

This accumulation of secret human deformities, compounded by the intense guilt that accompanies a morbid self-consciousness, begins to torture Peter. It is why he feels "his mind so often turning upon himself" (Chappell 8).

The downstairs salon has—as has everything in the house—its own invisible substance comprised from feelings, ideas, and the life stories of its former inhabitants. In *Dagon* this substance is not passive and waiting for the possibility of speaking to a sensitive individual, but rather active and insidious. For Peter, the salon represents an unknown place and he desires to penetrate its secret, but he does not realize that he is, in fact, entering his own forgotten history. He perceives the room as somebody else's body, a place which is, in a way, connected with death. When he sits down on the sofa, the odor submerges him and his spirit seems to be "drowning in the smell" (8). Peter accepts the room—and through it, the entire house—into himself. It becomes a part of his body and soul. Other symbolic objects in the salon include a "silly little ashtray," a "dark secretary," a "diseased and disordered" piano, and a big doily, which "looked like a fishnet" (9, 12), ready to catch a susceptible visitor. Peter gradually realizes that the room's still-living inhabitant "was not simply the impersonal weight of dead personality but a willful belligerence, active hostility" (12–13).

In chapter two, Peter and Sheila decide to have a picnic near the farmhouse. This time the setting is predominantly natural and almost bucolic, but Peter still worries about his surroundings. Perhaps it is because the "big ugly house" sits "almost in the center of the wide farm, the four hundred acres shaped vaguely like an open hand" (15) and thus dominates all of the surrounding landscape. It is no coincidence that the farm reminds one of a trap. Even in this Elysian garden of fresh milk, sweet honey, and wild flowers, the secret signs of corruption and threat are hidden. "A slow dark stream" is "serpentine" and "sluggish" (16), and it reflects no light. According to Sheila, however, the stream looks "nice and cool" (16). Peter's wife is so rational, self-confident, and happy that she easily fails to notice all the cautionary signs encircling her. She still believes in a stable order of things and a nobility of past events. Nevertheless, the sinister details of this earthly Paradise suggest that it is only a dream, like the one depicted on the sofa pillow in the house. The water in the nearby brook, with its joyful movement and light, should represent life. But in Peter's farmland it appears as an opposite symbol of powerlessness and death. As with the biblical serpent metaphor, the farm (garden) brings to Peter the promise of forbidden knowledge. This temptation is soon materialized in the obese tenant farmer Ed Morgan, who encounters the young couple during their idyllic picnic. His face is "like a balloon, red as catsup from wind and sun," and his grin is "so fixed" (22) that it can be painted. He wears overalls and no shirt, the fat on his chest moving "with a greasy undulation" (22).

Similar descriptions are typical when Southern literature depicts the lives of impoverished mountain folk from the mostly agrarian

Appalachian region. These inhabitants of the Southern mountains and deep forests may not always be a source of disgust, pity, or fear. In some literary sources they are celebrated as brave Anglo-Saxon descendants of truly American pioneers living in the cultural and economic isolation of some kind of a natural utopia. Richard Gray portrays this type as "self-sufficient but also hospitable and loyal, simple but also wise, undemonstrative and taciturn but also deeply attached to certain pieties and people" (237). Apart from this noble mountain frontiersman, however, we can identify another cultural form of the mountain inhabitant—the degenerate beast. This mountaineer is no more a pious Christian than a superstitious and guileful pagan. The simplicity of a life closely connected to the soil is replaced by an idiocy coming on after many years of inbreeding. Romulus Linney in his novel *Heathen Valley*, published in 1962, describes these people as "haunted by hallucinations and night spirits, obsessed by lunacy and death, hungry and violent, celebrating their passions and fear in wild, amoral sprees, wandering barefoot with ancient homemade long rifles . . . and speaking a curt, blunt language, occasionally obscured by forgotten words" (Gray 281). Morgan and his family firmly belong to this heathen land and its bestial tribe. He drinks from the same poisonous spring as the nameless mountain rapists of James Dickey's *Deliverance* (1970) or as the poor necrophiliac Lester Ballard of Cormac McCarthy's *Child of God* (1973). Lovecraft's influence on Chappell should be remembered here. Lovecraft repeatedly and consistently portrays degenerate peasants in their New England milieu. For example, in "Beyond the Wall of Sleep," he scornfully describes one of the mountain inhabitants and his society:

> His name, as given on the records, was Joe Slater, or Slaader, and his appearance was that of the typical denizen of the Catskill Mountain region; one of those strange, repellent scions of a primitive colonial peasant stock whose isolation for nearly three centuries in the hilly fastnesses of a little-travelled countryside has caused them to sink to a kind of barbaric degen-

eracy, rather than advance with their more fortunately placed brethren of the thickly settled districts. Among these old folk, who correspond exactly to the decadent element of "white trash" in the South, law and morals are non-existent; and their general mental status is probably below that of any other section of the native American people. (11–12)

In this light, it is questionable whether the literary source and inspiration of the brutish Morgan family is Southern Gothic, Lovecraftian imagination, or a mixture of both. Because the Lovecraft influence otherwise remains obvious in the novel, Chappell may have indeed read this story. But as Chappell grew up in the South, it is just as possible that he was reacting to, while repeating, a common stereotype about all lower classes of rural areas, particularly his own. In any case, these figures represent the prominent source of the uncanny, albeit sometimes on the very verge of parody.

In the hideous interior of Morgan's cabin, with its "hot and viscous" air (27), pestilent swarms of flies, and the "smell of rank incredibly rich semen" (28), Peter sees the enormously fat body of the farmer's wife, whose great torso reminds the reader of the prehistoric fertility idol of Mother Earth. Casey H. Clabough sees her as a "symbol of primitive and powerful, though unthinking and inarticulate, female sexuality" (59). Along with multitudes of flies as symbols of evil and the reek of semen, which refers to excessive and unbridled copulation, Morgan's wife manifestly stands against Peter's strict and ascetic Christian tradition. However, this corpulent matriarch does not constitute the real spiritual center of Morgan's household. It is in fact his daughter Mina, a strange and highly sinister creature who steadily watches Peter with extremely large eyes. Contrary to her mother, she represents the sexual force which is not procreative but infertile. She never seems to become pregnant and her sex with men is a part of a degrading inhuman ritual, which is doubly sinful to the Puritan mindset. Mina's fixed gaze suggests something about secret psychic powers with which she controls Peter, because he has to "use his whole will to take his eyes off her" (29). He is also worried by other signs in the appearance of the girl. She has almost no nose, and he notices something fishlike in her flat face. Mina reminds him not only of a fish but also of a snake. In keeping with the idea of a hungry temptress, she literally tells him that she could just eat him up. After this bizarre confrontation Peter leaves Morgan's cabin, but he cannot expel Mina's image from his mind. His meeting with the girl can be seen as the next step in his dark initiation into the cult of Dagon.

The third chapter recalls Peter's typical ministerial service and reveals his inner motives for it. He has always been haunted by his familial Puritanical tradition, so "his black imagination force[s] him to take everything all too seriously" (31). His tormented mind has been predominated by the anxious "fantasies about his father, who had died when Peter was so young that he could not at all remember him" (31). The mysterious death occurred when Peter lived on the farm and his mother categorically refused to speak with him about it. Therefore, he never found out how his father died and only captured sparse and blurred remarks about some "terrifying disease" (32):

> So that in his dark mid-adolescence he had begun to imagine that this disease was probably hereditary, had begun to wonder when it might overtake him also. He would imagine it as sudden and painlessly fatal, a black stifling area of wool dropped over him abruptly; or he would think of it as gradual and excruciating, a blob of soft metal dissolving in acid. (32)

Peter's visions and phantasmal fears aptly pick up the threads of Lovecraft's work and disprove the notion that the main difference between Chappell and Lovecraft lies in their source of literary horror. According to John Lang, Lovecraft identifies the source of horror in the external (i.e., cosmic) powers, while Chappell locates it in the internal empire of the "individual psyche" (Lang 34). However, Lang never takes fully into account that Lovecraft's horror maliciously infiltrates the very core of a man. His protagonists often fiercely scrutinize genealogical records of their old families in order to find out that they are the true descendants of "corrupted blood" (Lévy 78).

This hereditary interiorized menace cannot be escaped by any means. What are all the horrors of the immeasurable cosmos in comparison with our own internal corruption leading inevitably to physical and mental degradation? In some cases these "horrors of heredity" (Lévy 73) may lie in real degeneration and gradual transformation of humanity into the beast, but in others they may lead to unimaginable marvels. Chappell's most mysterious and malevolent figures, Ed Morgan and his daughter Mina, only herald the coming of this inevitable fate. In Chappell's novel as in Lovecraft's stories, monstrous forces act through familial heredity. As expressed by Maurice Lévy: "Evil is in us" (74). This laconic statement accurately corresponds to Peter's Puritanical doctrine of original sin.

The inherent evil in a person is also why Peter chose this theme for his scholarly study of the Puritans. In one of his sermons, he refers to the Old Testament pagan deity Dagon, worshipped by the Philistines. He reveals to his congregation that the invocation of this fallen fertility god has been brought to America and lurks under its Christian surface. At the end of his lecture Peter compares the Dagon cult to the American commercial culture, with its "endless irrational productivity, clear analogue to sexual orgy" (38). The entity secretly worshipped in the Appalachian Mountains is not the same as the biblical fish-man deity of Peter's interest. As will be explained later, the name Dagon from the title of Chappell's novel mainly refers to a figure from the pantheon of the Lovecraftian mythos.

Chappell himself has said that he invented the myth "that there was a secret cult that still worshiped [Dagon] that went on all through American history" (Lang 35). Nevertheless, this authorial statement is only partially true: the idea in fact also originates from Lovecraft's body of work, though even Lovecraft himself did not invent it. He was inspired by a classic study written by Margaret Alice Murray, published in 1921 and titled *The Witch-Cult in Western Europe*. Murray, a

British anthropologist, believed that witch rituals were manifestations of real pagan cults operating in the underground of the official Christian religion for centuries. This theory appears in Lovecraft's work, again closely connected with American Puritanism. In his essay "Dr. Margaret Murray and H. P. Lovecraft: The Witch-Cult in New England," Robert H. Waugh explains it as follows:

> According to this analysis Puritanism rebels against the political order in the name of imagination and personal desire; but the freedom that promises to gratify desire instead represses it and in a wilderness that models the interior darkness transforms the landscape into a dream, a fantasy impoverished and distorted because it no longer has the support of traditional institutions and culture. In this impoverishment the person is devoured by instincts of individual and prehistoric origin which civilization had held in check; imagination and desire overcome individual autonomy. (115)

The same desire may have once overcome Peter's grandparents, too. One way or another, Morgan and his family seem to be members of a primal witch cult older than Western society.

The fourth chapter depicts Peter tortured by wild dreams. It is symptomatic that his sleep is not peaceful in this weird environment of terrible secrets, where the past pervades the present. Peter's nightmares, along with his increasingly frequent hallucinations, are of course characteristic of the Gothic genre. The dreams signify the fusion of different realities and the surrender of the diurnal world to the nocturnal. Peter's psyche is not yet ready to accept the truth of his destiny, however, so he is not able to remember the dreams properly. He wanders about the house and the face of Mina constantly appears in his mind. His connection to the ancestral edifice grows stronger. In this tormented state of mental distress he slowly realizes that he had "missed something central" about his grandparents, something "that he could discover in himself" (Chappell 44–45) and that is not only "soured Puritanism" but "something even darker" (45). These ruminations again refer to

Lovecraft's frequent motifs of sleeping and of suddenly reactivated unclean hereditary tendencies, strangeness, and monstrousness hidden in the individual. In a trunk, Peter finds some obscure correspondence with exotic words such as "Nephreu," "Yogg Sothoth," and "Cthulhu" (45). The words reveal—with the exception of the novel's enigmatic epigraph—the story's first original traces of Lovecraft's Cthulhu Mythos.

At this time, it is appropriate to mention briefly the basic philosophical characteristics of Lovecraft's pseudomythology. Lovecraft was an atheist and mechanistic materialist, and he was "totally devoid of any dualistic belief" (Mosig 14) in any supernatural phenomena of a religious nature. At the center of Lovecraft's literary work is not humanity, but rather man's total insignificance and meaninglessness in the infinite, insensitive, and unknowable—and therefore seemingly purposeless—cosmos, whereas the ultimate horror is the very realization of this fact. Such a cosmos is not anthropocentric and a man does not bear God's image. The Cthulhu Mythos is constituted by thematically interconnected stories that include, particularly as aesthetic devices, a group of alien entities called gods by ignorant humans. Lovecraft's characters are not able to understand these mighty beings from outer space or other dimensions, "so either worship their greatness as divinity or exorcise their threat to human security and peace of mind calling them devils" (Price 249). The most widely known entities are Azathoth, Yog-Sothoth, Nyarlathotep, and Cthulhu.

Azathoth, a blind, idiot god, serves as a symbol of primeval chaos at the center of the indifferent cosmos. Yog-Sothoth, a titanic profusion of toothy mouths, goggle eyes, and swirling tentacles, is a colossal cosmic or extra-dimensional being that functions as a "gate" to other worlds. Nyarlathotep serves as a messenger of these extraterrestrial entities, called the Old Ones, and is a harbinger of apocalypse. Finally, Cthulhu—associated with the sea-deity Dagon from a homonymous Lovecraft short story—is a gigantic octopus-like monster that came to Earth from the stars before the dawn of man and dwells in the ancient sunken city of R'lyeh at the bottom of the Pacific Ocean. This fabulous city is supposed by Lovecraft's mythos to have sunk like Atlantis millennia ago, and the cosmic entity Cthulhu waits for the proper star conjunction to obtain its former power and glory again. This monstrous character and a corresponding short story—Lovecraft's "The Call of Cthulhu" (1926)—is referenced by the otherwise indecipherable epigraph in Chappell's *Dagon*: *"Ph'nglui mglw'nafh Cthulhu R'lyeh wgah'nagl fhtagn."* The phrase is usually translated as "In his house at R'lyeh dead Cthulhu waits dreaming" (Lovecraft, "The Call of Cthulhu" 150). Dead but still dreaming, Cthulhu embodies the hidden cursed past that lurks to infest the present.

In connection with *Dagon*, it is useful to remember that even the Lovecraftian characters that are most acquainted with the Old Ones and their power "cannot face the terrible human-minimizing implications of the existence of the overshadowing aliens and [they therefore] take superstitious refuge in religion, deifying the Old Ones as gods who care about their human worshippers and will reward them" (Price 249). This appears to be the case with Peter's grandparents and quite certainly with Mina and her backwoods relatives. The poor tenant family seems central to the Dagon cult in this novel, but their optimistic belief in Dagon as a fertility deity is only a delusion, as is Peter's fatalistic belief in the Christian God of death. The confused cultists from New England or Appalachia worship not gods but extraterrestrials. To this extent, the Cthulhu Mythos is in fact an atheistic pseudo-mythology with no real parallel in Christianity or any other dualistic theology. There is no supernatural conflict between the forces of good and the forces of evil because the cosmos, shorn of false anthropocentrism, is exclusively amoral. Only substantial "misunderstanding of Lovecraft's intent led his followers to write a kind of religious fiction" (Price 250). But by direct use of the innovative and highly original motifs from Lovecraft's oeuvre in *Dagon*, Chappell also transposed Lovecraft's philosophical conceptions.

Peter Leland, like Lovecraft's courageous searchers, uncovers glimpses of a maddening truth in the correspondence of his grandparents. The letters that provide him with strange names and sinister quotations written in an "unknown language of despair" (Chappell 86) are magical objects that seize the life of their readers and transform them mentally through fantastic dreams the words evoke. Indeed, the letters are accomplices of the house.

The chapter culminates when Peter enters the attic. The room is buried under "tons of dust" (46) which, according to Lang, suggests the "detritus of the past and of mortality" (35). In this mysterious place Peter discovers a "queer arrangement of chains" (47) with attached iron bands. After he tries one of the bands, he locks his right wrist in it and cannot to open it again. In this pivotal scene the attic appears like an enchanted chamber, the center of a castle from a traditional Gothic novel. After some time, it comes to light that Peter is strangely connected with this place of horror—it once served as a scene of a torture—and that it is prepared just for him. He suddenly realizes that it was this room "where his father had died" (50). This recognition calls for attention more and more insistently:

There wasn't evidence, his mind didn't need evidence, the whole house was full of the fact. His mind was full of the house. The cuff fitted exactly. The image in his head was an event he had already experienced; had stood here with both arms chained, fallen against the hot wall and sweating furiously in the clothes he had fouled all over. . . . His father, not mad, but furiously raging in inhuman anger, with the sweat all over him like yellow paint. His shattered eyes. What was it they had wanted him to see? (50)

The father's martyrdom in chains resembles the tragic death of Miss Rosa's father in William Faulkner's iconic Southern Gothic novel *Absalom, Absalom!* (1936). It is clear that the attic functions as a place of initiation. Whether in Faulkner or in Poe, whoever enters into such a place submerges into it, succumbs to its power, and sometimes never leaves, entombed by its history. However, this time Sheila comes and releases Peter from the dark grip of his hereditary past. At first Peter feels relief and pity for her because she found him in such a state. Then, when the lights in the house return after a blackout, everything looks naked and "they seemed naked too and turned away from each other as if in shame" (56). The sin has been introduced in the Garden of Eden and their mutual separation has begun.

In the fifth and the sixth chapters, Peter's alienation deepens further and he finally recognizes the true nature of his secret family inheritance: "Inheriting the farm he had inherited Mina, inheriting the house he had inherited chains" (58). The incident in the attic has convinced him that it is impossible to resist his fate; he can only be reconciled gratefully, and his passive mind then welcomes this recognition with a grim satisfaction. Sheila suspects that the farm is unhealthy place for Peter, but she cannot break the spell of this threshold, between this ordinary world and Mina's realm of unearthly horrors, which her husband already crossed. He looks dark somehow, "as if his body gathered some of the darkness of the furnishings, or as if it had been tinged by the thick obscurity of the attic" (66).

Peter is like any typical Gothic protagonist, figuratively infested by his ancestral past. It pervades his troubled sleep in the form of nightmares of "great deserted cities which flashed through his consciousness, gleaming white cities with geometries so queer and dizzying as to cause nausea" (66). These strange visions illustrate Mina's psychic control over an increasingly passive and submissive Peter. Peter's dreams furthermore resemble the bizarre dreams that torture many characters in Lovecraft's tales. In such dreams, the Old Ones usually communicate with mortals, offering them the marvelous and sinister vistas of their extraterrestrial architecture, which is described as the triumph of something unnamable by the dreamer, a vision so alien as to remain impossible to rationalize. Peter's dream continues with the appearance of a "milky-white odorous ocean" (67), a symbol of sexual orgies in honor of the fish-man god Dagon. This ocean, however, contains a level best understood through Lovecraft, as it also embodies his mythic sea of darkness, in which chaos rules, and from which apocalyptic beasts arise.

The new stage of Peter's dreaming includes his murder of Sheila. It can be considered as a direct instruction from Mina or as a reification of his own unconscious sense of guilt. In any case, Peter is slowly turning from the position of victim to a temporary position of victimizer. His descent into madness is accompanied by this outburst of seemingly unmotivated and blind violence. The next day, after a peculiar snake attack that leaves him even more ashamed in front of his wife, he kills her in reality. As George Hovis reminds the reader, the horrible and incomprehensible night crime continues not only in the tradition of prominent Southern Gothic authors such as Edgar Allan Poe, Mary Flannery O'Connor, Erskine Caldwell, William Faulkner, or Truman Capote, but also draws its inspiration from the "darker earthy elements in the work of the frontier humorists" (33). According to Hovis, Peter's sociopathic behavior resembles "similar behaviors found in so many folk ballads of the Appalachian frontier" that "often examine the darker side of yeoman independence" (33).

This occasionally stubborn independence, leading in extreme cases to misanthropy and social pathology, can be applied more to Morgan's family than to the nearly apathetic Peter Leland. However, some folklorists identify in these folk songs an "uncanny fascination with violence and criminality for its own sake" (33). Hovis underlines the manifestly random character of the mountain crimes and equates Peter to the protagonists of these ballads, because he is, like them, "never capable of or much interested in understanding the social ramifications of his act" (34). Appalachian ballads may very well testify of the "young mountaineers' problems with intimacy" (34), but Peter's crime should be considered in the context of his dark spiritual quest as well. Chappell's *Dagon* is, among other things, an initiation novel. Peter's naive arrival at the inherited farm, his search inside his grandparents' house, his imprisonment in the attic, and the final murder of his wife constitute the inevitable steps toward his spiritual initiation.

As both Southern Gothic and initiation story, *Dagon* follows one of two motifs central to literature of initiation. Popular in Southern fiction from Mark Twain to Dorothy Allison, initiation literature can focus on physical maturation, or coming-of-age. Peter Leland's coming-of-age, however, is spiritual. His process of spiritual initiation entails many trials, including symbolic death and resurrection. Also characteristically, he must suffer physical breakdown in order to be prepared for his spiritual initiation. The protagonist's road to knowledge leads through the labyrinthine outer world into the inner space of his soul. On this arduous road, protagonists of initiation literature often meet the figure of the initiator, who helps the protagonist, sometimes even against his will, to be ritually cleansed and to enter the inner sanctuary for the highest trial: the ritual and the transformation. The spiritual initiation—or its black parodic variation—is a common motif of the Gothic novel, too. However, Peter's initiation quest resembles a descent into hell.

After he literally murders his wife, Peter finds his way through the darkness of the night into Morgan's cabin where he meets Mina, this time alone. She offers him a mug of liquor and he thirstily drinks. This symbolic act, a parody of the communion, releases Peter from any residual commitments to his former life and delivers him to the hands of his initiators, members of the Dagon cult. The room is even filled with a yellow "warm dank religious light" (Chappell 80). It is the color of Peter's sick dreams ironically connected not with the forces of good, health, and life, but with the minions of evil and death. It resembles urine or bile polluting the blood and epitomizes the sickness and corruption of the soul.

The second part of the novel begins with Peter in the old tenant's shack, where he has found a new asylum. The cabin, "always full of movement" (83), stands as a renitent counterpart of Leland's farmhouse forever frozen in the past. There, lying in the "shabby shaggy bed" (83), Peter is constantly fed with the moonshine by Mina. He rapidly degrades into a pitiful human ruin. Deprived of the last remnant of his dignity, he rolls "like a pig on the floor" (85). During an immense summer storm he goes out onto the porch, and in a sudden flash of lightning he experiences an almost mystical revelation, which he attributes to God. Peter's vision seems to be a prophetic one, because he sees himself as dead: he "had to be killed first" (90), and then resurrected.

Peter finds a broken handle of a water pump and attaches to it emotionally. The dysfunctional object is interpreted by Lang as a symbol of Peter's lost masculinity and as a peculiar "emblem of the sterility of the world" he inhabits (38). In one lucid moment Peter realizes that his humanity has disappeared. He again feels the "presence of other systems, other universes, to which humanity—his humanity—was irrelevant" (Chappell 123). It almost seems that he is able to penetrate the mundane world with its trivial human superstitions and take a look into the cosmic void, though he is not yet ready. His only compensation for the life he once knew is the liquor from Mina. His only friend is an imaginary one, a snake—an appropriate representation of the fallen human condition:

> We live as serpents, sucking in the dust, sucking it up. The stuff we were formed of, and we ought to inhabit it. We ought to struggle to make ourselves secret and detestable, we should cultivate our sicknesses and bruise our own heads with our own heels. Where's the profit in claiming to walk upright? There's no poisonous animal that walks upright, a desecration. (121)

No wonder that such a concept leads Peter to an utterly fatalistic attitude. He acknowledges that there is "nothing to escape from" because he is only "his own prisoner" (129), and the only way to escape is to die. The above quotation clearly stands as evidence of a residual Christian guilt that has not yet been won over in Peter by that recurring sense of wholly alien universes. It is possible to blame him for his passivity and lack of resistance, but the reader has to take into consideration that, if understood through the Cthulhu

Mythos, Peter is predisposed, by incomprehensible cosmic forces, to this situation. He is bound by his heredity working behind the scene.

Mina takes Peter from their native mountains to the coastal town of Gordon, where they settle with some other members of the cult in an abandoned house. He is again locked in chains, this time for the purpose of passing through a preparatory ritual that includes a total deadening of his body by painful tattooing. The proximity of the sea corresponds to Lovecraft's sinister imagery in his short story "The Shadow over Innsmouth," in which a nameless traveler arrives at a decaying New England port only to discover that almost all of the town's population is a product of crossbreeding between humans and mysterious undersea creatures. The peak of horror comes when the protagonist finds out that the corrupted inhuman blood runs in his own veins, too. Peter's unhappy fate remarkably mirrors that of Lovecraft's anonymous narrator. Equally, the fish-stench covered and polluted Innsmouth, sheltering the Esoteric Order of Dagon and inhabited by fishlike humanoids, resembles Mina's loathly odor and noseless face.

The tattooing sessions grow in intensity; Peter believes these ritual operations will lead to some "horrifying climax," but he is lacking in the willpower to stop them. His body has no contact with the world because "it had been absorbed entirely into another manner of existence" (170). His physical identity has been replaced by the symbolic system of signs. Only then is he ready to meet the deity, because signs work better between different species. The place where this sacred event occurs is a "low weather-stained shed" (171), a diminished version of Peter's inherited farmhouse and Morgan's backwoods cabin. In this primitive sanctuary stands a "silly altar" (172) before which Peter is left alone. There, the very substance of space is changing, creating "a circle of blackness" (172), and the alien god comes forth:

> Reptilian. Legless. Truncated scaly wings, flightless, useless. The god Dagon was less than three feet long. Fat and rounded, like the belly of a crocodile. He couldn't see the mouth hidden away under the body, but

he knew it: a wirelike grin like a rattlesnake's; double rows of venomous needles in the maw. On this side a nictitating eye, but he thought that on the other side there would be no eye, but merely a filmy blind spot, an instrument to peer into the marrow of things. (173)

The god Dagon, as the prominent bearer of initiation (the highest initiator), appears like a union of opposites, like an abstract principle transformed into a being. Peter recognizes an idiot in him. He is omnipotent but without intelligence. He embodies a "naked will uncontrollable" (173). After this abysmal encounter with the blind chaos of the universe, Peter welcomes Mina's knife. As R. H. W. Dillard reads it, he becomes "his own executioner" (18).

The story does not end here. The closing sixth chapter of the second part introduces Peter in a "new mode of existence" within an "undefined bright space," into which he "came through death" and "from which he could look back upon this little spot of earth and there see the shape of his life in terms not bitterly limited by misery and fear" (Chappell 175). By facing Dagon, the extraterrestrial messenger from the infinite cosmic oceans, he maintained his former identity and simultaneously obtained the mystical knowledge of universal human destiny. From his luminous dwelling out of time, Peter looks back at his past miserable life and he laughs "without rancor and without regret" (175), because he has finally apprehended his existence:

> He understood suffering now and the purpose of suffering. In an almost totally insentient cosmos only human feeling is interesting or relevant to what the soul searches for. There is nothing else salient in the whole tract of limitless time, and suffering is simply one means of carving a design upon an area of time, of charging with human meaning each separate moment of time. Suffering is the most expensive of human feelings, but it is the most intense and most precious of them, because suffering most efficiently humanizes the unfeeling universe. (175–76)

The governing principle of this sublime afterlife is metaphor itself, and Peter's only task is to select and "take his likeness in every possible form in the universe" (176). Inspired by the galactic ages, he takes the form of Leviathan, the great fish "some scores of light-years in length" (177). Full of calm and joy he wallows and sports "upon the rich darkness that flows between the stars" (177). Such an epilogue can be easily interpreted as some kind of an absolution in life after death, which is in strong opposition to the Lovecraftian mechanistic materialism and his bleak "cosmicism" that minimizes humanity to mere evanescent dust. Lang, for example, claims that the conclusion is "ill suited, unfortunately, to the brutal naturalism of Peter's earlier moral disintegration" (44). In some of Lovecraft's tales, however, this kind of conclusion is not uncommon. In specific cases his characters do not "resign themselves to the ineluctable" but rather "go eagerly to their downfall" (Lévy 77). Even the exact nature of Peter's spiritual afterlife is dubious, because Lovecraft himself sometimes describes similar modes of existence as being in another dimension with non-Euclidean geometry.

If we consider *Dagon* as a novel primarily compounded out of the two contextual levels, first Gothic—closely connected with a Christian pervasive sense of original sin—and the second bleakly Lovecraftian, then in the breathtaking epilogue Chappell unexpectedly produces a third level. This third level of meaning is radically new because in its context, a human being achieves something quite apart from both former world views. Peter is not deluded into religiously worshipping an alien intelligence, nor does he go insane from his realization of the inhuman core of the cosmos. He experienced the authentic god Dagon, so different from the biblical pagan deity of his sermon; instead of perishing from the weight of that knowledge, he has found the ultimate creative freedom of metaphor.

And so, analogous to the Great Cthulhu, Peter Leland is dead but still dreaming in the infinite space between the stars, the resemblance of an immortal poet. Nevertheless, unlike Lovecraft's protagonists, he helps to fill the cosmos with meaning. In a sense, he has ascended into heaven.

Works Cited

Bizzaro, Patrick, ed. *More Lights than One: On the Fiction of Fred Chappell.* Baton Rouge: Louisiana State UP, 2004. Print.

Chappell, Fred. *Dagon.* New York: Harcourt, 1968. Print.

Clabough, Casey Howard. *Experimentation and Versatility: The Early Novels and Short Fiction of Fred Chappell.* Macon: Mercer UP, 2005. Print.

Dillard, R. H. W. "Letters from a Distant Lover: The Novels of Fred Chappell." Bizzaro 6–26. Print.

Gray, Richard. *Southern Aberrations: Writers of the American South and the Problems of Regionalism.* Baton Rouge: Louisiana State UP, 2000. Print.

Hovis, George. "Darker Vices and Nearly Incomprehensible Sins: The Fate of Poe in Fred Chappell's Early Novels." Bizzaro 28–50. Print.

Joshi, S. T. *I am Providence: The Life and Times of H. P. Lovecraft.* New York: Hippocampus P, 2010. Print.

Lang, John. *Understanding Fred Chappell.* Columbia: U of South Carolina P, 2000. Print.

Lévy, Maurice. *Lovecraft: A Study in the Fantastic.* Trans. S. T. Joshi. Detroit: Wayne State UP, 1988. Print.

Lovecraft, H. P. "Beyond the Wall of Sleep." *The Thing on the Doorstep and Other Weird Stories.* Ed. S. T. Joshi. London: Penguin, 2002. 11–20. Print.

___. "The Call of Cthulhu." *The Call of Cthulhu and Other Weird Stories.* Ed. S. T. Joshi. London: Penguin, 2002. 139–169. Print.

___. "The Picture in the House." *The Call of Cthulhu and Other Weird Stories.* Ed. S. T. Joshi. London: Penguin, 2002. 34–42. Print.

Mosig, Dirk W. "H. P. Lovecraft: Myth-Maker." *Dissecting Cthulhu.* Ed. S. T. Joshi. Lakeland: Miskatonic River P, 2011. 13–21. Print.

Price, Robert M. "Lovecraft's 'Artificial Mythology.'" *An Epicure in the Terrible: A Centennial Anthology of Essays in Honor of H. P. Lovecraft.* Ed. David E. Schultz and S. T. Joshi. Rutherford: Fairleigh Dickinson UP, 1991. 247–56. Print.

Waugh, Robert H. "Dr. Margaret Murray and H. P. Lovecraft: The Witch-Cult in New England." *A Century Less a Dream: Selected Criticism on H. P. Lovecraft.* Ed. Scott Connors. Holikong: Wildside, 2002. 112–23. Print.

Gothic Fear and Anxiety in Cormac McCarthy's *Suttree* _____

Christopher J. Walsh

Much like the history of Southern Gothic as a distinct imaginative and critical practice, Cormac McCarthy's *Suttree* (1979) is ambiguous, fragmentary, and elusive. Southern Gothic is a contested discourse, and it is hard to apply a singular, all-encompassing definition to it (as other contributions to this study have insightfully acknowledged). Is it strictly rural, or can it have urban manifestations? How can we speak of a Gothic tradition in a culture bereft of ruins, mysterious Catholic practices, and a decayed and decadent aristocracy? Does Southern Gothic have to engage with the legacy of slavery in order to be legitimate, or can it explore the repressed racial nightmare of the South (and the nation for that matter) in other ways? How can a text be haunted when it is produced from within a cultural narrative that stresses prosperity— "rationality"—and a belief that the past and the future can be shaped according to the desires of the individual will?

All of these questions are encountered when trying to formulate an approach to what exactly is meant by Southern Gothic. If the Gothic seeks to distort hierarchies, interrogate cultural assumptions, and destabilize categories of order and identity, then a good case can be made that *Suttree* is a fine representation of Southern Gothic. But *Suttree* itself is something of a relic, a text that was published in 1979 but had been composed, left alone, and returned to over a number of years (it is the fourth of McCarthy's early Appalachian novels, and McCarthy had been working on it while the other three were published). Yet for its author and its central protagonist, *Suttree* is a novel of departures; after its publication, McCarthy moved west (physically and imaginatively), where critical and commercial success eventually followed. McCarthy's first three Southern/Appalachian novels—*The Orchard Keeper* (1965),*Outer Dark* (1968), and *Child of God* (1973)—received very little attention, so the author (much like many of his characters) lit out for the territories where popular book clubs and film adaptations followed. All of this might suggest that the Southern Gothic mode had perhaps exhausted itself for McCarthy.

The Gothic and McCarthy seem like a natural fit, however. Many Gothic novels frustrate when one attempts to impose singular readings upon them, and this is certainly true of McCarthy and his multifaceted style. So while *Suttree* may not be an archetypal Gothic novel, it does contain a series of Gothic motifs and themes. Indeed, it is useful to bear in mind Catherine Spooner's application of the Gothic to works like *Dubliners* (1914), *The Waste Land* (1922), and *The Heart of Darkness* (1899) as it is very much true of *Suttree*: "Gothic becomes, rather than the determining feature of the text, one tool among many employed in the service of conjuring up interior terrors. These texts contain Gothic incidents, episodes, imagery, moments, traces: Gothic, we might say, haunts them" (40). It is therefore my intention here to demonstrate how the following themes from the novel reveal how Gothic does indeed haunt the text: McCarthy's contribution to the development of the urban Southern Gothic tradition; his use of the uncanny and a series of hauntings that center on the chief protagonist's fear of death; the entrenched Oedipus conflict between father and son; and his depiction of the abject, principally via the character of Gene Harrogate. Susan Castillo has insightfully observed that in Southern Gothic the "unpalatable realities the South has repressed in its own vision of itself" are articulated (487). In *Suttree*, this is most memorably achieved via the portrayal of Mother She, an elderly African American character who (according to significant critical responses) either liberates Suttree through her counterhegemonic powers or is a crudely reductive character who bespeaks Suttree's (and his culture's) racial terror. Finally, this essay will consider whether it can be claimed that a semblance of order is restored at novel's close, although it is not achieved (as in many conventional Gothic texts) through an endorsement of existing cultural and social power structures, but through a repudiation and flight from them.

A familiarity with the *Suttree*'s plot is necessary to understand and discuss the novel's themes. The central protagonist in McCarthy's fourth novel is Cornelius Suttree, the son of a respected attorney who eschews his family's privileged (although certainly not aristocratic) background, including a university education, for what he sees as a more authentic lifestyle in Knoxville, Tennessee, where he lives along the city's destitute riverfront community in the early 1950s. What principally drives Suttree's denial of his domestic family circumstances is not simply a nascent oppositional or perhaps even emerging artistic sensibility. Instead, it is his crippling fear of death—instilled by the knowledge of his stillborn twin—that propels him on his dread- and death-infused Gothic or existential quest to find an authentic way of living. Importantly, these attempts to permanently shake off this "dread other" result in a series of passages in which Sigmund Freud's notion of the uncanny clearly functions, which makes a vital contribution to the novel's Gothic credentials. Fred Botting maintains that many Gothic texts are narratives of transgression, and *Suttree* certainly adheres to this paradigm as it is a novel full of them.

One such example (and a cause of a Gothic-like anguish in many readers of *Suttree*) is that McCarthy transgresses conventional novelistic patterns of ordering, linearity, and resolution. The novel can be read as a kind of bildungsroman, but it is not entirely clear what kind of new knowledge Suttree receives at novel's end (although I will try to prove otherwise in this discussion). *Suttree* can be read as picaresque in parts, but these scenes remain somewhat fragmentary and disjointed, never to coalesce in a definite sense of things being resolved. Suttree appears to challenge notions of power, control, and order in the book, but it is never clear what he would replace them with. Finally, it is often difficult for clarity to be established in a novel where inanimate phenomena compete for attention on an almost equal footing with the characters who can be attributed with agency (although this can often be difficult to assign in any McCarthy novel).

Suttee and the Urban Gothic Tradition

Setting and spatial representations are of great importance in any novel, but it can be argued that they have a heightened importance in Gothic texts. Many foundational Gothic texts are located in what were considered remote or exotic European locations where mysterious Roman Catholic practices and customs were prevalent. Archetypal Gothic locations include isolated or ruined castles, remote graveyards, and all manner of desolate and decaying physical structures that engender feelings of imprisonment and claustrophobia. As the genre developed, spatial representations became more sophisticated—as in the ideological negotiation between civilized centers and wilderness spaces in novels such as *Frankenstein* (1818) and *Dracula* (1897)—as authors operating within the Gothic mode looked for more subtle ways to interrogate cultural anxieties in their work.

One of the most significant contributions to the development of the urban Gothic was made via the depiction of London in Robert Louis Stevenson's *The Strange Case of Dr Jekyll and Mr Hyde* (1886). Stevenson's novella initiated a tradition of writing about the city that collapsed boundaries and that made the savage and civilized, order and disorder, acceptable and unacceptable exist in a location (nineteenth-century London) that was supposedly the epitome of reason and order. One of the most enduring examples of the Gothic in London to be found in Stevenson's novella comes when he describes Soho as like "some city in a nightmare" (23), and this nightmarish urban atmosphere pervades McCarthy's text. As the critic Robert Mighall has observed, Stevenson's spatial representations contemporized how the mode retained the capacity to horrify as he "dispenses entirely with the distancing devices of the traditional Gothic," situating the text in the London of his day and locating "horror *within* a respectable individual" (Introduction xvii). McCarthy achieves a similar effect in his novel, and the representations of the city make a significant contribution to the novel's Gothic atmosphere.

The material historical realities that account for this key spatial representation also feed into the novel's Gothic credentials, as this articulates a deeper lying cultural and indeed political concern. The majority of the urban scenes in the novel (and the place of Suttree's residence) is the waterfront communities of Knoxville and the district of McAnally Flats, a densely populated area of the city that was home to hundreds of displaced workers, petty criminals, and scores of marginalized figures. Much of the displacement was caused by the Tennessee Valley Authority (TVA) decision to flood substantial portions of traditional rural areas surrounding the city to protect against further flooding, but this of course had the effect that hundreds of families were displaced from their traditional homes. Many of the displaced fled to Knoxville and to riverfront districts and communities such as McAnally Flats. The abject poverty that existed in these precincts presents a very real social problem, and the squalid physical conditions of these areas juxtaposes with Suttree's internalized existential, death-haunted battle.

The Gothic motifs associated with McCarthy's spatial representations are announced in the novel's prologue. Indeed, the overtly Gothic feel evoked in the prologue (it is significant that it stands *outside* of the text proper as the world it depicts falls under increasing civic control as the narrative develops) will erode as the narrative develops. The "*ruder forms*" announced will not be able to survive—they stand outside of textual and civic control here (McCarthy 5). The italics of the prologue also evoke a sense of mystery as they are temporally ambiguous, and the narrative consciousness works to create a sense of disquiet that surrounds this "*encampment of the damned*," this "*city constructed on no known paradigm*" (3). The Gothic seems to have found an ideal spatial site here, as it is as jumbled, slippery, and elusive as the imaginative practice itself. Awareness of spatial and geographical representations in Gothic texts is vital, as it allows readers to see, in a genre where psychological criticism dominates, other districts or memories that a culture seeks to repress or deny (Mighall, *Geography* x).

It is worth quoting from a remarkable, if somewhat lengthy, passage from the prologue here. If an archetypal feature of the Gothic is taken as a presentation of death- and dread-infused landscapes, then the prologue to *Suttree* undoubtedly fulfills that criteria. Before being introduced to the central protagonist, readers are presented with an anachronistic city setting (one that seems so unlike what would be expected of a 1950s American city, even by Southern standards) that is haunted and shadowed by the presence of death itself as a psychological terror. Moreover, the combination of archaic rhetoric (*maugre, muerngers, carder, deadcart*) with personal address (*Dear friend*) makes readers somehow complicit in the metaphysical and social hauntings that are about to unfold. There is also a degree of irony in the final warning offered by the narrative consciousness here as Suttree does relentlessly dwell on this phantom knowledge (i.e., his awareness of his own mortality) in a series of morbid, hyperaware meditations. It is also symbolic that the narrator draws attention to the *righteous* who look down on this vista *from carriage or car*, as they have an elevated optical and moral position it would seem, sealed safely above the uncivilized scene below them. It is also notable that Suttree walks whenever he can in the novel, another Gothic rebuke to prevailing cultural norms:

> We are come to a world within the world. In these alien reaches, these maugre sinks and interstitial wastes that the righteous see from carriage and car another life dreams. Illshapen or black or deranged, fugitive of all order, strangers in everyland. The night is quiet. Like a camp before battle. The city beset by a thing unknown and will it come from forest or sea? The muerngers have walled the pale, the gates are shut, but lo the thing's inside and can you guess his shape? Where's he's kept or what's the counter of his face? Is he a weaver, bloody shuttle shot through a timewarp, a carder of souls from the world's nap? Or a hunter with hounds or do bones horses draw his deadcart through the streets and does he call his trade to each? Dear friend he is not to be dwelt upon for it is by just suchwise that he's invited in. (4–5)

The Gothic elements evident in the prologue's spatial descriptions of the city and its bedraggled citizens are maintained in the text proper. Many aspects of the novel's Gothicism can be attributed to a deeper exploration of psychological, cultural, and indeed racial anxieties, but certain (albeit limited) descriptions of the city are on the brink of lapsing into something resembling Gothic local color or Gothic by numbers. This is particularly evident in a series of scenes set around Knoxville's Market House, a center for commercial exchange and a seeming magnet for all manner of grotesque characters. Although not the real concern, even the commercial practices conducted within the Market House (predicated on barter and exchange and not completely dependent on a cash economy) are somewhat Gothic; they are out of kilter with the larger cultural and economic narrative of the 1950s, which witnessed the robust development of advertising, marketization, and corporate hegemony. Yet McCarthy presents a tableau of "maimed humanity," a gallery of grotesques where "every other face [is] goitered, twisted, tubered with some excrescence" (67). Once again, readers are drawn to McCarthy's powerfully evocative language, especially "goitered" and "tubered," in this passage, which conjures images of swollen, distorted physical forms that blur the boundary between normal and abnormal, human and inhuman—all of which destabilizes identities and categories of order, a hallmark of Gothic texts. It is also significant that Suttree chooses to associate with a case of "derelicts, miscreants, pariahs, poltroons . . . and other assorted and felonious debauchees," as "the bodies of savages, criminals and degenerates provided a new location for the unwelcome past to survive into and threaten the civilised present" (McCarthy 457; Mighall, *Geography* xxiii).

Many discussions of the novel examine how the urban spatial representations are, quite literally, full of rubbish. This is incredibly significant for Gothic readings of the text as it not only indicates much about the historical conditions of Knoxville at the time, but it also anticipates how spatial representations can be read within Julia Kristeva's notion of the abject—a theory that has illuminated (and arguably even reinvigorated) many recent critical discussions about the Gothic. Kristeva's theory of the abject is principally announced in her *Powers of Horror: An Essay on Abjection* (1982), and although undoubtedly complex, they are worth considering here. The abject can be traced to a subject's innate desire to establish an independent identity that is separate from the maternal but, at the same time, includes a wish to return to the state of non-identity in which the subject is half inside and half outside the womb. For Kristeva, the abject is "a border; abjection is above all ambiguity" (9). Abjection is therefore associated with waste (in physical, moral, social, or cultural terms) and with things that are marginalized and banished. Crucially, this banishment is notable because it presents a challenge to established order and hierarchies, and *Suttree* offers such challenges throughout.

The subject of the abject can be revisited when examining the character of Gene Harrogate, but for Gothic representations that align with spatial readings, the abject enables better understanding of the trash motif. It should come as no surprise that this theme is announced in the prologue description of the river, which is full with "*dread waste*" and "*fecal matter*"; the reference to things expelled from the body is significant here as its abject status represents a challenge to order and stability (McCarthy 4). The river in the prologue is overloaded with discarded material to the extent that it is described as being "*afreight with the past*" as it flows through this abject area of the city (4). This abject description of a natural phenomenon also feeds into a more conventional Gothic theme as Suttree will struggle to escape from the burden of his psychological and familial past throughout the novel—a struggle that is conducted against urban vistas replete with "slagheaps of trash" (81). This layering of rhetorical detail adds to the impression of the city as a labyrinth that resists attempts to order its spaces rationally. These environmental details, particularly the "attention to filth and stench," is, for Mighall, "an important characteristic of the Urban Gothic Mode" (*Geography* 66).

So far, discussions of how spatial representations of the novel contribute to its Gothicism have centered on urban scenes and passages. Although these undoubtedly dominate, Suttree's wilderness sojourn needs attention because it contains a series of abject and oppositional images; these images foreshadow the deranged phantasmagoric passages that McCarthy creates at novel's close during Suttree's near-fatal duel with typhoid fever. Suttree's wilderness trip takes him into the mountains surrounding Knoxville and eventually to North Carolina, but it is significant that he sets out for unmapped territories as these become increasingly scarce as the novel progresses. This relative wilderness excursion is replete with abject and carnivalesque figures that parade before Suttree—including "squalid merrymakers" and, somewhat disturbingly, a "gross and blueblack foetus clopping along in brogues and a toga" (McCarthy 287–88). Free from the claustrophobic and overtly grotesque city environment, Suttree is able to glimpse how his identity will be stabilized and though "everything had fallen from him. He could scarce tell where his being ended or the world began nor did he care" (286). This is significant as it hints at a synthesis that eludes Suttree in the urban setting; the carnival motif is worthy of attention as, in the theory of the Gothic and grotesque (especially in the work of Mikhail Bakhtin), "the carnival meant reconnecting with the earth and earthiness," which Suttree accomplishes in the passage above (Hurley 142).

Spatial representations are vital in adding to *Suttree*'s Gothic credentials. The prologue announces how depictions of the city of Knoxville will be haunted by a palpable sense of death, a macabre shadow that will follow Suttree throughout the narrative. The overt Gothicism is alleviated to an extent when Suttree makes his wilderness sojourn, but even this is temporary as his increasingly hallucinatory imaginings are filled with abject and carnivalesque imagery. Nevertheless, what is clear is how McCarthy inscribes all of the significant spatial settings in the novel with a distinctly Gothic flavor.

Suttree and the Uncanny/Hauntings

In addition to the significant contribution that Kristeva's theory of the abject has made toward contemporary approaches to the Gothic, another foundational text that has made an immeasurable contribution to the understanding of the inner workings of the Gothic mode is Sigmund Freud's "The Uncanny," which was published in 1919. Principally structured around a reading of E. T. A. Hoffmann's 1817 short story "The Sandman," Freud's essay can be read as a Gothic text itself since it denies easy categorization as it merges Freud's interest in aesthetics and psychoanalysis. It is concerned with returns, disturbances, and phenomena that unsettle whatever constitutes reality for a subject. As Hugh Haughton observes, "psychoanalysis after the First World War increasingly conjures up a Gothic closet, an uncanny double, at the heart of modernity," and Haughton maintains that, despite its slipperiness, Freud's essay can be read as a "theoretical commentary on the power of strangeness" (xlii–xliii).

Two aspects of Freud's theory of the uncanny reveal how motifs of the Southern Gothic play a key role throughout *Suttree*. These are his notion of *das Unheimlich* (the unhomely) and the fragmentation of the individual psyche when a sense of the uncanny is experienced. This results in a fear of the double or some kind of deeply unsettling haunting presence, both of which afflict Suttree. For Freud, "the term 'uncanny' (*unheimlich*) applies to everything that was intended to remain secret, hidden away, and has come into the open" (132). Of course, the opposite of *unheimlich* is *das Heimlich* (the homely), and Suttree's progress through the narrative can be read as one long flight from the home and all that it represents, even if the central point of resolution in the novel (such as it exists) forces him to confront these deep-rooted anxieties. He flees from the stable, respectable middle-class home of his father and lives in a houseboat, the most undomesticated kind of existence he can possibly achieve; there are numerous scenes in the novel where he eschews even this liminal form of domesticity (as in his sojourn to the mountains or when Suttree wakes up following a night of wild drinking).

So Suttree is unhoused and unhomely for the majority of the text, and a main cause of his experience of the uncanny can be attributed to his fear of the double, which Freud regards as "an uncanny harbinger of death" (142). Many foundational texts of the Gothic canon—one primarily thinks of *Frankenstein* and *Dracula*—provide overt representations of some kind of monstrous double that obliquely articulate deeper cultural and social concerns; in *Suttree*, however, the double relates to a morbid fascination with death imprinted on his psyche from childhood. This is primarily related to the knowledge of his stillborn twin *and* his internalized longing for an archaic, mystical insight, which is denied by the prevailing rationalism of his contemporary circumstances. This conforms to David Punter's conception of the uncanny as it can be attributed to phenomena that hearken back to "something archaic, something which indeed lies within our psyche but at a level so deep that we know it only phantasmally," and the uncanny sends reminders from "a world which antecedes us" (131, 136). Thus, Suttree's psychic trauma from childhood is conjoined with his acute awareness of an emptiness at the heart of modernity; both contribute to an uncanny sense of some kind of double and a sense of self that, as recognized by Freud, has become "duplicated, divided and interchanged" (142). Of course, the distinction from earlier Gothic texts is that these figures are not personified in some kind of supernatural form and instead haunt Suttree in more subtle, unsettling, and distinctly psychological ways. If the Gothic can be read as a narrative of returns, then Suttree's experience of the uncanny can be directly linked to this phenomenon.

One final aspect of Freud's conception of the uncanny helps to illuminate McCarthy's novel. Freud claims that the uncanny "is represented by anything to do with dead, dead bodies, revenants, spirits and ghosts" (148), and *Suttree* is a novel full of them. As already seen in the prologue, death itself has a palpable presence in the novel, and the text proper opens with a suicide victim being fished from the river. The novel is littered with dead bodies and all manner of things—both animate and inanimate—in various forms of degeneration and decay. The uncanny aspect of such passages is also enhanced by McCarthy's penchant for layering rhetorical detail so that inanimate matter competes for narrative attention with the figures who supposedly retain some kind of agency, a narrative trope that has an unsettling effect on readers and characters alike. The following passage exemplifies this technique; the narrative consciousness follows Harrogate on one of his walks through the city, but his perspective is nonexistent as the narrator draws attention to the inanimate matter that surrounds him. Punctuation is used sparingly, but detail after detail assails the reader:

> Harrogate came batting his way through the jungle of kudzu that overhung the bluffs above the river until he found a red clay gully of a path going down the slope. He followed along through lush growths of poison ivy and past enormous mummy shapes of vinestrangled trees, banks of honeysuckle dusted in the ocher, into a brief cindery wood in which grew black sumacs, pokeweeds gorged with sooty drainage. . . .
>
> . . . By and by he came upon two fishbutchers slick with blood by an old retaining wall, holding a goodsized carp between them. . . . They stayed their gorestained hands a moment to study him while the fish bowed and shuddered. (McCarthy 91)

The knowledge of Suttree's haunting is announced at an early stage in the narrative when his uncle John visits him in his houseboat. Domestic or conventional familial scenes are a rare thing indeed in McCarthy, and this is no different; it is a tense exchange compounded by John's tipsiness and Suttree's disdain for what he sees as his uncle's simplistic understanding of his father's class biases and social pretensions. The exchange is significant, however, because it is the first instance where Suttree's stillborn twin is alluded to, the knowledge of which is the genesis of his psychic trauma (17). From the abject moment of his coming into the world, Suttree had, from a young age, "already begun to sicken at the slow seeping of life" (136). The narrative consciousness reveals the highly Gothic nightmarish terrors that used to afflict Suttree at night as a child: "He himself used to wake in terror to find whole congregations of the uninvited attending his bed, protean figures slouched among the room's dark corners in all multiplicity of shapes, gibbons and gargoyles, arachnoids of outrageous size" (149).

It is perhaps the knowledge of his double—a knowledge that operates at a subterranean level of his unconscious—that most unsettles Suttree's sense of selfhood and destabilizes his identity. This, of course, is an instance of the Gothic in the narrative, representing yet another moment of ghostly or spectral return, another instance where a buried life erupts to disturb the reality in which Suttree is attempting to function. This is most strikingly revealed in his isolated trip into the mountains, where he is haunted by the presence of "some doublegoer, some othersuttree" that "eluded him in these woods" (287). This persistent sense of being haunted ensures that Suttree is troubled throughout and, to return to Freud, something that should have been hidden away "has come into the open." Suttree's unconscious psychic memory and his longing for access to a deeper mystical knowledge (one that is directly opposed to the prevailing rationalism of his contemporary circumstances) ensures that there are many significant uncanny moments throughout the novel. The dissolution of the self is a central Gothic trope, and *Suttree* is not alone in tracing "the fragmentation of the unified subject, [which makes] visible the fracture lines that are always present within the formation of the post–Enlightenment subjectivity" (Baker 166).

Oedipal Trouble

Another stock motif of many Gothic texts is conflict generated between oedipal figures and their progeny in biological, cultural, or social terms. This is certainly true of *Suttree* (and many McCarthy texts for that matter, as insightfully discussed by critics such as Jay Ellis), where the central protagonist reacts against the overbearing influence of his father *and* the hegemonic patriarchal control of his own culture as represented by figures of control and authority. Much like his treatment of the uncanny, readers can see how McCarthy employs a major Gothic theme by exploring a dual process whereby the personal and the cultural, the psychological and the political, are explored using this fundamental Gothic trope.

Much like the "othersuttree," Suttree's father functions as a haunting and repressive figure throughout the narrative. Indeed his only appearance in the text is a somewhat ghostly one, and it comes via his letter to his son, which is treated with overt disdain. The letter also aligns the novel with some from the early Gothic canon; it was a common stylistic feature in these foundational texts for a mysterious letter or document to be discovered that initiated the rest of the narrative action. This is certainly true of the father's letter in *Suttree* as it very much resembles a Gothic artifact, a contemporized version of a conventional Gothic narrative that, rather than bringing the son back into the family fold, actually provides him with the mandate to continue the denial of his father's will. In the letter, it is not difficult to see how Suttree rebels against his father's smug bourgeois values and belief in his strictly empirical conception of life: "If it is life that you feel you are missing I can tell you where to find it. In the law courts, in business, in government. There is nothing occurring in the streets. Nothing but a dumbshow composed of the helpless and the impotent" (McCarthy 13–14). The irony is that the son views his father's creed as monstrous, an existence that attempts to elide by repression rather than confronting its fears and anxieties, which is what Suttree is attempting here.

Although biographical readings are not the concern here (and of course are perhaps even more fraught with danger when applied to the Gothic mode with its inherent slipperiness, which is possibly more pronounced than with other genres), the relationship between McCarthy and his father, Charles Joseph McCarthy, should briefly be considered here. McCarthy's father was a senior attorney for the TVA and was actively involved in the displacement of traditional communities by vast federally sponsored programs. Many of these purchases were conducted using the legal tactic of eminent domain, which meant that those who were moved were powerless to oppose, and it seems that McCarthy championed the cause of the dispossessed in this case, a cause that feeds the challenge to patriarchal control documented in the novel. Indeed, Jay Ellis has commented that the novel can be read as "an apology for, rather than to, the father" (147), which reveals how the anxiety related to biographical and ideological patriarchal hauntings and control feeds into the text.

While the relationship with his own father can be read within the critique of patriarchal power structures often dealt with by Gothic texts, Suttree's relationship with Ab Jones goes someway to countering the negativity. Suttree's anxieties about fatherhood have obviously been engendered by his relationship with his own father and compounded by the fact that he is an absent father to his own child, who dies in the course of the narrative. The reaction of Suttree's ex-wife and mother-in-law when he arrives at their home to attend the child's funeral tells readers all they need to know about their thoughts about his performance as a father. Yet Suttree's relationship with Ab Jones, an African American character who is marginalized by the hegemonic power structures that Suttree's father pronounces such faith in, tells readers much about his willingness to engage with the Other in society. Ab's culture (and the tradition of American Gothic for that matter) portrays him as the physical and moral personification of blackness, yet it is from Ab that Suttree learns a moral code that enables him to work through his episodes of psychological trauma. When Ab tells Suttree, "I got no use for a man piss backwards on his friends" (McCarthy 203), an authentically simple moral lesson is inculcated in Suttree, a genuine mandate for existence that is found in a subject so clinically marginalized by the world of power and control that Suttree's biological father represents.

Mother She and "Racial Terror"

While Ab Jones presents a positive treatment of culturally excluded Others, the character of Mother She poses some more difficult questions. Does she grant Suttree access to pre–Enlightenment forms of mystical knowledge through hallucinatory substances that are regarded as taboo, thereby making a significant contribution to Suttree synthesizing the knowledge of his uncanny "doublesuttree" into a unified sense of self? Or does her representation bespeak a larger cultural misogyny and fear of blackness in racial and spiritual terms?

These are indeed complex questions. What the depiction of Mother She allows readers to see is the sophisticated working out of the archetypal Gothic theme of transgression. It is, of course, problematic that Mother She is denied full agency within the novel and that she only really serves as a mystical auxiliary in Suttree's quest to heal his abject and divided Gothic subjectivity along with his sense of self; Mother She is not alone, however, in being denied full mimetic narrative agency in this overwhelmingly fragmentary text. Karissa McKoy is one of a number of critics who have remarked on this ambiguity, claiming that in one of the visions Mother She conjures "blackness appears as a nightmarish threat to the intact white self" (96). It must be acknowledged that Suttree's sense of self has *never* been intact thus far in the novel, and it is the encounter with Mother She that plays a significant role in ensuring that his divided Gothic identity is indeed ultimately reconciled.

Arguably nobody else, either individually or institutionally (certainly not the Roman Catholic Church, in whose doctrines Suttree was schooled, but which itself operates as an obsolete Gothic-style relic in the text), has attempted to "read the weathers in your heart" as Mother She does (McCarthy 424). It is impossible to argue that the most intimate, graphic descriptions of Mother She are anything but unsettling and abject, but it is through Suttree's confrontation with such an ideologically marginalized Other, an abject figure who rightly challenges its master, to borrow from Kristeva, that Suttree moves toward a reconstituted self. The descriptions of Mother She in Suttree's bizarre and hallucinatory sexual confrontation with her— in which he is threatened to be subsumed by her "shrivelled cunt puckered open like a mouth gawping"—fuse Suttree's most acute physic, maternal, and perhaps even racial fears (427). Mother She's lack of agency can be attributed to the imbalance and lack of fidelity to realistic techniques found in narratives where Gothic tropes play a key role, as opposed to bespeaking a deeper lying authorial prejudice. This graphically liminal abject moment ironically moves Suttree toward unification as opposed to dissolution, a function of the abject as outlined by Jerrold Hogle: "Whatever threatens us with anything like this betwixt-and-between, even dead-and-alive condition, Kristeva concludes, is what we throw off or 'abject' into defamiliarized manifestations, which we henceforth fear and desire because they both threaten to reengulf us and promise to return us to our primal origins" (7). This premodernistic, primal moment ultimately allows Suttree to access the forms of archaic knowledge that have been denied him elsewhere.

Gene Harrogate and the Abject

Another striking representation of an abject and marginalized character in *Suttree* is provided through the description of Gene Harrogate. Suttree's dealings with Mother She work toward reconstituting his fractured subjectivity in a troubling and racially ambiguous primal scene, but the treatment of the same theme through Harrogate is, on a superficial level at least, a more humorously subversive one. But readers should not lose sight of the ideological function of Harrogate's character as he articulates another deep-seated cultural or social anxiety (a central trope of many Gothic texts), and it relates to the novel's concern with the fate of dispossessed white working-class southerners.

Harrogate appears in a series of often-grotesque comedic scenes that seem to align him, as noted by many critics, with the subversive tradition of Southwestern humorists such as George Washington Harris. Yet, in a very unique way, his own Gothic marginalized status is announced when he is introduced in the novel as he sexually couples with a farmer's patch of watermelons (McCarthy 32). The arrest for this offense results in a stint in the workhouse and Harrogate's introduction to Suttree, and the latter serving as a kind of surrogate father despite the fact that he informs Harrogate that "you look wrong. You will always look wrong" (60). It is this very wrongness, Harrogate's almost "monstrous" quality—if monstrosity is understood in this context as a representation of all that a culture seeks to deny, categorize, and marginalize—that marks him out as a character who tells readers more about his culture's anxiety than his initial impressions may suggest.

His Gothic oppositional function is more fully realized in the scene where he attempts to blow his way into the vaults of Knoxville's banks via series of explosions and the city's system of subterranean sewage pipes. Harrogate is a character who internalizes his culture's rational narratives, particularly its emphasis on an individual's ability to achieve material success through willful self-purpose, but he lacks the social apparatus or intellectual ability to fully realize this culturally prescribed role; in other words, Harrogate offers a critique of the fate of society's dispossessed. It should come as no surprise that one of the most memorable episodes is therefore associated with waste as this underground man dismally fails to complete his task. After he detonates the series of explosions he hopes will lead to his material improvement, Harrogate is instead "engulfed feet first in a slowly moving wall of sewage, a lava neap of liquid shit and soapcurd and toilet paper from a breached main" (270). There are no archaic vocabulary choices or complex rhetorical strategies employed here as the association between Harrogate and abject forms of waste are explicitly apparent. The narrative consciousness notes that Harrogate "became without boundary to himself" when he is lost underground following these botched explosions; this symbolically confirms how one of the novel's abject, borderless, and "monstrous" characters is able, in characteristically Gothic mode, to challenge existing forms of cultural control (275).

Order Restored?

It is not easy to talk about neatly packaged, singular conclusions to Gothic texts, especially one as fragmentary as *Suttree*. Critics have discussed how some of the most foundational texts of the Gothic canon explore new sources of horror and terror, but always seek to restore order in the conclusion; indeed Allan Lloyd-Smith has observed that "Gothic tends to reinforce, if only in the novel's final pages, culturally prescribed notions of morality and propriety" (5). Other critics have noted that Gothic oscillates between revolutionary and reactionary impulses depending on the text's moment of production. So what of *Suttree*? Is order restored and linearity asserted, or does fragmentation and chaos triumph? Does it radically critique existing political and cultural hierarchies and hint at the birth of new institutions, or does it endorse the status quo?

The one area where it is clear that some kind of order has been restored is in Suttree's psyche. The dread other—the nightmare inducing "othersuttree" that has haunted him throughout—has been banished and a succession of casting-offs take place "until there was nothing left to shed," and confirmation of a fully synthesized subjectivity is confirmed when Suttree states that he has learned that "there is one Suttree and one Suttree only" (McCarthy 468, 461). And yet this is juxtaposed with the modernistic and bureaucratic transformation of the riverfront and McAnally, the very outlaw spaces that have allowed this Gothic quest to take place, as they become subject to "scenes of wholesale razing" (464).

So while the psychological battle has been won, another has not and perhaps can never be. Suttree's "dumbshow" life on the streets—the squalid Gothic existence so deplored by his father—has resulted in a psychic transformation in Suttree, but perhaps the more chilling aspect is that the coldly rational and progressive modernistic world of his father is the one that wins the cultural and spatial battle here. This raises some wider ideological questions about the novel's conclusion as Suttree (albeit watched by the hounds of death) lights out for the territories at novel's end. In doing so, he forsakes the people (or at least those who remain behind, those who are not dead, imprisoned, or geographically relocated for economic opportunities elsewhere, reasons that all reveal much about prevailing ideologies) who have enabled this transformation.

But perhaps it is this very incoherence and unevenness that makes *Suttree* a representative text of the Southern Gothic tradition. The novel is very much one of transformations and returns, in spatial, psychological, and spiritual terms. It articulates some of its culture's most deep-seated fears and anxieties and, while it perhaps falls short from a strictly ideological perspective, a case could be made that this is not really Gothic's job anyway. As Steven Bruhm maintains, the end of the novel underlines why the Gothic is still important: "We need it because the twentieth century has so forcefully taken away from us that which we once thought constituted us—a coherent psyche, a social order to which we can all pledge allegiance in good faith, a sense of justice in the universe—and that wrenching withdrawal, that traumatic experience, is vividly dramatized in the Gothic" (273). Perhaps above anything else, *Suttree* represents the adaptability and relevance of the Gothic form; its innate slipperiness, its ability to reconstitute subjectivities, is perhaps called for now more than ever in a world that is increasingly borderless, unsettled, and abject.

Works Cited

Baker, Brian. "Gothic Masculinities." Spooner and McEvoy 164–75.

Botting, Fred. *The Gothic*. Oxford: Routledge, 1996. Print.

Bruhm, Steven. "The Contemporary Gothic: Why We Need It." Hogle 259–76.

Castillo, Susan. "Flannery O'Connor." *A Companion to the Literature and Culture of the American South*. Ed. Richard Gray and Owen Robinson. Oxford: Blackwell, 2007. 486–501. Print.

Ellis, Jay. *No Place for Home: Spatial Constraint and Character Flight in the Novels of Cormac McCarthy*. New York: Routledge, 2006. Print.

Freud, Sigmund. *The Uncanny*. Trans. David McLintock. London: Penguin, 2003. Print.

Haughton, Hugh. Introduction. *The Uncanny*. By Sigmund Freud. London: Penguin, 2003. vii–lx.

Hogle, Jerrold E., ed. *The Cambridge Companion to Gothic Fiction*. Cambridge: Cambridge UP, 2002. Print.

___. Introduction. Hogle 1–20.

Hurley, Kelly. "Abject and Grotesque." Spooner and McEvoy 137–46.

Kristeva, Julia. *Powers of Horror: An Essay on Abjection*. Trans. Leon S. Roudiez. New York: Columbia UP, 1982. Print.

Lloyd-Smith, Allan. *American Gothic Fiction*. London: Continuum, 2005. Print.

McCarthy, Cormac. *Suttree.* New York: Vintage, 1992. Print.

McKoy, Karissa. "Whiteness and the 'Subject' of Waste: The Art of Slumming in *Suttree.*" *Cormac McCarthy Journal Special Issue*: Suttree 5.1 (2005): 85–99. Print.

Mighall, Robert. *A Geography of Victorian Gothic Fiction: Mapping Histories Nightmares*. Oxford: Oxford UP, 1999. Print.

___. Introduction. The Strange Case of Dr Jekyll and Mr Hyde *and Other Tales of Terror.* By Robert Louis Stevenson. London: Penguin, 2003. Print.

Punter, David. "The Uncanny." *The Routledge Companion to the Gothic*. Spooner and McEvoy 129–36.

Spooner, Catherine. "Gothic in the Twentieth Century." Spooner and McEvoy 38–47. Print.

Spooner, Catherine, and Emma McEvoy, eds. *The Routledge Companion to the Gothic*. Oxford: Routledge, 2007. Print.

Stevenson, Robert Louis. The Strange Case of Dr Jekyll and Mr Hyde *and Other Tales of Terror.* London: Penguin, 2003. Print.

"Anything dead coming back to life hurts"[1]: The Double Murder of *Beloved*

Sharon Decker

Toni Morrison's fifth novel is difficult. From the subject matter to the violent, vivid, evocative language to the fragmented narrative structure, *Beloved* (1987) is wrenching. These elements, along with the novel's exploration of historical and social tensions, are the reasons why Morrison's work lends itself so well to the Gothic style. The novel contains several Gothic conventions: a haunted house, a ghost, incarceration, supernatural events, embedded texts, and multiple narrators. Morrison also uses *Beloved* to explore several cultural and social anxieties, a staple of the Gothic form: the anxiety of motherhood, of family, of identity, of community, and of freedom. What is most interesting about Morrison's use of the Gothic, though, is how she collapses binaries in many, if not all, of these areas, ultimately creating a work that celebrates elements from its Gothic forerunners, such as Horace Walpole and Mary Shelley, and that helps define American Gothic as it continues to move forward into its own space.

One of the reasons Morrison wrote *Beloved* was to tap into what she calls "the national amnesia" regarding the horrors of slavery (qtd. in Angelo 68). She attacks this subject slowly, disjointedly, having her characters unearth the trials that they have undergone at the hands of slave owners through the process of "rememory." Although many of her characters insist upon forgetting, Morrison compels them to remember, forcefully reclaiming and repositioning slavery, and effectively blurs the lines between fiction and history, imagination and reality. In doing so, Morrison is able to expose the amnesia, to open the cultural consciousness, and to dedicate *Beloved* to the "Sixty million and more" who have been suppressed in the vaults of memory. The fragmented form of the Gothic proves instrumental for Morrison; the disjointed narrative enables her to show the gaps in the recognition of slavery and to show the impossibility of re-creating a coherent whole when so many have been erased. Fragmentation is also of use because the distance it creates allows readers breathing room to explore the atrocities of families destroyed, bodies mutilated, maternity shunned, and babies split from ear to ear. The gaps provide space for readers to digest the enormity of the bloody collective consciousness that is American slavery.

Gothic Elements

From the very opening lines, Morrison establishes *Beloved* as a ghost tale worthy of J. S. Le Fanu, with a ghost, supernatural events, shattered families, and anxious characters:

> 124 was spiteful. Full of a baby's venom. The women in the house knew it and so did the children. For years, each put up with the spite in his own way, but by 1873, Sethe and her daughter Denver were its only victims. The grandmother, Baby Suggs, was dead, and the sons, Howard and Buglar, had run away by the time they were thirteen years old—as soon as merely looking in a mirror shattered it (that was the signal for Buglar); as soon as two tiny hand prints appeared in the cake (that was it for Howard). (3)

In these few lines, readers encounter the four main characters and are able to sense their daily struggles: Sethe and Denver, a mother and daughter trapped by an unknown force; the angry, vengeful baby, strong enough to scare off teenage boys and turn grown women into "victims;" and 124, a "spiteful" house. This carefully crafted paragraph also reveals the current boundaries in the household. 124 does not welcome men. It separates the women and the children. And it has removed Baby Suggs, the woman who fostered community until 124 drove that notion out of Baby Suggs's very soul: "Baby Suggs had danced in the sunlight. Before 124 and everybody in it had closed down, veiled over and shut away; before it had become the plaything of spirits and the home of the chafed" (Morrison 86–87).

Beginning the novel in medias res, Morrison does not indicate why the characters are so frightened and trapped. As the novel unfolds, readers enter a world of horror on many levels, entering characters' lives and, through flashbacks and interspersed narratives, following them over the course of several decades. The story focuses on the tale of Sethe, a mother of four, convicted of infanticide for killing her "crawling already" baby (Morrison 93). Sethe now lives a straightforward existence, refusing to confront many things from her past. She and her daughter, Denver, have been ostracized by the community; they live in 124 surrounded by the baby ghost's palpable anger. Paul D, Sethe's friend from Sweet Home, the plantation where many of the novel's wrenching scenes occur, turns up on 124's doorstep and battles with the baby ghost's spirit. Instead of listening to Paul D's cries—"Leave the place alone! Get the hell out! . . . She got enough without you" (18)—the ghost crystallizes into the human form of what can only be called Beloved, the young child Sethe murdered many years ago. Beloved proceeds to run Paul D out of 124, captivate and almost obliterate Sethe, force Denver to enter society to save her mother from the ghost's clutches, and, most importantly, give all of the characters space to reflect upon the experiences they have repressed in order to survive.

Given that readers are faced with a murdered child who turns into a vengeful ghost before manifesting as walking flesh, many focus on Beloved when discussing this novel. But that would be to ignore the power of 124 itself. As in many Gothic tales, the house is a character. While not as grand as Walpole's Otranto, as incestuous as Edgar Allan Poe's Usher, or as vicious as Shirley Jackson's Hill House, 124 is worthy of landing on the list of notable haunted houses in Gothic fiction. Denver is very aware of its status: "Denver approached the house, regarding it, as she always did, as a person rather than a structure" (Morrison 29). When she moved in, Baby Suggs had reconfigured 124 so that the back door was permanently shut; it was her attempt to ensure that the past—of slaves having to enter through a back door, of runaways sneaking in or out attempting to escape the Fugitive Slave Acts, of servants not allowed on the front porch with the owners—would no longer exist metaphorically or physically. The ineffectiveness of Baby Suggs's gesture should not be surprising, however, for one of the main anxieties in Gothic literature is the anxiety of the past. In *Beloved*, that anxiety crystallizes as everyone's pasts insidiously creep in, through 124's *front* door, and through all of the characters' memories.

Another aspect of 124 worth noting is its very name. The house is steeped in Sethe's deed, for she has killed her third child. It is this baby ghost who comes to reclaim the house and her mother, taking her place with her siblings—the third of four children in a 1-2-3-4 sibling pattern. The house has gone from the "cheerful, buzzing house where Baby Suggs, holy, loved, cautioned, fed, chastised, and soothed" (Morrison 86–87) to a house consumed by spirits, turning against all men in its quest for mother love. Even their male dog is destroyed by the house: "the baby's spirit picked up Here Boy and slammed him into the wall hard enough to break two of his legs and dislocate his eye, so hard he went into convulsions and chewed up his tongue" (12). The missing "3" of 124, the same unholy ghost who forced out Baby Suggs, only wants the female trinity: Sethe, Denver, and Beloved.

Even the very owners of 124, the Bodwins, are worthy of skepticism. While they have clearly helped many slaves, their motive is troubling: they had "goods and gear for runaways, because they hated slavery worse than they hated slaves" (Morrison 137). Denver is rather shocked to discover a statue of a black child in the Bodwins' house, "with his mouth full of money" and the words "At Yo Service" painted at the base (255). Susan Bowers raises another concern about the owners, noting that when Mr. Bodwin drives toward 124 at the novel's end, he is so transfixed by the site of a naked Beloved on the porch, that he does not realize Sethe is coming at him with an ice pick. Bodwin had been reminiscing about the "precious things" that he had buried at 124, and Bowers suggests that he equates Beloved with his "treasure," implying the beautiful black woman is viewed by Bodwin as his possession (Morrison 259; Bowers 41–42). Such representations are just one of the ways Morrison grounds her fictitious story in the historical nastiness that is slavery.

124's haunting by Beloved blurs the line between life and death. Beloved, the undead, is the living representation of the fear that the past can resurface. The narrator's description of Ella's fears eloquently voices everyone's: "Ella didn't like the idea of past errors taking possession of the present" (Morrison 156). This Gothic trope works brilliantly in the novel on two levels: as the tale of a family struggling with its own demons and of a nation struggling with its own past. The repressed memories of Sethe, Paul D, Beloved, and many others provide the channel for Morrison to wade into the pool from which the specter of Beloved rises. These repressed memories ultimately make "readers to shift their focus away from the fantastic elements like the haunted house and the ghost toward the 'real' gothic elements of the text: slavery itself and those who systematically perpetuated it" (Spaulding 63).

Fragments and Memories

Beloved is a series of digressions. The novel is composed of flashbacks, embedded narratives, songs, colloquial conversations, narrative interruptions, and small sections of poetry. In other words, it is not a coherent, linear form, but rather many pieces of many forms interconnected to form a stunningly, painfully, evocatively beautiful whole. This fragmented composition in some ways evokes the older, meandering Gothics in which digressions were an important part of the narratives. Digressions allow readers to inhabit the spaces in the stories where their minds can wander. A singular clear line would not allow readers space to explore ideas, but just carry them forward (just as Sethe had been doing with her life from the time of Beloved's murder to her reappearance). Marilyn Sanders Mobley explores time as nonlinear, explaining that Morrison changes the slave narrative with this technique: "*Beloved* meanders through time, sometimes circling back, other times moving vertically, spirally out of time and down into space. Indeed, Morrison's text challenges the Western notion of linear time that informs American history and the slave narratives" (192). Mobley's idea augments the notion of fragmentation. By not presenting things in a linear way, Morrison gives those unfamiliar with the deeper horrors of slavery time to slow down, connect, process—understand—the tragedies laid out in her pages.

Fragments, little pieces of the narrative that force the reader to connect, make the most sense with Morrison's topic; indeed, the piece *must* be fragmented if for no other reason than the history of slavery is fragmented. Too many of the "sixty million" have been removed. In order for the text to work, the fragments have to come together, combine, just as Beloved did. But if it were to cohere in a clear, linear narrative, it would be too harsh. Beloved-as-form is too much to handle. This tension is evident in the text. Beloved-in-fragments when she is haunting 124 is at least something that can be dealt with. But when Beloved materializes, when the full reality of Sethe's actions stand in front of her, the tenuous balance of 124's inhabitants is thrown into chaos.

Sethe is not the only one afraid to piece her narrative together: Paul D, Halle, and several others struggle valiantly to hide in those narrative gaps in order not to face their past actions or, as is often the case, their inactions. Paul D relies upon his "tobacco tin lodged in his chest," believing "nothing in this world could pry it open"; the figurative space to hide his memories of "Alfred, Georgia, Sixo, Schoolteacher, Halle, his brothers, Sethe, Mister, the taste of iron, the sight of butter, the smell of hickory, notebook paper" (Morrison 113) is shut up as tight as Paul D can make it, for when it opens, Paul D turns to drinking and running. He cannot face his fears alone.

Halle, Sethe's husband at Sweet Home and the father of her four children, is similar to Paul D. Halle understands the value of freedom, but he also knows the horrors of slavery. Halle tries to live in the gaps, to even rewrite the gaps, by working extra hours to buy freedom for his mother, Baby Suggs. But when the reality of his lack of authorship over his own life becomes clear—when Halle realizes he will never be able to purchase freedom for himself, his wife, and his four kids—he begins to splinter. Clearly a smart man, Halle is capable of finding the time to work extra for his mother, to learn arithmetic, and to plan an escape. But when the fragments come together and Halle sees that, no matter what he does, he cannot protect all the members of his family, he snaps. The day Halle views Schoolteacher instructing two young boys to hold Sethe down and take her milk irreparably changes Halle. As Paul D later tells Sethe,

> You said they stole your milk. I never knew what it was that messed [Halle] up. That was it, I guess. All I knew was that something broke in him. Not a one of them years of Saturdays, Sundays, and nighttime extra never touched him. But whatever he saw go on in that barn that day broke him like a twig.

The honest, full reality is simply too much to bear, and Halle ends up "sitting by the churn. He had butter all over his face" (Morrison 68–69). The white men finally break Halle's spirit, and Halle ends up with his identity, his face, covered with something belonging to slave owners that is a color of their own.

Morrison seems to imply through these examples that the reality of slavery needs to be gathered from the fragments. She does not want the past buried: Baby Suggs and Mr. Bodwin try to do that, and one ends up dead and the other is almost slain by an ice pick. Instead, Morrison suggests that the veil over the stories and memories of slavery needs to be lifted slowly—that a community is necessary to piece the fragments together and to catch those who tear apart when they confront the horrors. The anxiety for the reader, then, is connecting the bodies, the scars, the "sixty million" voiceless voices, and forming a coherent whole. Readers need fragments to digest, to work through, to remember. And when Sethe has the courage to say, "No more running—from nothing. I will never run from another thing on this earth" (Morrison 15), readers have to put aside their amnesia and stop running, too.

The very concept of memory, or "rememory" as Sethe calls it, is fragmented in this novel. Memories are often thought of as something belonging to a person, an individual's notions. But Sethe redefines memory as a shared experience:

> If a house burns down, it's gone, but the place—the picture of it—stays, and not just in my rememory, but out there, in the world. . . . Someday you be walking down the road and you hear something or see something going on. So clear. And you think it's you thinking it up. A thought picture. But no. It's when you bump into a rememory that belongs to somebody else. (Morrison 36)

In Sethe's theory, each person has a little piece of shared memory, and in this novel, it takes the community working together to allow the full story to be told. Paul D, Sethe, Stamp Paid, Ella, and Beloved all share partial stories that the reader is able to piece together in a form of collective remembering. The problem, though, is that the remembering opens up tobacco tins; it sheds light on a husband's face smeared with butter; it reminds a black man that he did not really "give" his wife to his white owner because she would have been taken anyway; it reminds a slave woman of her "puberty spent in a house where she was shared by father and son" (257). Eventually, that collective memory becomes a physical beast that must be acknowledged. It becomes Beloved, in every strange, titillating, horrifying, beautiful, worrisome aspect of that word.

When speaking of this novel, Morrison said, "I thought this has got to be the least read of all the books I'd written because it is about something the characters don't want to remember, I don't want to remember, black people don't want to remember, white people don't want to remember" (qtd. in Angelo 68). The excruciating act of remembering and its accompanying horrendous images that the community of characters and the community of readers are able to piece together, though, succeed in lifting the veil on the national amnesia. As Bowers notes, this novel is " about collecting fragments and welding them into beautiful new wholes, about letting go of pain and guilt, but also recovering what is lost, and loving it into life" (42).

What's in a Name? Characters and/as Monsters

One thing to "recover" and "love into life" in this novel is one's sense of identity. Another trope of Gothic literature is the quest for lineage and roots. In one passage, Paul D reflects upon family:

> He had already seen his brother wave goodbye from the back of a dray, fried chicken in his pocket, tears in his eyes. Mother. Father. Didn't remember the one. Never saw the other. He was the youngest of three half-brothers (same mother-different fathers). . . . Once in Maryland, he met four families of slaves who had all been together for a hundred years: great-grands, grands, mothers, fathers, aunts, uncles, cousins, children. Half white, part white, all black, mixed with Indian. He watched them with awe and envy, and each time he discovered large families of black people, he made them identify over and over who each was, what relation, who, in fact, belonged to who. (Morrison 219)

Paul D's fascination with family, with "identifying," echoes throughout his journey to find something to call home. Sweet Home is anything but sweet, but at least there he has a sense of brothers and of community. When Mr. Garner, their owner, dies and Schoolteacher replaces him, the slaves' sense of family and identity is slowly undermined. Paul D's brothers are destroyed—Sixo burned alive and Paul A beheaded and hanged—and Halle is driven insane. Sethe is Paul D's only remaining family, so his reaction when he sees her makes sense: at first, Paul D "simply wanted to move, go, pick up one day and be somewhere else the next. Resigned to life without aunts, cousins, children. Even a woman" (221). But when he sees Sethe at 124, "the closed portion of his greased head opened like a closed lock" (41). Paul D realizes that he and Sethe can make a life together. He can move from being one of many Pauls—a name which means "small"—to being a man with a family, children, a house. It is not surprising when Paul D tries to fight Beloved's presence in the house, nor is it shocking when, as Beloved's power gets stronger and Paul D feels as if he is being shut out, he says to Sethe, "I want you pregnant Sethe. Would you do that for me?" Paul D's fragmented sense of self finds comfort in establishing an identity with Sethe, in "document[ing] his manhood" (128).

A similar quest for identity plays out in many of the individual narratives in the novel, particularly with regard to names. A common practice amongst slave owners was renaming their slaves after themselves or giving them Christian names, as we see with Paul Garner naming several of his slaves "Paul." This lack of individuality strikes Baby Suggs as she crosses the river to the free side and finally finds the courage to ask about her name:

> "Mr. Garner," she said, "Why you all call me Jenny?"
> "Cause that what's on your sales ticket, gal. Ain't that your name? What you call yourself?"
> "Nothing," she said, "I don't call myself nothing."
> . . . "What do you answer to?"
> "Anything, but Suggs is my husband name."
> . . . "What did he call you?"
> "Baby."
> "Well," says Mr. Garner . . . "Mrs. Baby Suggs ain't no name for a freed Negro."
> Maybe not, she though, but Baby Suggs was all she had left.
> (Morrison 142)

Their exchange underscores the notion of the loss of identity through slavery. For years, Baby Suggs had been called the wrong name but been too afraid to question, and later, when given the chance to claim her identity, she simply does not have one, other than to name herself after a slave who had been ripped away from her and sold.

What is interesting about Baby Suggs's choice, though, is its connection with the past. While her name reminds her of her husband, it also represents the horror. Her identity claim is similar to Stamp Paid's. As Stamp notes, "They called me Joshua . . . [but] I renamed myself" after his wife was taken from him for a year to be a sex slave to the plantation owner (Morrison 233). So although Stamp and Baby Suggs have different rationale, both choose not to replicate white names and instead call attention to the atrocities of broken families and people without names. Their choices, then, underscore slavery's destruction of lineage and of self. In an interview, Morrison notes, "The novel is not about slavery. Slavery is very predictable. There is it and there's [information] about how it is, and then you get out of it or you don't. [The novel] can't be driven by slavery. It has to be the interior life of some people, and everything that they do is impacted on by the horror of slavery, but they are also people" (qtd. in Rothstein). Stamp Paid's and Baby Suggs's choices show how their "interior lives" were suppressed for many years.

An important question to consider regarding identity is why Beloved does not have a name. Prior to her death, she is almost two years old and "crawling already," so she should have had a name. On a literal level, readers know that Sethe simply does not have enough money so she sells herself to get her daughter's headstone chiseled: "Ten minutes for seven letters. With another ten could she have gotten 'Dearly' too? . . . for twenty minutes, a half hour, say, she could have had the whole thing, every word she heard the preacher say . . . 'Dearly Beloved'" (Morrison 5). Metaphorically, readers come to realize Beloved is unnamed because she cannot be named. In representing an idea, Beloved is more sublime than one name can encompass; she is beyond the ability to name because she is so horrific. In Mary Shelley's *Frankenstein*, for example, the monster is never named because he is undead, an unspeakable other. Beloved is the same. Yet, she is "beloved" because she *is* each individual. She *is* each one's past. "Beloved" is an apt word for the main source of anxiety in this text: love. Maternal love, spousal love, sibling love, friendship, self-love—all of these bonds are denied. So the very idea of a slave having something that is beloved is loaded with anxiety. *Beloved*'s epigraph states, "I will call . . . her beloved, which was not beloved." She is owned and not owned. A perfect notion for a novel about slaves.

Beloved is several things at once, a fragmented essence. She is the baby girl Sethe murdered; she is a slave remembering her Middle Passage; and she is a figurative representation of all slaves. As such, Beloved is both helpful and dangerous for Paul D, Sethe, and Denver. She opens them up to their past—the tobacco can, the rememory, the silence—but she also *opens up* their past to these numerous things that they do not wish to face. And she consumes them: Paul D physically, Sethe emotionally and physically, and Denver emotionally. Beloved, then, exists in that liminal state between fear and hope for these characters. She is Gothic in its essence, defying life and death, defying memory and understanding.

As Beloved morphs from the spectral to the concrete, Morrison ensures that characters can no longer "beat back the past" (218). Beloved stands there, corporeal, forcing others to see their pasts: Halle with butter smeared on his face, Paul D with a bit in his mouth, Sethe's back as canvas for Schoolteacher's chokecherry tree. Beloved, the representation of all that is not beloved, births herself from each character's repressed consciousness—a spirit rising out of the waterhole of the African American community and revealing how slavery upended both the American and the African American narratives—and now demands recognition.

Through her, readers can experience the Middle Passage, understand abandonment (of a person and a race), and grasp the terror of dislocation and ownership. The monster that is Beloved thrives on the fears and repressed memories of the African Americans who have somehow lived through slavery. Morrison posits that this monster needs to be addressed and reclaimed in order for Sethe—and by extension, all—not to live in fear that Schoolteacher will show up at her door at any moment.

The Monstrous Mother

Beloved-as-past connects Sethe with Beloved-as-character on multiple levels. They represent several elements of slavery: the role of women, the inevitability of severed maternal bonds, and the destruction of family lines. They are also both monsters. Beloved, the terrifying, needy, soul-swallowing phantom reveals the monstrous reality of slavery; Sethe, while not a ghost, is also terrifying, needy and all-consuming. Their connection—motherhood—is clearly understood by Sethe, as is evident by her ironic thoughts regarding Paul D's request to father his child: "unless carefree, motherlove was a killer" (Morrison 132).

The anxiety of motherhood as a direct result of slavery surfaces in several characters' stories. Often caused by the inability to control what happens to the female body, as well as the fear of what will ultimately happen to one's children—especially the female children—motherhood for slaves is rife with problems. The narrator voices Baby Suggs's despair at Halle's birth, noting how her life as a slave effectively strangles her natural maternal response:

> [Halle was] the last of her children, whom she barely glanced at when he was born because it wasn't worth the trouble to try and learn features you would never see changed into adulthood anyway. Seven times she had done that: held a little foot; examined the fat fingertips with her own – fingers she never saw become the male or female hands a mother would recognize anywhere. (Morrison 139)

Ella's anxiety is more body specific. Like Baby Suggs, she refused to view her child at birth. But Ella's refusal was based more on hatred than despair: "She had delivered, but would not nurse, a hairy white thing, fathered by 'the lowest yet'" (Morrison 258–59). After years of being held as a sex slave by a father-son team, Ella's refusal to use her body to continue the line of "the lowest yet" speaks to her complete disassociation from the maternal. Her owners' actions had killed her motherly impulse to nurse the child, leaving her furious and "beaten every way but down" (258).

Slave owners preyed upon female slaves in another way: using their bodies as commodities to produce further stock for their farms. Schoolteacher brazenly evaluates Sethe's womb, calculating what she has produced and what is still in vitro: "maybe with the breeding one [Sethe], her three pickaninnies, and whatever the foal might be," he could have enough slaves to make "Sweet Home worth the trouble it was causing" (Morrison 227). Schoolteacher doesn't even know her name, and his reference to her unborn child as a "foal," as well as his many other references throughout the text to Sethe as an animal, shows his outright disregard for the notion of motherhood for slaves being anything other than an economic boon for the owners.

This disrespect for the institution of motherhood has a direct consequence on the children. Similar to Paul D, Sethe suffers from a lack of familial connection, specifically the maternal. She does not remember her mother, the woman who had to be "pointed out to her by an eight-year-old child who watched over the young ones" (Morrison 30). Eventually, her mother pulls her aside to show Sethe where she was branded so that Sethe would know her body. All that Sethe remembers, though, is the hat her mom wore, and she would spend hours seeking that hat. When the hat disappears from the fields, Sethe knows her mom has been hanged, and she is drastically altered by it: Sethe "stuttered after that" for many years, (201), and more importantly, Sethe becomes obsessed with raising her own children and with her desire to mother as she wished to have been mothered. Ironically, the very things slavery attempted to suppress become stronger in Sethe. Given her status as slave, though, Sethe's maternal desires are not permissible or tolerated and eventually cause the ultimate perversion of motherhood: infanticide.

The tension of becoming a mother is demonstrated throughout the text, but most noticeably in Sethe's painful, terrifying flight from Sweet Home to the other side of the Ohio River. Her own safety and comfort are not even considered as long as she can get milk to the child who needs it. Her journey almost destroys her feet, her back is ripped raw from her recent whipping, her breasts are painfully full and leaking because she has not been able to nurse her child, and she is wracked with contractions from the new child about to be born. Indeed, Sethe almost dies. But she carries on, for two reasons: "Nobody will ever get my milk no more except my own children" and "I wouldn't draw breath without my children" (Morrison 200, 203). Sethe cannot contemplate a world where her body is owned by anyone but her own children or a world where she would be separated from her children. She would rather die—or kill those children herself—than be forced to live as a slave.

After her excruciating journey, Sethe is given a reprieve. Baby Suggs and the community embrace Sethe, and she spends her days with her four children, finally giving and receiving a maternal embrace. But then, Sethe looks up and "recogniz[es] Schoolteacher's hat." So she "collect[s] every bit of life she had made, all the parts of her that were precious and fine and beautiful, and carri[es], push[es], drag[s] them through the veil, out, away, over there where no one could hurt them" (Morrison 163). Sethe does her best to make sure the "dirty white things" do not get her children, cutting the two boys, attempting to slam the life out of the infant, and severing the baby's throat with a saw.

While Gothic texts often struggle with the anxiety of motherhood, and the parallels in *Beloved* to earlier Gothics are clear—trapped female character, impregnated out of wedlock, seeking the best outcome for her child—Morrison's character is not rescued from a vault or found to be innocent. Sethe's decision to kill her own child turns Sethe into a monstrous mother. But Morrison has clearly indicated that Sethe is not at fault. The word "decision" never appears, and the implication is that Sethe is forced to kill her child. For, similar to Beloved, it is slavery that has made Sethe a monster.

The result of Sethe's actions for readers, then, is a blurring of the line between monster and mother. While most likely horrified by the thought of anyone taking a hacksaw to a young child's neck, readers can also see that Sethe is, in some ways, the ultimate mother. To Sethe, her "big love" for her children means protecting through sacrifice. As Cedric Gael Bryant posits, "Sethe . . . embrace[s] the power at the margins unapologetically, defiantly" (548). In doing so, Bryant believes Sethe becomes something "new," something that "lies outside all the familiar social constructions of normal, human, mother, woman, lawful, blackness and whiteness" (548). That is not to say that Morrison is condoning Sethe's action. The fact that Sethe is haunted by an unsettled ghost for decades clearly expresses some form of disapproval. Further, the language in the infanticide scene reduces Sethe to an animal: when she recognizes Schoolteacher's hat and realizes he is coming to put into effect the Fugitive Slave Law, she flies "snatching up her children like a hawk . . . her face beak[s]. . . her hands work[ing] like claws" (Morrison 157). Sethe becomes a creature, reverting to what some could view as animalistic passion. This scene shows the collapse of the human/animal binary and the history/narrative binary, leaving readers uncomfortably processing whether infanticide is perhaps justifiable when laws position people as animals that other people can possess.

Along with these unsettling concerns is the question of whether Sethe is successful. Whereas Halle snapped before he could rewrite his family's future, Sethe does succeed in rewriting. She has made it such that "whites might dirty *her* all right, but not her best thing, her beautiful, magical best thing—the part of her that was clean" (Morrison 251). The infant she murdered will not be sullied by slavery. She also protects her other three, for upon seeing Sethe covered in blood, Schoolteacher gives all of the children up for either dead or insane and leaves them in Ohio. Upon his leaving, Denver the newborn needs to eat, so Sethe nurses her; in doing so, "Denver took her mother's milk right along with the blood of her sister" (152). This aberration of mother's sustenance, this blurring of life and death, protects Sethe's "best thing." So not only has Sethe rewritten her future, but her children's as well. She has rewritten in milk and blood. Using her body, her power as a mother, and her big love, Sethe authors change. And the image of Sethe perverting the maternal in this scene entwines the past with the present, motherhood with slavery, and breaks down the binaries that society has attempted to establish to distance itself from the reality of slavery.

But this act, and the community's response to it—they abandon Sethe—forces her to live linearly. As a result, Sethe buries her voice and her history. In blocking her memories, all that remains of Sethe is her body as text: her milk, her tree, her breasts, and her children. That is why motherhood is so important to her. It is her "best thing." It is from her body, which is all she has left. This type of mothering is not healthy, as we see from 124 shutting out all men and the community shunning Sethe. Also, Sethe's perversion of maternal desire effectively shuts out the most maternal figure in the novel: Baby Suggs. Known as the woman who mothers all, Baby Suggs's "great big old heart began to collapse twenty-eight days after her daughter-in-law arrived" (Morrison 89). Fittingly, in the space of a woman's menstrual cycle, slavery has replaced Baby Suggs, mother, with Sethe, monstrous mother. The malignant seed is birthed, lives for eighteen years, and finally is challenged with another shocking birth: when Beloved appears, "Sethe's bladder filled to capacity. . . . the water she voided was endless. . . . there was no stopping water breaking from a breaking womb" (51).

At first drawn to Beloved simply because Sethe is compassionate, slowly Sethe begins to realize that Beloved is the daughter she lost. This "timeless present" thrills Sethe (Morrison 185), and she lets the reborn past feast on her food, her stories, her body. But Beloved-as-monster is insatiable, and Sethe slowly becomes smaller while the gluttonous past consumes her to the point where Sethe stops eating and sits quietly in a corner without any strength. Sethe's repression of her maternal desire, her anger at being milked, her desire to love without permission, have left her defenseless against Beloved. Like the tree on her back, Sethe is numb. However, after eighteen years, she notes that her tree "could have cherries too now for all I know" (16). This line underscores Sethe's maternal power. What has been deadened in her for eighteen years since the infanticide is alive. But again, Morrison blurs the lines, for the chokecherry tree is poisonous for animals, and while it is closely related to the sweet cherry, the chokecherry produces a bitter fruit. So the berries that may be growing on Sethe's back attest to her motherhood but also her bitterness and her ability to kill.

Beloved capitalizes upon this split in Sethe, growing bigger daily. Critic Philip Goldstein suggests that Beloved grows in stature because she is "pregnant with Paul D's child" (4). It can also be argued, however, that Beloved grows because she is showing Sethe the monstrosities of thwarted, perverted motherhood. She is growing as Sethe decreases because Beloved is becoming the monstrous mother as Sethe is cannibalized. The only way to stop this horror, then, is to join forces against the past, to stop that amnesia, and to have the community recognize the forces within. That is the only way to reclaim Sethe's body—from slavery, from master, from whites, from past, from repression, from Beloved.

"Anything dead coming back to life hurts"

As the novel draws to a close, Beloved has forced the community to face their beasts within: Ella remembers her "hairy white thing;" Paul D has relived the many things that have given him a permanent "tremble;" Stamp Paid reveals the nightmare behind his name; and Sethe has spoken of her beating, of being milked, of running, and of murdering. Their bodies testify to the truth: Ella with "scars from the belt were as thick as rope around her waist" (Morrison 258); Paul D with shackle scars on his ankles, wrists, and neck; Sethe with her chokecherry tree; and countless other bodies broken, battered, and branded by slavery. In remembering, they help readers piece together the fragments. And readers, too, must remember the atrocities many have sanctioned.

When the women gather in the front yard of 124, they do so to reclaim Baby Suggs's maternal space that Sethe had perverted, to drive out the evils of the past into the light where it can be recognized. They pray and then revert to just sound: "in the beginning was the sound, and they all knew what that sound sounded like" (Morrison 259). Sethe recognizes that sound, and once again, a birth occurs: "it was a wave of sound. . . . It broke over Sethe and she trembled like the baptized in its wash" (261). The community gives Sethe a chance at life, a chance to leave the hatred that holds her hand on that porch and embrace the community. Once again, Morrison blurs the lines, though, for Mr. Bodwin appears and Sethe confuses him for Schoolteacher. Thinking he is coming to take her children, Sethe flies from the porch with her ice pick, leaving Beloved behind, but is tackled by a "pile of people" (262). Although they are physically restraining Sethe, the community is also helping her—keeping her out of jail, taking her from Beloved, embracing her. And when it is done, Beloved is gone.

Morrison's monsters in *Beloved*—the characters, institutions, fears—reveal the depth of many cultural anxieties. While each character struggles to address his or her own demons, the past itself cannot be changed. Therefore, Beloved, in her multiple meanings, must be destroyed for other characters to move forward. To do so, Morrison kills Beloved twice: once by the institution of slavery as Schoolteacher's imminent arrival drives Sethe to murder Beloved and then again by the black community as they are determined *not* to be haunted by what white society has created. These killings are bookends: an opening of the wound of the past and a sense of closure for that wound. The latter destruction is not erasure, though, for the characters have now *seen* the specter of the past, lived with it, embraced it, fought with it, and reclaimed it. The scars, both physical and mental, remain, but the power of the past to fragment and consume the future no longer holds.

Notes

1. Morrison 35.

Works Cited

Angelo, Bonnie. "The Pain of Being Black: Toni Morrison, Winner of the Pulitzer Prize for Her Gritty Novel *Beloved*, Smolders at the Inequities That Blacks and Women Still Face." *Time* 22 May 1989: 68–70. Print.

Bowers, Susan. "*Beloved* and the New Apocalypse." *Modern Critical Interpretations: Beloved*. Ed. Harold Bloom. Philadelphia: Chelsea, 1999: 27–43. Print.

Bryant, Cedric Gael. "The South Has Bandaged Moments': Reading the African American Gothic in Wright's 'Big Boy Leaves Home,' Morrison's *Beloved*, and Gomez's *Gilda*." *African American Review* 39.4 (2006): 541–53. Print.

Goldstein, Philip. "Black Feminism and the Canon: Faulkner's *Absalom, Absalom!* and Morrison's *Beloved* as Gothic Romances." *Faulkner Journal* 20.1 (2004): 133–48. Print.

Mobley, Marilyn Sanders. "A Different Remembering: Memory, History and Meaning in Toni Morrison's *Beloved*." *Modern Critical Views: Toni Morrison*. Ed. Harold Bloom. Philadelphia: Chelsea, 1990: 189–99. Print.

Morrison, Toni. *Beloved*. New York: Plume, 1988. Print.

Rothstein, Mervyn. "Toni Morrison in Her New Novel Defends Women." *New York Times* 26 Aug. 1987: C17. Print.

Spaulding, A. Timothy. *Re-Forming the Past: History, the Fantastic, and the Postmodern Slave Narrative*. Columbus: Ohio UP, 2005. Print.

RESOURCES

Other Works on Southern Gothic Literature_____

Long Fiction
The Grandissimes: A Story of Creole Life by George Washington Cable, 1880
The Awakening by Kate Chopin, 1899
God's Little Acre by Erskine Caldwell, 1933
Other Voices, Other Rooms by Truman Capote, 1948
Wise Blood by Flannery O'Connor, 1952
The Night of the Hunter by Davis Grubb, 1953
To Kill a Mockingbird by Harper Lee, 1960
The Keepers of the House by Shirley Ann Grau, 1964
Deliverance by James Dickey, 1970
A Confederacy of Dunces by John Kennedy Toole, 1980
The Thanatos Syndrome by Walker Percy, 1987
Bastard Out of Carolina by Dorothy Allison, 1992
Souls Raised from the Dead by Doris Betts, 1994
Swamplandia! by Karen Russell, 2011

Short Fiction
"A Struggle for Life" by Henry Clay Lewis, 1843
"Parson John Bullen's Lizards" (originally as "Sut Lovingood's Lizzards" by George
    Washington Harris, 1857
"Life in the Iron Mills" by Rebecca Harding Davis, 1861
"No Haid Pawn" by Thomas Nelson Page, 1887
"Jordan's End" by Ellen Glasgow, 1923
"Sweat" by Zora Neale Hurston, 1926
"Noon Wine" by Katherine Anne Porter, 1937
"Desire and the Black Masseur" by Tennessee Williams, 1967
"Anse Starkey at Rest" by Mark Steadman, 1971
"The Child Who Favored Daughter" by Alice Walker, 1974
"Coming Close to Donna" by Barry Hannah, 1978
"The Honored Dead" by Breece D'J Pancake, 1981
"A Party Down at the Square" by Ralph Ellison, 1996 (posthumously)
"Stay Awake" by Poppy Z. Brite, 2000

Bibliography

Bayer-Berenbaum, Linda. *The Gothic Imagination: Expansion in Gothic Literature and Art*. Rutherford: Fairleigh Dickinson UP, 1982. Print.

Bienstock Anolik, Ruth, and Douglas L. Howard, eds. *The Gothic Other: Racial and Social Constructions in the Literary Imagination*. Jefferson: McFarland, 2004. Print.

Brabon, Benjamin A., and Stéphanie Genz, eds. *Postfeminist Gothic: Critical Interventions in Contemporary Culture*. New York: Palgrave, 2007. Print.

Byron, Glennis, and David Punter, eds. *Spectral Readings: Towards a Gothic Geography*. New York: St. Martin's, 1999. Print.

Costello, Brannon, and Qiana J. Whitted, eds. *Comics and the U.S. South*. Jackson: UP of Mississippi, 2012. Print.

Davis, Thadious M. *Southscapes: Geographies of Race, Region, & Literature*. Chapel Hill: U of North Carolina P, 2011. Print.

Downing, David, and Susan Bazargan, eds. *Image and Ideology in Modern/Postmodern Discourse*. Albany: SUNY P, 1991. Print.

Edwards, Justin D. *Gothic Passages: Racial Ambiguity and the American Gothic*. Iowa City: U of Iowa P, 2003. Print.

Ellis, Kate Ferguson. *The Contested Castle: Gothic Novels and the Subversion of Domestic Ideology*. Chicago: U of Illinois P, 1989. Print.

Flora, Joseph M., Lucinda H. MacKethan, and Todd Taylor, eds. *The Companion to Southern Literature: Themes, Genres, Places, People, Movements, and Motifs*. Baton Rouge: Louisiana State UP, 2002. Print.

Gray, Richard, and Owen Robinson, eds. *A Companion to the Literature and Culture of the American South*. Oxford: Blackwell, 2007. Print.

Gray, Richard J. *The Literature of Memory: Modern American Writers of the American South*. Baltimore: Johns Hopkins UP, 1977. Print.

___. *Southern Aberrations: Writers of the American South and the Problems of Regionalism*. Baton Rouge: Louisiana State UP, 2000. Print.

Greeson, Jennifer Rae. *Our South: Geographic Fantasy and the Rise of National Literature*. Cambridge: Harvard UP, 2010. Print.

Gross, Louis S. *Redefining the American Gothic: From* Wieland *to* Day of the Dead. Ann Arbor: UMI Research P, 1989. Print.

Hobson, Fred. *Tell about the South: The Southern Rage to Explain*. Baton Rouge: Louisiana State UP, 1983. Print.

___. *The Southern Writer in the Postmodern World*. Athens: U of Georgia P, 1991. Print.

Hoeveler, Diane Long, and Tamar Heller, eds. *Approaches to Teaching Gothic Fiction: The British and American Traditions*. New York: MLA, 2003. Print.

Hogle, Jerrold, ed. *The Cambridge Companion to Gothic Fiction*. New York: Cambridge UP, 2002. Print.

Jackson, Robert. *Seeking the Region in American Literature and Culture: Modernity, Dissidence, Innovation*. Baton Rouge: Louisiana State UP, 2005. Print.

Jones, Suzanne W., and Sharon Monteith, eds. *South to a New Place: Region, Literature, Culture*. Baton Rouge: Louisiana State UP, 2002. Print.

Kilgour, Maggie. *The Rise of the Gothic Novel*. New York: Routledge, 1995. Print.

King, Richard H. *A Southern Renaissance: The Cultural Awakening of the American South: 1930–1955*. Oxford: Oxford UP, 1980. Print.

Lloyd-Smith, Allan. *American Gothic Fiction: An Introduction*. New York: Continuum, 2005. Print.

MacAndrew, Elizabeth. *The Gothic Tradition in Fiction*. New York: Columbia UP, 1979. Print.

Martin, Robert K., and Eric Savoy, eds. *American Gothic: New Interventions in a National Narrative*. Iowa City: U of Iowa P, 1998. Print.

Mishra, Vijay. *The Gothic Sublime*. Albany: SUNY P, 1994. Print.

Moreman, Christopher M., and Cory James Rushton, eds. *Race, Oppression and the Zombie: Essays on the Cross-Cultural Appropriations of the Carribean Tradition*. Jefferson: McFarland, 2011. Print.

Nelson, Victoria. *Gothicka: Vampire Heroes, Human Gods, and the New Supernatural*. Cambridge: Harvard UP, 2012. Print.

O'Connor, Flannery. *Mysteries and Manners: Occasional Prose*. New York: Farrar, 1969. Print.

O'Connor, William Van. *The Grotesque: An American Genre and Other Essays*. Carbondale: Southern Illinois UP, 1962. Print.

Powell, Anna, and Andrew Smith, eds. *Teaching the Gothic*. New York: Palgrave, 2006. Print.

Punter, David. *The Literature of Terror: A History of Gothic Fictions from 1765 to the Present Day*. New York: Longman, 1980. Print.

___. *Gothic Pathologies: The Text, the Body and the Law*. New York: St. Martin's, 1998. Print.

___, ed. *A New Companion to the Gothic*. Malden: Wiley, 2012. Print.

Purves, Maria. *The Gothic and Catholicism: Religion, Cultural Exchange and the Popular Novel, 1785–1829*. Cardiff: U of Wales P, 2009. Print.

Ringe, Donald. *American Gothic: Imagination and Reason in Nineteenth-Century Fiction*. Lexington: UP of Kentucky, 1982. Print.

Scott, Niall, ed. *Monsters and the Monstrous: Myths and Metaphors of Enduring Evil*. New York: Rodopi, 2007. Print.

Snodgrass, Mary Ellen, ed. *Encyclopedia of Gothic Literature: The Essential Guide to the Lives and Works of Gothic Writers*. New York: Facts on File, 2005. Print.

Spooner, Catherine, and Emma McEvoy, eds. *The Routledge Companion to Gothic*. New York: Routledge, 2007. Print.

Stecopoulos, Harilaos. *Reconstructing the World: Southern Fictions and U.S. Imperialisms, 1898–1976*. Ithaca: Cornell UP, 2008. Print.

Whitt, Jan. *Allegory and the Modern Southern Novel*. Macon: Mercer UP, 1994. Print.

Wilson, Charles Reagan. *Flashes of a Southern Spirit: Meanings of the Spirit in the U.S. South*. Athens: U of Georgia P, 2011. Print.

___, ed. *The New Regionalism: Essays and Commentaries*. Jackson: UP of Mississippi, 1998. Print.

About the Editor

Jay Ellis teaches in the Program for Writing and Rhetoric at the University of Colorado Boulder, where he is a fellow of the Center of the American West. His teaching emphasizes narrative rhetorics of evidence, electronic scholarship, and composing nontraditional stances in both interdisciplinary scholarship and rhetorics of civic engagement. His curricular and faculty development advocates creative nonfiction, student-centered computerized classrooms with course management systems that alleviate workload inequities for composition instructors, and variations in rhetorical stance to address problems of gender bias and class exclusion in disciplinary scholarship. He has taught literature and composition in the English and the Expository Writing Departments of New York University, where he completed a dissertation on Cormac McCarthy, and at the University of Texas at Dallas.

Research interests include Southern Gothic, spatial configurations in American literature and culture, and feminist aspects of post–World War II literature of the American West. Publications include "'Do you see?' Levels of Ellipsis in *No Country for Old Men*" in *Cormac McCarthy: All the Pretty Horses; No Country for Old Men; The Road* (2011); and chapters in *Rhetorical Democracy: Discursive Practices of Civic Engagement* and *Bloom's Modern Critical Views: Cormac McCarthy*. He has contributed to the *Rocky Mountain Review of Language and Literature*, *Negations: An Interdisciplinary Journal of Social Thought*, *Concho River Review*, *Sulphur River*, and *Chelsea*. His first book, *No Place for Home: Spatial Constraint and Character Flight in the Novels of Cormac McCarthy* (2006), remains in print. Works in progress include a second novel, *A Fixed Heart*; a creative nonfiction essay, "My Dark Places: Southern Gothic, Texas"; and *Don't Fence Me In: Reading, Watching, and Living in American Spaces*. A professional jazz musician for many years, he has performed extensively in Boston, New York, his native Dallas, and Colorado's Front Range, including Red Rocks Amphitheatre outside Denver.

Contributors

Bridget M. Marshall is an associate professor and associate chair of the English Department at the University of Massachusetts, Lowell. Her book, *The Transatlantic Gothic Novel and the Law, 1790–1860*, was published in January 2011, and her co-edited collection *Transnational Gothic: Literary and Social Exchanges in the Long Nineteenth Century* will be published in 2013. She teaches courses on the Gothic, nineteenth-century American literature, witchcraft trials, and disability in literature. Marshall has published articles on gambling addictions in Gothic novels, Hawthorne's use of the Gothic, and phrenology and physiognomy in the Gothic novel. Her article on witch tourism in Salem appeared in the collection *Spectral America: Phantoms and the National Imagination* (2004).

Christopher J. Walsh holds a BA honors degree in American studies from the University of Wales, Swansea. He stayed at Swansea to complete his PhD (titled *"You Talk Like A Goddamned Yankee": Cormac McCarthy and East Tennessee Exceptionalism*), which explored McCarthy's relationship to the Southern literary tradition. Walsh has published a number of articles on McCarthy, and 2010 saw the publication of his book *In the Wake of the Sun: Navigating the Southern Works of Cormac McCarthy*. Chris has taught at Hull University and the University of Tennessee, Knoxville, where he has taught a wide variety of modules related to American and European literature. He currently works in academic administration in London and lives in Cambridgeshire with his wife Nikki and son, Billy.

Henry L. Carrigan, Jr. is assistant professor and senior editor at Northwestern University Press. He writes regularly on comparative literature and American literature for a number of national newspapers and magazines. His essays on Robert Walser, W. G. Sebald, Robert Musil, Reynolds Price, Kurt Vonnegut, and others have appeared in Magill's Literary Survey, and his article on Albert Camus and W. G. Sebald appears in *Critical Insights: Albert Camus* (2010).

Jay Ellis teaches in the Program for Writing and Rhetoric at the University of Colorado, where he is also a fellow of the Center of the American West. Ellis began performing on drums in shopping malls, Veterans of Foreign Wars (VFW) halls, stock shows, and theaters at age eleven and studied performance and jazz composition and arranging at Berklee College. He earned his masters in interdisciplinary literary studies at the University of Texas at Dallas, and his PhD in American literature at New York University. He writes novels, creative nonfiction, and scholarship on Southern Gothic and Western American literature. Publications include *No Place for Home: Spatial Constraint and Character Flight in the Novels of Cormac McCarthy* (2006).

Ronja Vieth teaches at South Plains College and at Texas Tech University, where she holds a PhD in American Gothic literature. She received her MA in English from the University of Louisiana at Lafayette; and an MA in American literature, linguistics, and psychology from TU Carolo Wilhelmina at Braunschweig, Germany. Publications include "The Critical Reception of Cormac McCarthy" for *Critical Insights: Cormac McCarthy* (2012) and "A Frontier Myth Turns Gothic—*Blood Meridian, Or the Evening Redness in the West*" for *The Cormac McCarthy Journal* (2010), "The Mad Trickster—Or How Harriet Jacobs Subverts Madness in *Incidents in the Life of a Slave Girl*" in *Gender and Sexual Identity* (2010), and "Theron and the Eves of Modernism: The Feminine Influence as the Candle Illumination in *The Damnation of Theron Ware Or Illumination* (1896)" in the *University of Bucharest Review* (2006).

Julieann Veronica Ulin is the assistant professor of British and American modernism at Florida Atlantic University. She holds her PhD in English from the University of Notre Dame, MA in English from Fordham University, and BA in English from Washington and Lee University. She authored the introduction to *Race and Immigration in the New Ireland*, which she also coedited (2013). Her work has appeared or is forthcoming in *American Literature, Joyce Studies Annual, James Joyce Quarterly, Women's Studies Quarterly, Hungry Words: Images of Famine in the Irish Canon, Richard Wright: New Readings for the 21st Century*, and *Open Graves, Open Minds: Representations of Vampires and the Undead from the Enlightenment to the Present.*

Tanya Carinae Pell Jones is an English teacher and department chairperson at a charter high school near Charlotte, North Carolina. She holds a MEd from Queens University of Charlotte and a BS in education from Slippery Rock University of Pennsylvania. She has written chapters for multiple publications, including *The Mythological Dimensions of Neil Gaiman*, the *Journal of the Short Story in English*, and an academic collection on the *Resident Evil* franchise appearing in 2013. She is currently coediting a collection on the use of Gothic fairy tale motifs in children's and young adult literature. Her scholarly interests lie in Gothicism, fairy tales, Celtic and Nordic folk tales, and the paradox between science and the supernatural in literature. She lives in Charlotte with her husband. They are expecting their first baby in the spring of 2013.

Tanfer Emin Tunc is a faculty member in the Department of American Culture and Literature at Hacettepe University, Ankara, Turkey. She holds a PhD in American history from the State University of New York at Stony Brook, and specializes in Women's Studies and American Cultural Studies, with an emphasis on gender, race, and the South. Tunc has authored two books, edited four essay collections, and has written over fifty book chapters, reference book entries, book reviews, and journal articles, most of which have appeared in internationally-renowned publications such as *Rethinking History, Asian Journal of Women's Studies, Foreign Literature Studies, Women's History Review, Historical Journal*, and *Journal of Women's History*. She is a member of the editorial advisory board of *Medical History* (SSCI), vice president of the American Studies Association of Turkey (ASAT), and a member of the European Association for American Studies (EAAS) Women's Caucus Steering Committee.

David J. Rothman is director of the poetry concentration in the MFA in creative writing at Western State Colorado University. He also teaches at the University of Colorado at Boulder, Denver University, and Lighthouse Writers Workshop of Denver. He holds degrees from Harvard, the University of Utah, and New York University. His second book of poems, *The Elephant's Chiropractor*, was runner-up for the 1999 Colorado Book Award. His fourth collection, *Part of the Darkness*, is due out in fall 2012, and a fifth, *Go Big*, comes out in 2015. In 2013 he will publish *Living the Life*, a collection of essays about mountains and mountain towns. With Stanley Rothman and Stephen Powers he has also coauthored a book on film, *Hollywood's America* (1998), and his essays and book reviews on subjects from modern poetry to Restoration satire, film theory, education, music, ski mountaineering, and other subjects appear widely.

Michal Svěrák graduated from the Faculty of Law of the Masaryk University in Brno, Czech Republic. His interests include American (especially Southern) literature, philosophy, and religious studies. He translated Cormac McCarthy's novel *Outer Dark* into Czech and published a book-length monograph *Svět v hrsti prachu: Kritická recepce díla Cormaca McCarthyho* (*The World in a Handful of Dust: Critical Reception of Cormac McCarthy*) in 2011. Currently he lives in Prague, Czech Republic.

Sharon Decker is an assistant professor of English at Centenary College in Hackettstown, New Jersey. She teaches as a generalist in Centenary's undergraduate program, and serves as the eighteenth century specialist for the graduate students. Her latest coursework includes "Late Eighteenth Century Women Novelists in their Quest for the Mother" and "Gothic Literature: Horace Walpole to Poppy Z Brite." Sharon's current research interests are the development of the family through the eighteenth century, motherhood and maternity, female education, monsters, and identity theory. She has written about Elizabeth Inchbald's plays and novels, penned a short biography of Linda Pastan, and is currently working on gothic elements in Clara Reeve's works.

Index

murder, 150, 245
Musgrove, Clement (*The Robber Bride-groom*), 137–138
names and naming, 246, 252–254
"Narcissus as Narcissus" (Tate), 186
narratives, nonlinear, 247
New Criticism, 188
New South, conflict with Old South, 93, 100, 105–107
New Southern scholarship, xxxi
New Testament, 99
O'Connor, Flannery, 28–31, 36, 38
odes. *See also* poetry
"Ode Sung on the Occasion . . ." (Timrod), 184–185
"Ode to the Confederate Dead" (Tate), 183–187
oedipal relationships, 162, 234
Oedipus Rex (Sophocles), 176
Old South, conflict with New South, 93, 100, 105–107
Old Testament, 99
order, 113, 114, 131
pagan spirituality, 207
Paradise Lost (Milton), 189
Parker, O. E. (Obadiah Elihue) ("Parker's Back"), 40
"Parker's Back" (O'Connor), 40
Paul D (*Beloved*), 251
pederasty, 168
physical disfigurement and disabilities, 40. *See also* freaks; grotesque, the
plantations, 6–8, 67
Poe, Edgar Allan, xxiv, 23–25, 180, 181
poetry, 173–200
Pointer, Manley ("Good Country People"), 42–43
postapocalyptic world, 49–71
"Prelude to an Evening" (Ransom), 187–193
Puritanism, 203–204, 208–210

race relations, 86, 91
racism, 87, 90
Ransom, John Crowe, 183, 187
rape, 138
"Raven, The" (Poe), 173, 180–181
Reconstruction, 85–90, 112–115
religious references
    Faulkner and, 97–100, 108
    Southern Gothic and, 97–100
rememory, 243, 250
revelation, 38–40
Reverend Shegog (*The Sound and the Fury*), 107
Road, The (McCarthy), 49–71
Rosamond (*The Robber Bridegroom*), 134–141
"Rose for Emily, A" (Faulkner), 117
Salome (*The Robber Bridegroom*), 135–138
scientist archetype, 157
secrecy, 145
serpent imagery, 205, 208, 215, 217
Sethe (*Beloved*), 256–260
settings
    boardinghouses, 112, 115–116, 119–121, 128
    castles, 6
    haunted houses, 22, 203, 204
    house as the site of revelation, 39
    Natchez Trace, 147, 148
    plantations kc1, 6, 8, 64, 67
    urban, 225, 226
    Yoknapatawpha County, 26, 93
sex
    bestiality, 195
    female sexuality, 135–136, 139, 142
    homosexuality, 165, 168
    pagan sexuality, 207
    pederasty, 168
    rape, 138
    sex crimes, 9